Value Innovation Portfolio Management

Achieving Double-Digit Growth Through Customer Value

Value Innovation Portfolio Management

Achieving Double-Digit Growth Through Customer Value

Sheila Mello, *Managing Partner and Principal*
Wayne Mackey, *Principal*
Ronald Lasser, Ph.D., *Principal*
Richard Tait, Ph.D., *Associate*

Product Development Consulting, Inc.
(www.pdcinc.com)
Boston, Massachusetts

ISBN-13: 978-1-932159-57-8

ISBN-10: 1-932159-57-6

Printed and bound in the U.S.A. Printed on acid-free paper
10 9 8 7 6 5 4 3 2 1

Library of Congress Cataloging-in-Publication Data

Value innovation portfolio management : achieving double-digit growth through customer value / by Sheila Mello ... [et al.].

p. cm.

Includes index.

ISBN-13: 978-1-932159-57-8 (hardcover : alk. paper)

ISBN-10: 1-932159-57-6 (hardcover : alk. paper)

1. New products--Planning. 2. Product management. 3. Strategic planning.
I. Mello, Sheila, 1943-

HF5415.153.V35 2006

658.8′01--dc22 2006019186

Direct all inquiries to J. Ross Publishing, Inc., 5765 N. Andrews Way, Ft. Lauderdale, FL 33309.

Phone: (954) 727-9333
Fax: (561) 892-0700
Web: www.jrosspub.com

TABLE OF CONTENTS

PREFACE

We decided to write this book because, in our consulting practice at Product Development Consulting, Inc., we too frequently observed companies of all types making misguided decisions about the products in which they invested and then suffering major disappointments—and sometimes outright failures—as a result of those decisions. Our experience in implementing the Market-Driven Product Definition (MDPD®) process defined in Sheila Mello's earlier book, *Customer-Centric Product Definition—The Key to Great Product Development*, revealed that most of our client companies did not include a customer value dimension in their portfolio management, but rather simply reacted to customer demands. Such reactions across a firm's product portfolio lead to the prevalence of product disappointments and failures.

In addition, as we realized when implementing the MDPD process in client companies, to fully achieve the potentially enormous benefits of the process, organizations needed to change their methods for managing the broader issue of company portfolios. We watched many of our clients make MDPD an integral part of their product development processes, then go on to use the resulting database of customer value information as input to their portfolio processes. Thus was born our idea of providing a new methodology, philosophy, and criteria for evaluating changes to the portfolio *before* making portfolio decisions and committing company resources.

Portfolio decisions based solely on financial projections are often inaccurate, misleading, and result in far too many costly failures. Companies operating with a rigid, prescriptive portfolio management process based on milestones, gates, and hurdles don't consider the dynamic nature of portfolio management. Others with misaligned goals, objectives, or strategies experience hit-or-miss results. We came to believe that there is a better way: a portfolio management process based on repeatable, verifiable, and documentable facts.

During the past few years, we brainstormed around these concepts and developed a methodology that we tested, researched, and sharpened. The results are in this book.

WHO SHOULD READ THIS BOOK?

Any company that desires to improve its method of portfolio management should embrace the ideas presented in this book. Senior managers, especially, will benefit from reading this book by developing a thorough understanding of VIP management. The book will help guide their decisions before, during, and after they implement a development project or program. They will see how their decisions affect the company's product development activities. The individuals and teams involved directly in the product development process will benefit from the guidance the book provides for creating a robust and thorough product definition process aligned with the portfolio management of the enterprise. This book also is a must for anyone in sales or marketing. Infusing VIP management principles into the business processes of your company is a differentiator in itself and can be a significant competitive advantage. Lastly, professors should include this book as required reading for students in engineering and business curricula.

We look forward to future work that further refines our understanding of how to help deliver product portfolios that surprise and delight even the most demanding consumers. We challenge you to take the VIP journey, first by reading this book and then by putting its ideas into practice at your own company.

Sheila Mello, *Managing Partner and Principal*
Wayne Mackey, *Principal*
Ron Lasser, Ph.D., *Principal*
Richard Tait, Ph.D., *Associate*
Product Development Consulting, Inc. (www.pdcinc.com)
Boston, Massachusetts

ABOUT THE AUTHORS

SHEILA MELLO (LEAD AUTHOR)

Sheila Mello is the managing partner of Product Development Consulting, Inc. She is a widely known and well-respected expert in consulting who combines many years of executive and hands-on experience in product development, hardware engineering, software development, manufacturing, marketing, sales, service, and quality with strong analytical and organization skills.

Ms. Mello has developed methodologies to deliver unique, measurable value to her clients, having led dozens of cross-functional teams to institutionalize best-in-class product development and product definition methodologies for faster time to profit and market acceptance. An authority on portfolio management and product definition practices, as well as product development process improvements, she serves as an advisor to the International Institute of Research and The Management Roundtable. She is the author of *Customer-Centric Product Definition: The Key to Great Product Development* (first published in 2001 by AMACOM, now available from PDC Professional Publishing).

Before joining PDC in 1993, Ms. Mello held director and vice president positions at Bolt, Beranek and Newman, Wang Laboratories, Palladian Software, and Distribution Management Systems in engineering, software and hardware development, and manufacturing and was a principal consultant with Arthur D. Little, Inc.

Ms. Mello earned a B.S., magna cum laude, in mathematics from Tufts University. She is a member of the Institute of Electrical and Electronics Engineers (IEEE), the American Marketing Association, the Product Development Management Association (PDMA), and the American Society for Quality (ASQ). She has been active in the Center for the Management of Quality (CQM) and has taught the CQM's senior executive management course.

WAYNE MACKEY

Wayne Mackey's expertise is grounded in more than 20 years of hands-on management of large engineering, manufacturing, and procurement organizations. His management consulting focuses on product/service development, especially in areas of collaborative design, metrics, supply chain management, and business strategy implementation.

Mr. Mackey has been a Principal with Product Development Consulting, Inc. since 1997. Prior to joining PDC, he worked for 20 years in the high-tech, aerospace, and automotive fields. A natural change agent and leader, he has counseled Fortune 500 companies, major universities (Stanford, MIT), and government agencies in product development, supply chain management, and rapidly implementing enterprisewide change. He also has worked as a senior scientist, material operations manager, program manager, engineering manager, and systems engineering manager.

Mr. Mackey has been a keynote speaker on rapid organizational change and a featured speaker on performance improvement, metrics, voice of the customer, supply chain management, and product development. He has hosted forums and served on expert panels for numerous organizations. He has been an invited chairman for many conferences and is an industry advisor for The Management Roundtable and the International Association of Product Development. He recently contributed a chapter titled "Metrics for the Real World" to PDMA's forthcoming third edition of the *PDMA ToolBook for New Product Development.*

Mr. Mackey earned a B.S. in electrical engineering and economics from Carnegie Mellon University and an M.S. in engineering from Loyola Marymount University. He is a senior IEEE member and a member of the International Council on Systems Engineering (INCOSE), the IEEE Engineering Management Society, the IEEE Information Theory Society, the Society of Concurrent Engineering (SOCE), and the Product Development and Management Association (PDMA). In 1997, he was leader of the Nationwide Metrics Task Force and has participated in the following organizations: Stanford University's Integrated Manufacturing Association/Global Supply Chain Forum, the American Society for Quality (ASQ), and MIT's Lean Aircraft Initiative.

RONALD LASSER, PH.D.

Ron Lasser has worked at PDC since 2000 and specializes in helping clients quickly recover from product development problems. He is able to increase his clients' ability to deliver projects on time and on budget by applying his years of experience managing engineering organizations.

Mr. Lasser has improved time to market for leading-edge product developments in robotic semiconductor test equipment, private line analog and digital modems, and imaging devices. His client work centers on delivering products that meet customer needs using innovation management methods, focusing projects and resources by setting strategic direction and portfolio planning, and performing beyond the enterprise with remote collaborative product development techniques. He also works to close the gap between business, technology, and product development.

Mr. Lasser started his career in telecommunications and computers developing Unix and MS-DOS-based systems and networks for AT&T Bell Laboratories. He worked in DuPont's electronic prepress business developing scanners, document processing, and color imaging products. He also was the director of engineering at General Scanning responsible for medical imaging and printing technologies.

Mr. Lasser has a Ph.D. from Carnegie Mellon University and holds M.S. and B.S. degrees in mechanical engineering, also from Carnegie Mellon University. He has completed the executive education Strategic Marketing Management program at the Harvard Business School and is a lecturer at Tufts University for courses in the Entrepreneurial Leadership Program and for the electrical engineering/computer science department. Ron is a member of Sigma Xi, a research society for learning and science, the American Society of Mechanical Engineers (ASME), and the Institute of Electrical and Electronics Engineers (IEEE).

RICHARD TAIT, PH.D.

In his role with PDC, Mr. Tait focuses on Accelerated Implementation Model (AIM™) and Product Development Process (PDP) projects. He brings a wide range of consulting insights and expertise to his work with clients.

Mr. Tait's accomplishments are highlighted by a 22-year research, management, and consulting career with DuPont that included positions as senior research physicist for DuPont Central Research and Development, planning manager for DuPont Corp. R&D Planning, and R&D lab director for DuPont Diagnostic Imaging. He also was a founding member and innovation manager for the DuPont Center for Creativity and Innovation. Mr. Tait was a codeveloper of the Institute for Inventive Thinking for the National Inventors Hall of Fame.

Mr. Tait has done extensive work with a number of companies in the chemicals industry. As a principal consultant with DuPont Consulting Solutions, he led DuPont's Corporate New Product Network and implemented rapid cycle-time product development processes in several DuPont business units. He helped lead the effort to develop and implement DuPont's Business Initiative Process for managing business growth initiatives, and he was instrumental in establishing DuPont's Asia-Pacific Venture Support Team.

Mr. Tait holds a Ph.D. in physics from Cornell and a B.S. in physics from the University of Virginia. He is a member of the American Chemical Society (ACS), the Product Development and Management Association (PDMA), and the Commercial Development and Marketing Association (CDMA). He is a certified New Product Development Professional (by the PDMA) and is a certified facilitator for the Bottom Line Innovation creative problem-solving process (by BLI Associates, Inc.).

ACKNOWLEDGMENTS

The creation of this book was due in no small measure to the dedication of our customers, who helped us explore the ins and outs of the process and allowed us to learn from their experiences.

We would like to thank all of the companies we have worked with to implement MDPD as part of division-wide or companywide standard practices. We would especially like to thank those individuals we interviewed or who informally contributed regarding their and their companies' experiences with the MDPD process and their extension of this process into portfolio management. Their quotes may or may not have made it into the final rendering; however, their input shaped every aspect of the book. Our special thanks goes to the following individuals: J. C. Paradise of Avaya Inc.; Steve Sichak of Becton Dickinson and Company; John Fowler of CNH; Deirdra Dougherty of Dade Behring, Inc.; Tony Frencham of The Dow Chemical Company; David Miller of DuPont Electronics; Lucia Buehler of Ethicon Endo-Surgery, Inc., a Johnson & Johnson Company; Deborah Nelson of Hewlett-Packard Company; Tom Luin of IBM; Kurt Schilling and Frank Konings of Johnson & Johnson; Pat Clusman of Kimberly-Clark Corporation; Don DeLauder of Medrad, Inc.; Anthony Carter of Motorola Corporation; James Euchner of Pitney Bowes, Inc.; Frank Bauer of Teradyne, Inc.; Will Hill of The Stanley Works; and Jane Mockford of Uniqema.

Thanks also goes to the following companies whose enthusiasm has helped us evolve our MDPD and VIP management processes as we've helped them with implementation: Abbott Laboratories; Agilent Technologies; Avaya Technologies; BASF; Becton Dickinson and Company; bioMerieux, Inc.; BioRad, Inc.; C.R. Bard, Inc.; Cisco Systems; Dade Behring, Inc.; Eastman

Kodak Company; Educational Testing Service; Hewlett-Packard Company; Honeywell, Inc.; Intermec Corporation; IPC Information Systems; JLG Industries, Inc.; Keithley Instruments, Inc.; LDM Technologies; Lifeway Christian Resources; LinuxCare, Inc.; Lucent Technologies; Luminex Corporation; Medrad, Inc.; Medtronic, Inc.; Mentor Graphics Corporation; Minitab Inc.; New Pig; Philips Medical Systems; Reynolds & Reynolds, Inc.; Teradyne Corporation; Tektronix, Inc.; The Chinet Company; The Nasdaq Stock Market, Inc.; The Stanley Works Corporation; Tundra Semiconductor Corporation; Uniqema; and Western Digital Corporation.

We also would like to recognize PDC's own Lyse Fontaine for her contribution to making all of these customers successful. She has worked with nearly every customer to provide support and insights on their qualitative and quantitative data.

Creating a process such as VIP management is an iterative journey. A special thanks to John Carter, founder of PDC, for the initial white paper on the value-based portfolio management practice area before he retired, and to Lyse, whose proficient skills in performing the interviews for this book made the book come alive with real stories and examples from best-in-class companies.

We are all exceptionally lucky to have such depth of knowledge in our consulting practice. Having four people actively involved in writing this book created some special challenges for our editor, Audrey Kalman. We have been blessed to have her talents and enthusiasm driving us to complete this book. This book would not have happened without Audrey's countless hours of editing, rewriting, and encouragement. Audrey's patience and gifted writing skills enabled us to collaborate successfully.

Finally, we would like to thank Lawrence Smetana, for all his insight and contributions toward the development of this book by challenging and refining all our thoughts from the large set of data we used as source materials and input. His marketing expertise, business experience, and willingness to research lent the insights of a discipline that complemented each of our backgrounds. Although we all worked as a team, the very start of the book would not have been possible without Larry's support. We owe much of the material to his interests, and we all look forward to continuing our discussion about the benefits of the combination of customer value and innovation in portfolio management with him. Thank you, Larry, for being part of this collaboration.

At J. Ross Publishing we are committed to providing today's professional with practical, hands-on tools that enhance the learning experience and give readers an opportunity to apply what they have learned. That is why we offer free ancillary materials available for download on this book and all participating Web Added Value™ publications. These online resources may include interactive versions of material that appears in the book or supplemental templates, worksheets, models, plans, case studies, proposals, spreadsheets and assessment tools, among other things. Whenever you see the WAV™ symbol in any of our publications it means bonus materials accompany the book and are available from the **Web Added Value™ Download Resource Center at www.jrosspub.com.**

Downloads available for *Value Innovation Portfolio Management: Achieving Double-Digit Growth Through Customer Value* consist of articles on collecting the voice of the customer and creating a framework for measuring innovation.

INTRODUCTION

MANAGING THE PRODUCT PORTFOLIO FOR CUSTOMER VALUE: TRANSFORMING BUSINESS DRIVERS FOR NEW PRODUCT DEVELOPMENT

Every executive who has sat through presentations by eager product managers touting hockey stick growth curves for proposed products knows that financial projections alone may not provide a meaningful assessment of a product's potential market success. Yet, given no viable alternatives, most will either shoot from the hip or resign themselves to simply going by the numbers, using metrics such as projected market share and growth, net present value, and cost/benefit analysis—even when such economic measures involve an uncomfortable amount of guesswork.

There is a better and simpler way. The key to choosing products that contribute to sustainable profitability lies in changing the business focus of portfolio management from *financial metrics* to *customer value.* Paradoxically, by putting aside financial data and giving more weight to customer value data when making product portfolio decisions, companies can in fact improve financial performance by identifying products with the potential to delight customers. Customer value, defined as the customer's perception of how well a solution meets his or her needs, is the only proven course to drive profit: The greater the value of the solution to the customer, the more likely the customer will buy it—and pay a premium price for it. And, unlike many financial projections (and contrary to the beliefs of many executives), customer value is based on something real, which you *can* accurately measure to yield trustworthy results.

REDEFINING YOUR PORTFOLIO ALONG THE VALUE DIMENSION

Just as an individual's dogged pursuit of happiness for its own sake may in fact engender misery, a myopic quest for profit may not actually yield long-term profitability. So how can companies transform their approach to portfolio management from being profit-obsessed to customer value-driven?

The first step is to examine how the company defines portfolio management and how well—or poorly—its product portfolio meshes with its business strategy. In our work with scores of companies, we have encountered many that divorce portfolio management from business strategy. They consider only how much of the R&D budget they will allocate to each project to maximize the calculated value of the total portfolio. While R&D resources do have dollar values and efficient resource allocation is a valid concern, in our experience this view leads to overreliance on financial metrics and a narrow focus on individual products and their revenues and costs. By contrast, those companies that approach portfolio management holistically, considering how their allocation of resources maps to strategy, and include in those decisions all functions in the company, from sales and distribution to support and manufacturing, make sounder product portfolio decisions and create products that better match customer needs.

We have observed another serious problem. Portfolio management, product realization, and business strategy can become disconnected from each other when decisions about which products to build are divorced from the company's vision and mission. Several factors contribute to this disengagement:

- **Process.** Product development often is managed using the phase-gate review process, a methodology concerned with schedule and resource management. Phase-gate reviews can be isolated from the portfolio and unsuited to the dynamic nature of products and markets.
- **Turf.** Companies believe that product development is an R&D thing. R&D is not part of business strategy, which is a business thing. Product management is for lower levels of management. Departmental functions (often referred to as silos) in the

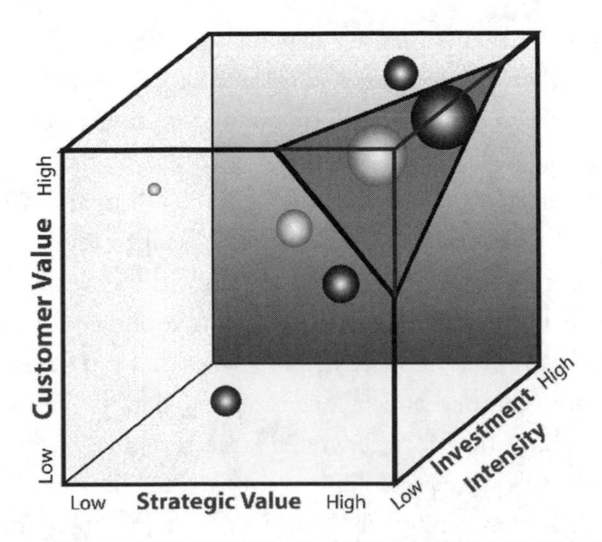

Figure I.1 Identifying the sweet spot for new portfolio projects at the intersection of high customer value, high strategic value, and optimal investment intensity.

organization take ownership of—or set up barriers to—successful product development efforts.

- **Personality.** Business managers think, *We're on the business side and product development is too technical.* R&D looks at marketing and thinks, *What do they know? Marketing is an art, not a science.* The overarching problem is that, for many companies, portfolio management is not aligned with new product development. Further, while many companies create cross-functional teams at the operational level, senior-level teams often *don't* operate cross-functionally.

When deciding which projects to fund in the portfolio, executives must consider not only cost but also the customer value delivered by the project in relationship to the company's strategic goals. As Figure I.1 shows, the intersection of high customer value, high strategic value (aligned with the strategy of the business unit or enterprise), and optimal investment intensity (the level and profile of resources invested in a new product or venture) is the *sweet spot* for new portfolio projects.

Optimal investment intensity depends on the specific product and the company's market. Sometimes a company needs to make a high level of investment—and do it quickly—to enter and dominate a new market or a new technology. If the new market or technology offers high customer value, high investment intensity is justifiable and desirable. Sometimes low investment intensity is right because creating an incremental product may be the right thing to do. For example, Apple's iPod Nano was a new product requiring a major investment in R&D and manufacturing tooling, while its predecessor, the 4 GB iPod Mini, was an incremental release that improved on its forerunner with more memory and a longer-lasting battery. Both met customer requirements—and therefore generated large revenues—with different levels of investment. A healthy portfolio is composed of a balance of products that span the range from new-to-the-world to incremental. Where a company finds its sweet spot depends on what it needs to do to solve the customer's problem using its core competencies or partnering with others.

The representation of various portfolio factors in three dimensions, with customer value assuming a place alongside strategic value and investment intensity, drives home the point that monetary investment should not be the sole barometer of new product development. "We can calculate all kinds of stuff out to 10 decimal places, 100 if you want," says Don DeLauder, director of product innovation and advanced development at Medrad, Inc. "But it's all gibberish. The degree of uncertainty in the inputs to those calculations is so high that it's almost nonsensical to make the calculations." Instead, DeLauder says, "You have to use a balance of judgment and some estimates driven by market research."

Finally, one of the biggest problems in the area of product portfolio management is poor or nonexistent guidance of the portfolio by senior management. Senior management too often ignores portfolio management altogether or ties it to an *internal* metric—profit—rather than an *external* one like customer value. This is a tempting trap, because profit seems easy to measure, while customer value seems far less tangible and much harder to quantify. However, you *can* in fact measure customer value and use it to guide portfolio decisions. This book is about why you should and about the mind-set, decisions, and business practices required to successfully align your portfolio along customer value dimensions.

GETTING TO VALUE: A NEW DEFINITION OF PORTFOLIO MANAGEMENT

Twenty-first-century portfolio management requires an integration of competencies, hierarchies, strategies, and tactics. It's an enormous management challenge, and one that companies can't afford to ignore. This book argues that mastering integrated, customer-centric portfolio management is the most important accomplishment any senior executive team can strive for—one that will pay off for years to come in better products, higher profits, and happier customers. We advance the idea that portfolio management will build greater competitive advantage and generate larger economic value if it is tied to customer value. This does not discount other approaches such as financial analysis, but it adds a vital and more significant parameter.

The ideas advocated in this book compose what we call *Value Innovation Portfolio™ (VIP) management*, which we believe is the key to building and sustaining a winning position in the marketplace. Why did we choose this title and name?

- **Value.** Because we believe the fundamental driver for decision making on where to go should be the value created for the customer
- **Innovation.** Because innovation is the ultimate output of your development activities—that is, the new value you want to introduce to the marketplace
- **Portfolio.** Because it is through the full basket of products, services, and related product life cycle, support, and delivery projects that you effectively create that value
- **Management.** Because none of this will happen without thoughtful, active senior management guidance and direction through a systematic and structured framework

This approach uses techniques that uncover customer value so corporate managers can base portfolio decisions on factual, objective data about what customers will value. Far more encompassing than the traditional portfolio management goals of allocating resources and choosing among proposed product ideas, the VIP approach to portfolio management leads to a product portfolio that

- Delights customers by delivering total solutions to customer problems
- Aligns new products with the strategic goals of the company
- Optimizes investment intensity to ensure the right amount of investment at the right time and in the right places depending on a product's role in the portfolio

The prevailing focus of portfolio management must expand to encompass more than just development resource allocation. Resource allocation—figuring out what R&D should do over the next year, how much money it needs, and how many people it requires—may have been a worthy overarching focus in a simpler business environment. But today, products are complex, competition is tough and multifaceted, differentiation is the mantra of success, and long cycle times cripple even the best products. The question becomes how to create economic value in the face of these challenges. The answer is to take a broader view of resource allocation, to make sure that senior management views portfolio management as a strategic, not tactical, tool, *and* to tie portfolio management explicitly to customer value.

The creation and success of FedEx Corporation exemplifies this. FedEx provides the same services as the U.S. Postal Service, but with greater speed, reliability, traceability, and accountability. It saves time, which its customers value and are willing to pay a premium to get. It also ensures that shipments arrive when specified, offering security in addition to speed. Creating services that reduce time and increase delivery reliability, traceability, or accountability has driven product development at FedEx. Developments such as wireless communications with portable computers, Internet tracking, bar coding, and radio frequency identification all offer opportunities to solve real customer problems, and therefore the potential to increase the value of FedEx services to the customer.

In the VIP approach, portfolio management never stands alone. Strategic planning, information gathering, and capability assessment precede it. Project

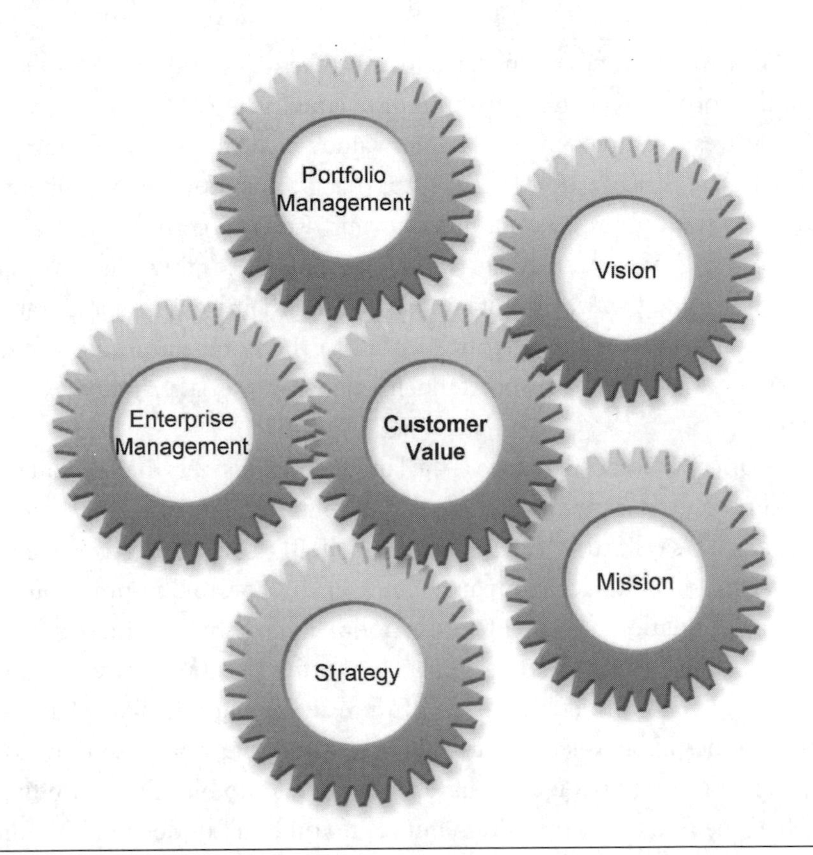

Figure I.2 This representation of the corporate environment as a planetary gear shows customer value as the central driver.

management, implementation, and risk mitigation follow it. The effectiveness of the VIP approach depends on the results of the new product development process and project management.

Figure I.2 shows a view of a corporate environment that embraces a VIP management approach. The center gear—customer value—provides the system's input, driving the motion of the other gears. This illustrates the interconnectedness of the portfolio management process with other key aspects of the business, its essential place among other strategic executive concerns, and the primacy of customer value as a driver for the other concerns. All other activities, whether internal processes such as sales metrics or externally focused ones such as competitive strategy, must mesh with the mission, vision, strategy, customer value, and management of the enterprise. If one area is not functioning well or is not aligned, it slips out of synch with adjacent areas and throws the corporate environment out of balance.

Executives must recognize customer value's rightful place at the nexus of the gear system, since a successful VIP approach to portfolio management is a strategic, integrated process that goes beyond R&D to connect with a company's core business strategy. As we describe in upcoming chapters, some executives operate this way intuitively, describing their work as comparable to juggling many balls without letting any fall to the floor. Rarely, however, do they explicitly acknowledge portfolio management as a primary executive concern.

"Historically, because finance is the language of business, before you make a decision as a general manager to do something it's mandatory that you have the financials," says Steve Sichak, president of BD Diagnostics-Preanalytical Systems, a medical device company. However, he goes on to point out that "there's a foundational element to portfolio management, which is a deep understanding of your customer and deep understanding of their requirements, and their future direction, and future requirements. If you have that, then it becomes much easier to prioritize and amongst projects, and by extension, your resources. If you don't have that, you end up blindly responding to IRR, NPV, the financial projections, but . . . if you don't understand customer needs, you run the risk of making flawed projections and flawed decisions."

WHAT YOU MEASURE GETS DONE: SENIOR MANAGEMENT IS NOT LINED UP BEHIND PORTFOLIO MANAGEMENT

To come into being, all of the potential projects in a portfolio must pass through a company's new product development process. New product development is the machine that transforms the portfolio into reality.

Senior managers rate portfolio management as a very important management concern.[1] However, despite this avowed commitment to portfolio management, only 34 percent of businesses built new product development metrics into senior managers' annual performance objectives. The best-performing companies measured 50 percent of management with new product development metrics. The worst reported including such metrics for a mere

14 percent.[2] Although management considers new product development vital to the continued success of the business, more than half of the companies studied don't use new product development as a metric to gauge senior management performance. There is dissonance between what senior managers *believe* is important and the actual factors that go into defining success and measuring performance.

A larger problem is that portfolio management often fails to appear at all on senior management's radar screen, perhaps because it has never delivered on its promise to help companies spend money on the *right* development projects.[3] By delegating portfolio management to lower levels of the organization, senior managers treat it as a tactical activity related to allocating product development resources, mitigating risk, and accelerating individual projects. The process of portfolio management is not always viewed as part of the strategic undertaking of meeting customer needs through valuable products and services.

One company that *has* elevated portfolio management to a strategic level is tool, security, and hardware company The Stanley Works. "I was VP of engineering and technology, which gave me the [necessary] influence—people listen when you report to the CEO and you're a corporate officer," says The Stanley Works' William Hill. "I see that as one of the things that is missing in so many companies. They push [portfolio management] down into the organization and say, OK, this is just another business process. Our CEO used to say 'new products are the lifeblood of any manufacturing company,' and I happen to believe that." Hill has more than his personal belief to go on; he has the company's phenomenal success. In 1996, according to Hill, the company sold $73 million in new products. Hill joined in 1997, with a mandate to increase the percentage of revenue from new products. "In the 2000 to 2001 time frame we did $300 million worth of new products. And the definition was much crisper at the $300 million point; they were products that were new in that year. They weren't line extensions, they weren't repackaging . . . In 1996 we got about $3 of new products out for every $1 we put in to engineering and technology. Through this [portfolio management] process, by 2001 we got close to $10 out for every dollar we put in." By putting portfolio management on the senior executive radar screen, The Stanley Works generated valuable solutions for customers, economic value for its shareholders, and the organizational robustness to weather the economic downturn of 2001 and 2002.

WHY THE STATUS QUO DOESN'T WORK

Portfolio management is not a new discipline. Yet many executives believe they don't do it well.[4] This certainly is not due to lack of advice. The literature is replete with methodologies that profess to help companies determine which products will be most successful: The Boston Consulting Group's Growth-Share Matrix[5] classifies products as cash cows, stars, dogs, or question marks. Bubble diagrams identifying the position of products in the portfolio help companies place products in their life cycle, clarify risk/reward relationships, rank projects in relation to one another, and compare costs. New software programs help manage, evaluate, and chart projects in the portfolio pipeline. At portfolio management conferences, companies espouse methodologies by describing improvements in process implementations for their portfolios.

Unfortunately, many of these tools offer lagging indicators that aid in classifying, comparing, and monitoring existing products, rather than determining the future composition of the portfolio. Such tools may be valuable for a retrospective view of the portfolio, but they may not integrate portfolio management with other activities such as innovation and don't address the issue of how to fill market gaps unfilled by existing products. The larger issue is that most of these tools are financially driven, using as one of the axes a measurement such as revenue, profit, net present value, R&D spending, or some other financial value.

Further, most literature and many methodologies and tools (usually software) address portfolio management only from an internal (company) perspective. Even those that appear to take an external (customer) view by advocating customer interviews or focus groups often are fooling themselves, because their approaches fail to capture the customer's true, deeply experienced needs. Simply talking to customers, which many companies believe is adequate for gathering customer input, does not rigorously capture the data necessary to use customer value as a yardstick for portfolio decisions.

One of the primary methodologies companies currently use to evaluate progress and help senior management stay involved is the *phase-gate review process*, during which management evaluates existing project plans and reviews schedule slips, budget metrics, and overall project plan execution. By itself, the phase-gate review process is useful for managing individual projects in the pipeline, but it can't help with the bigger questions of which projects or opportunities the portfolio should include unless it is tied to portfolio decisions. Further, when phase-gate reviews are not linked to a portfolio management approach such as VIP, schedule slips or cost overruns for one project may wreak havoc on the portfolio by disrupting resources for other projects.

If senior managers rely on a process such as phase-gate review, which is isolated from larger customer value concerns, as the sole mechanism for managing products in the portfolio pipeline, they may fail to take action at significant milestones. For example, Kimberly-Clark thought it saw an enormous potential market for premoistened toilet paper. (Yes—wet toilet paper!) Early in 2001 the company unfurled Cottonelle Fresh Rollwipes, spending $100 million on R&D. Two years later, Rollwipes was still in test marketing.[6] Perhaps, if those overseeing portfolio management at Kimberly-Clark had used a success metric that included customer value, the managers who continued to green-light Rollwipes development would have dropped the project before incurring a $100 million expense.

WHY THE VIP APPROACH TO PORTFOLIO MANAGEMENT WORKS

en·vi·ron·ment n.[7]

1. *The circumstances or conditions that surround one; surroundings.*
2. *The totality of circumstances surrounding an organism or group of organisms, especially . . . The combination of external physical conditions that affect and influence the growth, development, and survival of organisms.*

Just as the natural environment must be in balance to support life, so the corporate environment must be in balance to support the development and growth of new products. The planetary gear image in Figure I.3 is a variation of Figure I.2 in which the individual outside gears become a single ring gear representing the value innovation portfolio (VIP). In Figure I.3, representing business functions via the planetary gear captures more real-world complexity. Not only must the internal gears mesh, they must work together with larger internal and external issues driving the organization. The VIP encompasses mission, vision, strategy, the internal workings of the enterprise (new product development, project value propositions, resource requirements, pipeline portfolio, sales and operating metrics, product life cycles), and external environmental factors (customer needs, market dynamics, competitive and technological developments). This establishes the environment for the VIP approach to portfolio management. Customer value, the essential driver, remains at the center.

While process elements remain important, companies that can shift the conception of portfolio management from *process* to *environment* will be more successful. How you balance all the competing elements is the real test of whether the product portfolio environment is working. The price for an out-of-balance environment is waste and failure. Companies squander valuable time and financial, technological, and human resources at an alarming rate. Often projects consume and waste resources for far too long before anyone recognizes them as losers and cancels them. A VIP approach to portfolio management can avert or at least mitigate costly mistakes such as Kimberly-Clark's ill-fated Rollwipes. In fact, Kimberly-Clark has now adopted a customer-value-driven approach to portfolio management, which has helped them avoid such missteps and make the products they offer more relevant to customers.

The role of VIP management is to assist senior executives in identifying potential market opportunities and discriminating between successful and unsuccessful projects *as early as possible* to optimize portfolio decisions. VIP management, unlike more narrowly defined approaches to portfolio management, results in objective metrics that can be used throughout the selection and development cycle. It leads to thoroughly defining market/customer requirements in repeatable, measurable terms and reduces dependency on individual senior staff's knowledge and opinions. Because it is based on facts,

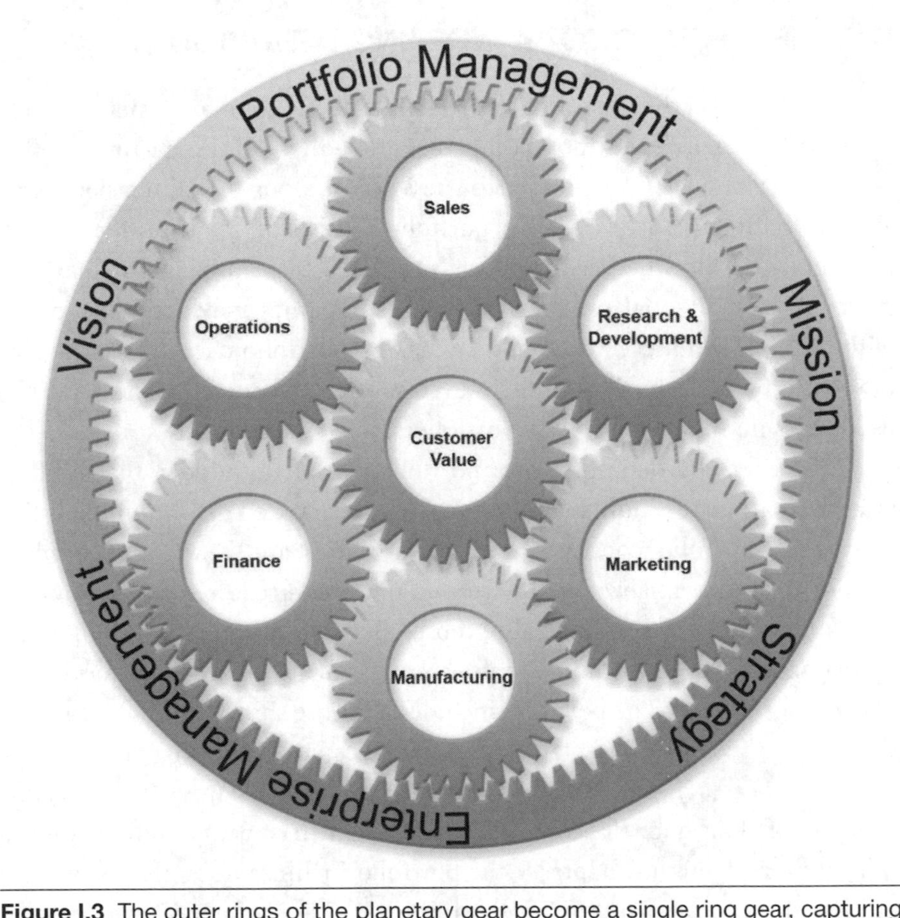

Figure I.3 The outer rings of the planetary gear become a single ring gear, capturing both the complexity and interconnectedness of the business functions.

not opinions, VIP management provides you with the necessary criteria to evaluate a product or service solution—not just whether it meets a set of internal specifications, but whether it provides customer value. Further, it can lead to the discovery of customers' latent requirements or delighters that can enable companies to introduce truly innovative products. And, as we outline throughout this book—but especially in Chapters 2 and 3—customer value and innovation can coexist, linked by corporate strategy.

WHAT IS A PORTFOLIO? A WORKING DEFINITION

As we indicated earlier, many companies view portfolio management too narrowly. In our experience, most companies also adhere to too narrow a definition of the word *portfolio*. This narrowness occurs along two dimensions: scale and depth. In the broadest sense, a portfolio consists of items to which a company must decide whether to allocate resources. Instead of just managing a portfolio of individual products, as small companies may, large companies with multiple product lines should be making portfolio decisions at the level of the product line, business unit, or even subsidiary company. The principles we discuss in this book apply to portfolio management on any scale.

To deepen the definition of a portfolio, we offer the idea that product portfolios are about more than products. This expanded definition holds that a product portfolio consists of all the products and services a company intends to commercialize *and* the related initiatives required to improve the company's ability to commercialize those offerings. A company selling packaged frozen food, for example, must conceive of its portfolio as more than plastic bags of peas. The portfolio includes all those things necessary to bring the peas to a consumer's table: processing capability, refrigerated trucks, refrigerator cases in grocery stores, and even in some instances the marketing campaign required to tell people why these are the best peas to buy. As we discuss in more detail in Chapter 8, the portfolio includes not only the product but also the associated technologies on which it's based, the infrastructure that supports it, and the marketing activities that impact it.

While the portfolio management process as we present it includes a wide range of activities, we want to clarify the demarcation between *portfolio management* and *product definition*, because many of the customer-oriented, value-seeking actions we identify for managing the portfolio also apply to product definition. Most significantly, the *overseers* and the *outcomes* of portfolio management and product definition are different. Executives are responsible for portfolio management (or ought to be), while high-level managers do not necessarily play a role in defining individual products. The output of the portfolio definition process can be thought of as the definition of a collection of *gaps in the market* that need to be filled (the portfolio roadmap described in Chapter 4), while the output of product definition is a *description of the fea-*

tures of a product that will fill the customer needs. Once a project's mission is clear at a portfolio level, each product development project can begin with its own initiative for gathering further customer data. Of course, portfolio management and product definition occur along a continuum, which is why the two-way communication we discuss in Chapter 6 is so important.

Finally, here's what we *don't* mean when we say the word portfolio: We don't mean a *financial* portfolio—stocks, bonds, and other financial investments. We don't mean a *project* portfolio, which, while it may contain projects related to the product portfolio, is more tactical and related to project management.

THE PAYOFF FOR MASTERING VIP MANAGEMENT

VIP management is the bridge between business strategy and realization. Companies build this bridge by executing project management, technical development, production, delivery, sales, and service. They traverse the bridge by meeting customer demand as customers perceive the product's value for solving a problem or eliminating pain. Without an environment in which strategy and tactics are connected, the momentum to cross the bridge remains latent. VIP management ensures this connection, releasing the energy needed to turn company strategy—the vision, mission, and objectives—into reality.

Defining a roadmap for future products in a VIP environment is difficult, but the payoff is a portfolio that optimizes value to the customer. It's an undertaking that rightly belongs to senior management to initiate, champion, and own. Making a commitment at the executive level to tie portfolio management explicitly to customer value can mean the difference between running a company that limps along into oblivion and one that grows impressively, returns great value to stakeholders, and stands out as best in class.

WHAT'S IN THE REST OF THE BOOK?

This book presents VIP management as essential to the environment in which twenty-first-century companies must operate to survive and grow. Drawing upon thousands of hours of direct experience with Product Development

Consulting, Inc. (PDC) customers and other best-in-class companies, as well as many hours of interviews, cross-industry benchmarking, and related research, this book will help senior managers focus their organizations and efforts to make cash flow, revenue, and risks more predictable—an undertaking that goes over well in every boardroom. Readers will come away with a thorough understanding of the essential elements of VIP management, how their companies measure up, and how a VIP approach can help increase the gap between their products and the competition's.

Chapter 1: Understanding Customer Value: The Grounded Portfolio

Even experts hold conflicting opinions about what makes for success in introducing new products. This chapter posits that the answer lies in unearthing what customers value and that delivering customer value is the foundation for the organization's existence, culture, markets, and operational framework. No matter the company's goals, it must consider portfolio management from the customer's perspective rather than from an internally guided point of view. This chapter examines what value really means to customers. We argue that companies can—and must—measure customer value, and that senior executives must take responsibility for the delivery of that value through the product portfolio.

Chapter 2: Understanding the Role of Innovation: The Relevant Portfolio

Most executives feel at a gut level that innovation somehow connects integrally with their companies' ability to excel in a chosen market and that selecting the most innovative products for their portfolios will bring success. Many senior executives will tell you they suffer no shortage of ideas, yet they often lack the ability to tell which ideas will become profitable new enterprises. The process of transforming an innovation into an attractive opportunity is complicated. This chapter is about setting the context for defining and executing that process. We look at the role of innovation in the portfolio, at whether innovation is always necessary, and if it is, how it can be transformed through the process of commercialization into something that delivers value to customers.

Chapter 3: Vision, Mission, Strategy, and Value: The Intentional Portfolio

When vision, mission, and strategy are aligned, unambiguous, and set a clear direction, they keep the business on course. This chapter reviews our definitions of these common business terms, explores what strategic value means in the context of a customer-value-driven portfolio, and considers vision, mission, strategy, customer value, and portfolio development as a continuing information loop with each part influenced by the others. From that perspective, companies need to understand how to achieve balance in the portfolio—not balance as usually defined, as simply risk/reward or investment/return on two sides of a scale, but balance in terms of bringing into equilibrium the various strategic purposes of the products you decide to finance. Finally, we look at outsourcing, a business practice that, when elevated to a strategic level, becomes part of the balancing of the portfolio related to investment intensity.

Chapter 4: Aiming for the Sweet Spot: The Optimized Portfolio

A sweet spot is that figurative juncture where a variety of factors come together to produce favorable conditions for success. Companies may aim to hit the sweet spot with product introductions, but studies show that *half the time*, companies fail to either identify the market sweet spot or to conduct business in such a way as to create a portfolio that targets it. In this chapter, we look at what goes into determining the sweet spot for your portfolio and the challenging process of whittling down the number of potential projects to pursue. By ensuring that projects are aimed at the sweet spot, then further filtering them based on criteria relevant to your company and market space, you can dramatically raise your portfolio batting average, spending precious resources on those projects destined to become market winners and killing early those that won't. We also take a fresh look at what it means to balance the portfolio.

Chapter 5: Accurate Customer Value Data: The Measured Portfolio

Preparation is a huge part of creating the VIP described in this book, and a big part of that preparation is gathering all the information you need to make informed decisions. This chapter is devoted to the framework and tools for obtaining accurate customer data. While you may be anxious to begin mapping out your portfolio, collecting and verifying customer data is the essential foundation of the VIP, without which your portfolio won't have staying power. This chapter offers an overview of the process of gathering quantifiable, reliable data on what customers value.

Chapter 6: Aligning the Organization: The Supported Portfolio

Only when the actions of everyone in the company are fully aligned to support the portfolio can the VIP come to life. At the moment of creation, your newly conceived portfolio may be the company's best-kept secret; only a handful of people outside of the management team that spearheaded the effort may know anything about it. It's impossible to achieve alignment when most of the company is in the dark! Now, senior management's job is to effectively communicate the portfolio—and the customer needs that spawned the portfolio—to the rest of the company. This chapter offers a way of simultaneously deploying and communicating the portfolio using the deployment tree, a method PDC has created (and successfully applied at numerous companies) for translating corporate strategy into relevant action.

Chapter 7: Elements of Realization: The Actionable Portfolio

It takes the actions of an entire organization, working together, to realize a goal such as the VIP. Getting there from where you are today means changing not only the way senior executives think about portfolio decisions, but changing the way everyone in the company thinks about their jobs and relationships. You need the right people working on the right tasks, following well-designed plans as part of competent and well-coordinated cross-functional teams, inspired and supported by senior management. This chapter considers the organizational and interpersonal elements of manifesting a VIP. Using established frameworks for evaluating personality types and work styles, we look at whether your organization may need to change to match your portfolio goals. And we highlight a key difference in the VIP approach that can make your cross-functional teams more successful regardless of the personality types that compose them.

Chapter 8: Appreciating Investment Intensity: The Fortified Portfolio

When you first identified the market sweet spot and began to construct your portfolio to target that sweet spot, you considered the issue of portfolio balance and analyzed what each potential project required, including investment intensity—that is, the level of resources required for success and the customer and strategic value this investment could create. Investment intensity is an ongoing concern that impinges on almost all areas of the company's operations. It always involves balancing competing priorities and considering the supporting elements to make the portfolio a reality. Paying the proper level of attention to these key supporting elements often spells the difference between a market winner and a failure. This chapter looks at these key supporting elements and their implications for the cross-functional team charged with transforming ideas and plans into tangible products and services.

Chapter 9: Keeping the Fires Burning: The Dynamic Portfolio

Any portfolio must be dynamic because it exists in a world of change. Your company may be blindsided without a dynamic portfolio review process. This chapter is about that process and about what's necessary to ensure that the portfolio, ablaze with possibility at the moment of inception, can adapt and thrive in a changing world. It looks at the changes in thinking you may need, as well as what's necessary to build synergies among projects and develop a culture that accommodates the dynamic nature of VIP management. We introduce the idea of dynamic governance, a process for making portfolio management part of a company's day-to-day operations, and explore the further use of deployment trees as they pertain to evaluating portfolio performance over time.

Chapter 10: A Talent for Change: The Sustainable Portfolio

Changing the business procedures and processes of any organization is a major undertaking. Usually, there's no shortage of good ideas about how to change business processes. The shortage is in the tools and ability to incorporate change into a company's daily operations. Success with VIP management requires more than simply recognizing it as a good idea. It requires a new approach to planning, executing, and measuring change. This chapter looks at how you can successfully introduce change to an organization. We examine ways that ensure your new portfolio management process makes it beyond the pilot stage by making your organization adept at the process of change itself. We look at how institutionalizing the VIP approach allows it to live on beyond its originators.

NOTES

1. Robert G. Cooper, Scott J. Edgett, and Elko J Kleinschmidt, *Portfolio Management for New Products* (New York: Perseus Books Group, 2001).
2. Robert G. Cooper, Scott J. Edgett, and Elko J Kleinschmidt, *Benchmarking Best Products in Product Innovation: The Role of Senior Management.* This study compares senior management commitment to new product development for best performers and worst performers.
3. According to a 2004 study by the PDMA (Product Development and Management Association), fewer than 20 percent of new product ideas reach commercialization. At each stage, however (idea screening, business analysis, development, testing), companies are spending money on which they receive no return if they eliminate the product before it reaches commercialization.
4. Robert G. Cooper, Scott J. Edgett, and Elko J Kleinschmidt, *Portfolio Management for New Products.*
5. See BCG's Web site: www.bcg.com/this_is_bcg/mission/growth_share_matrix.jsp.

6. Emily Nelson, "The Tissue That Tanked," *Wall Street Journal*, Classroom Edition, September 2002.
7. From www.dictionary.com.

1

UNDERSTANDING CUSTOMER VALUE: THE GROUNDED PORTFOLIO

Schering-Plough Corporation says that the U.S. launch of PEG-INTRON® (peginterferon alfa-2b) Powder for Injection and REBETOL® (ribavirin, USP) Capsules combination therapy has been the most successful new product introduction in the company's history, as measured by product sales.

—Product News in Brief, Drug Cost Management Report, January, 2003

The result of Titleist's process technologies, product design, and intellectual property protection efforts was the Titleist Pro V1. Introduced on the PGA Tour in fall 2000 and to the market in January 2001 to instant acclaim, the Pro V1 quickly became the most successful golf ball introduction in Titleist's and the game's history.

—From corporate press release: Titleist Pro V1 and Pro V1x Technology Leadership

Laserscope, a small maker of medical lasers and advanced fiber optic devices . . . saw revenues increase 63 percent in 2004. The product was a KTP (single-wavelength laser) system for treating enlarged prostates.

Sales of that product nearly tripled and company revenue increased to nearly $100 million.
—*"America's Fastest-Growing Small Public Companies," Fortune Small Business, July/August 2005*

Every company dreams of a category-busting new product, a launch that defies all expectations, an item that catches on with buyers, spreads like wildfire, and becomes a business legend. Such introductions don't arise spontaneously. They result from many factors, each of which may be necessary but not sufficient on its own to propel a new product into the sales stratosphere. Even experts hold conflicting opinions about what makes for success in introducing new products. Ask the question of product development professionals or executives responsible for product development and you'll get a variety of answers—everything from good management and a rigorous development process to Six Sigma and great development talent.

This chapter posits that the answer to that question lies in unearthing what customers value, and that delivering customer value is the foundation for the organization's existence, culture, markets, and operational framework. Whether a company strives for operational excellence, product leadership, superior customer service, or some other goal, it must consider portfolio management from the customer's perspective rather than from an internally guided point of view. We'll look at what value really means to customers. We'll argue that companies can—and must—measure customer value, and that senior executives must take responsibility for the delivery of that value through the product portfolio.

EVIDENCE OF THE LEADING CAUSE OF PRODUCT DEVELOPMENT FAILURE

Since conducting its first comprehensive study of new product development (NPD) practices in 1990, the Product Development and Management Association (PDMA) Foundation has offered evidence-based answers to the question of what causes new products to fail. PDMA conducted a second study in 1995 and a third in 2004. The findings reveal some thought-provoking insights into the relationship between portfolio management practices and product success.

The 2004 study[1] found that 55 percent of 416 respondents[2] had in place a well-defined, structured process for portfolio management. Forty-six percent had both a portfolio management process and a strategy. New development processes have increased dramatically in the past nine years, and cycle times and process efficiencies have improved. Cross-functional development teams are the norm.

These results sound great, until you consider some of the study's conclusions. Compared to 1995, in 2004:

- Overall *sales and profits* from new products *declined.*
- Incremental new products increased as a percentage of total projects in the portfolio *at the expense of more innovative new products.*
- Overall *success rates* of commercialized products had not changed. (In the 1990 study, 58 percent of new products were considered successful, versus 59 percent in the 1995 and 2004 studies. The success rate, as measured by sales and profits, remained essentially unchanged despite process improvements.)

Nor was this the total story revealed by the PDMA study. The respondents' varying degrees of success allowed PDMA to categorize them into "the best" (96 companies or one-quarter of respondents) and "the rest."[3] The best companies had considerably more success with NPD than their counterparts in the bottom three-quarters:

- The percentage of new products that were successful for the best companies was 75.5, compared to only 53.8 for the rest.
- 72.4 percent of new products at the best companies were successful in terms of profitability, versus 47.3 percent for the rest.
- New product sales as a percentage of total sales was 47.6 for the best and less than half that (21.4) for the rest.
- Profits from new products as a percentage of total profits was also higher: 49.1 percent versus 21.2 percent.

To us, these results say that process improvements, use of market research, and tools for engineering, R&D, design, and technology helped top-tier companies improve their performance. But while use of these tools and methodologies was necessary, it was not completely sufficient for success. Nearly 76 percent of the companies in the study significantly lagged behind their counterparts in NPD and portfolio management by every measure.

What accounts for this difference? The PDMA study itself concluded that the leading cause of product failure is "not understanding the customer."[4]

The experience of companies like Hewlett-Packard supports the corollary: Success arises from understanding the customer. "The more closely we work with customers in the development of a new product, the more successful we're going to be," says Deborah Nelson, vice president of Marketing and Alliances for Technology Solutions Group at Hewlett-Packard (HP). "So it's not just that you take customer input, you get an idea, you go away, you build the product and then bring it to market. It's much more of an iterative checking in with customers." Nelson states HP's commitment unequivocally: "Customers have to be the source of whatever we're doing. They have to. Whatever we're working on fundamentally needs to fulfill a customer need."

FISCAL FOCUS VS. CUSTOMER VALUE FOCUS

Companies that consistently deliver value to their customers with new products or services succeed. Those that do not deliver such value limp along or ultimately fail. Yet executives and managers often overlook this fact when managing company portfolios, as evidenced by another area examined in the PDMA study. One study question asked respondents to rank the tools and techniques they use for portfolio management, which they did as follows:

1. Rank ordering of projects
2. Discounted cash flow
3. Checklists
4. Scoring models
5. Strategic buckets
6. Option pricing or expected commercial value
7. Bubble diagrams or portfolio maps

Customer value is conspicuously absent. Although respondents may have implicitly incorporated customer value into these techniques, none *explicitly* cited—and therefore acknowledged the significance of—customer value as the driving criterion.

When evaluating their portfolios, too many executives rely on the analytical measures represented by the tools above such as financial projections, competitive positioning, market share, risk/reward, and time to market to decide among projects for the portfolio. They do so in the belief that evaluation by the numbers represents good business judgment. After all, most executive performance is evaluated by the numbers. The premier business schools in the United States and elsewhere teach that the numbers tell the story. Logically, executives look to select projects that deliver the greatest profit. Besides, they reason, what other factual data exist upon which they can base resource allocation?

The answer is *value to the customer*. Contrary to popular belief, value to the customer *can* be accurately measured based on facts. Using a documented, repeatable process, companies can collect information that represents the true voice of the customer (VOC). The process, which we describe in more detail in Chapter 5, involves interviewing techniques that use probing questions, digging down for the so-called golden nuggets, storytelling about customer problems, and using structured first-hand observation followed by quantitative Kano analysis.[5] With these methods, companies can determine the functionality that products must satisfy, as well as those features that delight, disgust, or elicit indifference in customers. With this data in hand, companies can separate potential winners from losers *before* launching into product development. Taking this method of analysis up a level to executive management allows companies to evaluate entire product portfolios using customer value as a yardstick.

The consumer packaged goods industry provides an enlightening portrait of what can happen when financial considerations trump customer focus. Beginning in the late 1800s, the industry provided good value and real returns for stockholders, customers, retailers, and other stakeholders. The industry grew with the population through the mid-twentieth century. Products proliferated. Companies such as Lever Brothers, Colgate-Palmolive, and General

Mills filled store shelves with an ever-increasing number of brands and incremental additions—new flavors of toothpaste, general cleaners, bath cleaners, specialized cleaners, breakfast cereals, stronger papers, tougher wipes, and clingier sealing wraps.

By the early 1960s, consumer packaged goods companies began focusing on increasing revenue growth and market share by pushing more products out the door each year to make the numbers. Incremental product development, an approach that became the norm and worked effectively through the 1960s and 1970s, began to falter during the 1980s and 1990s as the marketplace changed. New purchasing venues such as shopping clubs, super-retailers like Wal-Mart, and deep discounters were replacing traditional department stores and supermarkets as the major channels to consumers.

Not only were the consumer packaged goods companies losing pricing power, but also, more importantly, they were losing customers. Why? They lost sight of what customers valued. Brand proliferation was rampant, perhaps even out of control, confusing customers with a blizzard of brand names and messages. The companies' organizational structures also were out of control. Duplicate management teams, sales forces, warehouses, accounting systems, and manufacturing locations often worked at cross-purposes. Many companies were not operating with a unified vision, mission, or strategy, but simply were trying to outpace the previous year's revenue. Companies enhanced revenue through acquisitions and bolstered profits by cutting costs and restructuring. This model is still operating today at some of the largest consumer packaged goods companies. (Procter & Gamble acquired Gillette in 2005.)

A different story, however, is unfolding at The Clorox Company. Clorox focuses on building brands that make people's lives easier, healthier, and better by creating products that are the number one or strong number two brands in each market segment. During the heyday of the consumer packaged goods industry, the company built decades of success primarily on the strength of its number one and two leadership brand positions. This approach to success is still necessary, but no longer sufficient. According to former Clorox president and CEO Gerald E. Johnston, Clorox is also "all about winning . . . with consumers . . . with customers . . . with shareholders." That means owning a strong advantaged market position that delivers and sustains

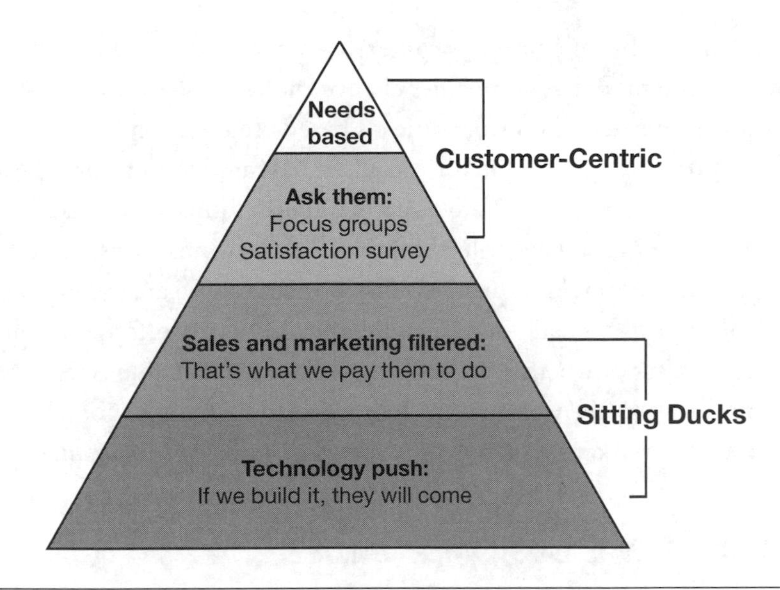

Figure 1.1 PDC's hierarchy of customer value.

exceptional returns. Now, as Johnston wrote in the firm's 2004 annual report (emphasis ours): "*Identifying and satisfying consumer needs* with brands and products is at the heart of everything we do . . . we believe this is about having *world-class consumer insights* . . . We then *deploy those insights* to develop consumer-preferred products . . . to better target consumer segments and to communicate with consumers." In 2004, Clorox evaluated its portfolios, businesses, and countries in which it operates. The management team targeted for removal weak brand positions that didn't have potential to win in the marketplace.

By defining products to include in the Clorox portfolio that can win in the marketplace because of their *value to consumers*, Clorox is undertaking a Value Innovation Portfolio (VIP) approach, albeit without labeling it as such. The essence of VIP is ongoing examination of products in the portfolio and potential investment in new product development driven by consumer needs.

Figure 1.1, our hierarchy of customer value, borrows from the ideas of psychologist Abraham Maslow, who proposed the theory that humans seek to satisfy progressively higher needs. As people's basic physiological needs are met, they seek to satisfy communal and spiritual needs, which appear at the top of the hierarchy. In a business context, this pyramid shows a kind of progressive enlightenment as companies change their focus from internal (technology push) to external (customer needs based) to create the VIP.

In proposing a new metric for executives facing difficult portfolio management decisions, we do not advocate the elimination of the business case. Rather, we introduce a new criterion project leaders must satisfy *before* allocating precious resources to projects. The question to be answered is simple: Will the new project create or increase the value of our offering to the customer? Regardless of whether the project is incremental, a line extension, cost reduction, a new-to-the world product, or a great R&D innovation, the fundamental question remains: *Will the customer value the offering and purchase it?*

WHAT EXACTLY IS CUSTOMER VALUE?

When a company decides to steer portfolio decisions using customer value rather than by financial analysis, management first must understand *exactly what customer value is.* This may seem obvious, but it needs clarification because, in our experience, too many companies *think* they are getting to the essence of customer value, when in fact their activities don't bring them any closer to understanding true customer needs.

The only way to deliver value to customers is to understand them at such a deep level that you know exactly what motivates them. What are their personal goals? What's missing in their ability to achieve those goals? What makes their lives frustrating, difficult, challenging, or impossible? Customer value is defined as *the solution that removes those frustrations, difficulties, challenges, or impossibilities from the customer's life.* Once you understand what drives customers crazy, you can start exploring the opportunity to fix it—which translates into customer value. You have found the *white space* or the *undiscovered country* in the market where nothing yet exists, enabling you to outstrip the competition by offering a solution first.

Products and services offer no intrinsic value to the customer. Value exists only in the extent to which a product provides the desired *results or outcome* the customer seeks. Clorox determined that people want a clean bathroom but hate carrying around a bunch of cleaning supplies and in response introduced

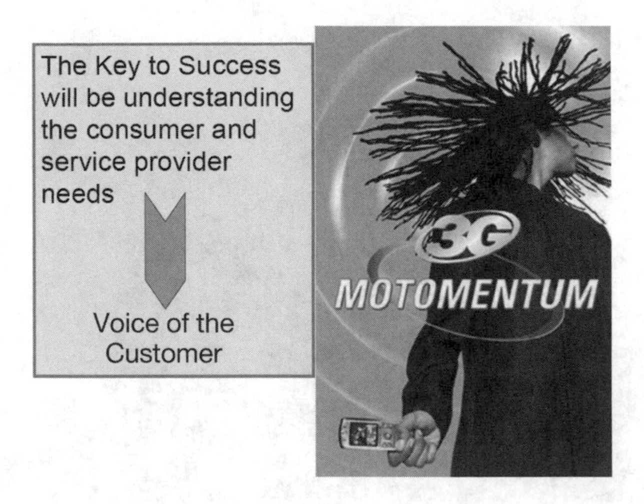

Figure 1.2 Example of Motorola's priority to understand the voice of the customer. (*Source*: Presentation by Anthony L. Carter, Motorola's senior director, new business development, at Management Roundtable's 2005 Voice of the Customer conference.)

the BathWand tub and shower cleaning system, which the company proclaims on its Web site will "replace the clutter of sponges, buckets, and bottles." In the trucking industry, desired results for customers (truckers) might include more hours on the road and fewer in the repair bay (provided by product characteristics such as reliability, uptime, maintenance, and ease of serviceability) and fewer accidents and greater driver comfort (provided by the features of visibility from the cab, ease of entry and exit).

Communications giant Motorola has integrated the process of unearthing customer value into its innovation process, as Figures 1.2 and 1.3 show. "One of the things that we've learned from a technology standpoint is that even though customers value many things, few things really have a core value that makes customers want to buy," says Anthony Carter, senior director of business development for Motorola, Inc. "You can look at a feature list and realize there's hundreds of features, but in reality, customers only buy because two to three features meet a core need . . . the rest is just pull through. One of the things that we really want to understand is: what are those two to three things that are really going to be the primary decision factors for the customer?" The idea of deciding what matters most to customers is the basis of the Kano rankings we describe in Chapter 5.

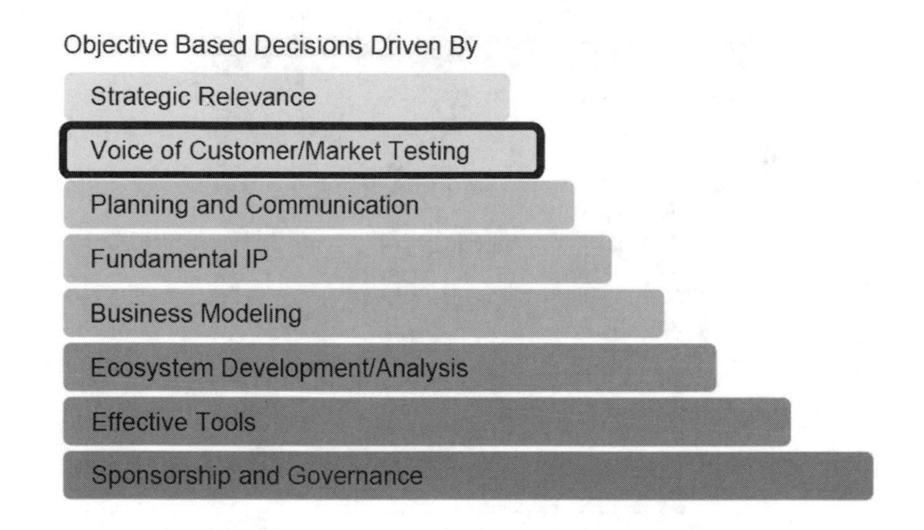

Figure 1.3 Where customer value fits in the innovation process at Motorola. (*Source*: Presentation by Anthony L. Carter, Motorola's senior director, new business development, at Management Roundtable's 2005 Voice of the Customer conference.)

Value from the customer's perspective extends beyond initial economics to encompass the product or service over the total life cycle and the total experience with the company. The truck fleet owner values *uptime*. If a vehicle is not operating for any reason, the fleet owner loses revenue. Reliability and quality of design and manufacturing are the characteristics that allow fleet owners to experience more uptime. Simplicity of maintenance and parts availability, which contribute to less downtime if something does go wrong, also factor into the equation. For cleaning aficionados, the ability to easily refill and dispose of the BathWand figures into the value they place on the solution along with ease of use and initial cost.

Customer value does not require disruptive innovation, although that kind of innovation can be an important consideration, as we discuss in Chapter 2. Apple's recently introduced iPod Nano did not create a new product category or add radically new capabilities to an existing one. Rather, it offered an innovative approach to providing an existing technology. A *BusinessWeek* article on the new player summarized the response of well-known designer Donald A. Norman: "the product sounds like the perfect compromise between the iPod Mini, which [Norman] finds to be slightly too large to be comfortable on his morning jogs, and that screenless iPod Shuffle."[6] Apple has understood perfectly the problems of the customer in getting his or her job done—in this case, jogging while listening to music or walking while wearing a skirt with small pockets.

WHY COMPANIES FAIL TO CAPTURE THE VOICE OF THE CUSTOMER

Executives who have invested heavily in customer relationship management (CRM) systems believe they are capturing the true voice of the customer. By tracking buyers and building a database of comments, complaints, returns, kudos, and extensive demographics, companies (incorrectly) believe they have the information they need to deliver customer value. Unfortunately, as with many processes that focus on the acceptance of product offerings or operational service levels, CRM does not address the value to the customer *before* the product or service is created—only after the fact, when investments have already been made. (See Figure 1.4.) Furthermore, CRM systems primarily deal with existing customers and not the untapped noncustomer potential in the market space. This is not to say that CRM is not a valuable tool; however, its purpose is not to identify what customers value. In contrast, the VIP approach to portfolio management focuses on customer desires, problems, and opportunities that exist in the market's white space. It provides executives a tool to evaluate the company portfolio *before* they commit vast company resources to product development.

PUTTING CUSTOMER VALUE IN ITS PLACE

Once you begin to conceive of your product in terms of what the customer values and are able to measure and rank customer value, you can see how sensible it would be to figure out which projects to fund by looking at their relative value to the customer. As a truck manufacturer, you might invest in the truck requiring fewest repairs. Yet as sensible as it seems to organize a portfolio around customer value, you must consider it in conjunction with company strategy and investment, as we describe in Chapters 3 and 4. This complex

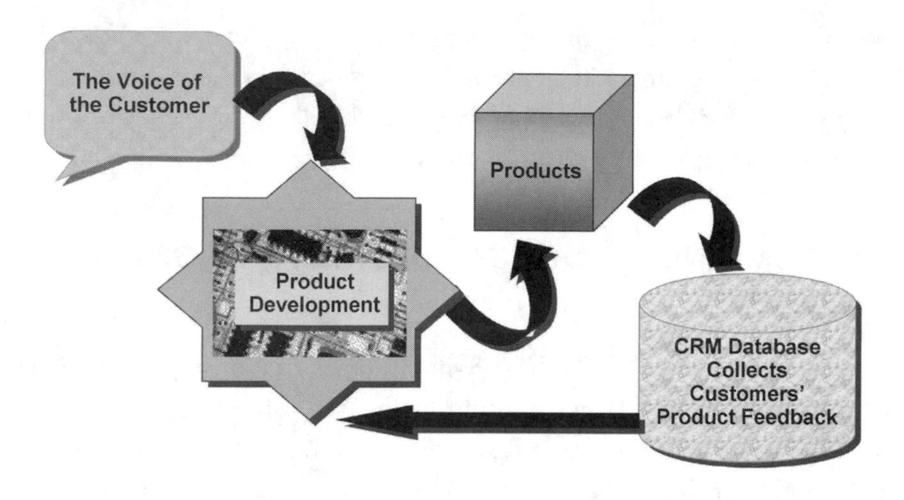

Figure 1.4 CRM does not equal VOC; VOC feeds product development and CRM collects the reactions to what you produced and loops back to product development.

interplay between a company's strategy and its product portfolio offers one of the most compelling reasons for top-level executive involvement in portfolio management. The process of evaluating and selecting products for the portfolio may lead to a reexamination of, and ultimate shift in, corporate strategy. To leave top management out of these decisions runs the risk of decoupling the portfolio from the strategy or letting portfolio decisions become de facto strategy decisions.

Even with executive involvement, we have identified two situations that can throw a portfolio off course. We call these the *Carved-in-Stone Scenario* and the *Market Downturn Scenario.*

The Carved-in-Stone Scenario

R&D and development organizations generate lots of ideas. When the development committee meets to present ideas at the executive level, there's often an assumption that the proposed new product idea *already has market acceptance.* Managers not directly involved in innovation assume that the innovators know the market. They fail to ask the fundamental questions about whether the innovation is connected to market needs and customer value. The idea appears to the executive team as if it had been carved in stone, with its direction already irrevocably determined. At this point, the project simply becomes an exercise in getting maximum payback from the financial investment. The product's success is hit-or-miss—maybe it hits the target of satisfying a customer need, maybe not.

The Carved-in-Stone Scenario shows that *senior executives charged with the responsibility of portfolio management must ensure that the project or program requesting resources aligns with the company vision, mission, and strategy and will create new or greater value for the customer.* Accountability at the highest levels is key. If you sit on a committee that approves new product ideas, if you meet regularly with VPs of development, it's part of *your* job to ask the hard questions about customer value. You can't assume that the people presenting the product ideas—no matter how intriguing or apparently compelling—have gone through the work required to determine what customers value and to align the resulting product with your firm's vision, mission, and strategy.

Executives need to arrive at such meetings armed with pointed questions about what the project means to the customer and with clear reiterations of the company's strategy, mission, and vision. As tempting as it may be to give a green light to the VP who says "I can save the company $20 million if we go forward with this project," that savings alone is not enough to justify the project.

The Market Downturn Scenario

When times get tough, the old adage goes, the tough get going . . . usually at slashing budgets and laying people off. Customer focus becomes a casualty of financial hardship. There's no longer money spent on visits to customer sites. The deep understanding of customers that may in the past have led to breakthrough new products gives way to reliance on old or sloppily collected data. The next new product isn't so new; it's a rehash of existing features. Management cuts staff across the board. Profits dwindle, and the company enters a downward spiral that may lead to its demise.

The Market Downturn Scenario shows that *instead of reducing costs arbitrarily in the face of financial pressures, companies need to sharpen their focus and husband their resources for the projects that will actually pay off.* At just the time when it seems that a deep understanding of what customers value is an extraneous luxury, it becomes one of the most vital keys to protecting the future value of the corporation. While slashing expenses 10 or 15 percent across the board in response to a business downturn may result in short-term savings, the long-term consequence is to cripple all projects in the portfolio pipeline. When the downturn ends, the company is left to struggle against stronger competitors with little in its reserves and few new and innovative ideas to fuel future growth.

Telecommunications company Avaya Inc. has grappled with this issue since it was spun off from Lucent Technologies in 2000. According to J. C. Paradise, Avaya's director of strategic marketing, "The catch-22 is the fact that, at least in our industry, you no longer have the resources of the go-go '90s to be able to throw at in-depth research, extensive voice-of-the-customer research. We have a constant push to do things as efficiently and as effectively as possible with the least amount of resources. Unfortunately, voice of the customer got the reputation for being incredibly valid, incredibly useful, very informative, but also very, very expensive to apply." Often, this reputation for being costly is undeserved. When viewed as a risk management tool and a percentage of overall projected development cost, the cost is minimal. As we discuss in Chapter 5, there are many ways to leverage customer research to get the most out of the money you do spend on it.

The bottom line is that whether portfolio changes are incremental or line extensions, are new to the world or the company, or represent cost reductions, executives must ask the same fundamental question: "Does the proposed product or service create or increase the value of the offering *to the customer?*"

CUSTOMER VALUE IN THE REAL WORLD

If products were developed in the corporate equivalent of a laboratory environment, where outside influences could be carefully measured and controlled, then separating customer value from financial considerations would be simple. The real world, of course, is never so clear-cut. Is a project that reduces the cost of producing a product or service intended to increase the value to the customer or simply to improve the profitability of the product?

THE NEED FOR A RIGOROUS METHOD TO UNDERSTAND CUSTOMER REQUIREMENTS

We speak in this chapter and others about *truly understanding customer requirements*. We must pause here to offer a more detailed explanation of what we mean, because in our experience many companies believe that they already understand exactly what customers need and want.

Companies may conduct surveys and focus groups. They may have a mechanism for accepting input from their sales and marketing staff. They may use the phrase *customer-focused* in their mission statements. However, none of these represent the rigorous, repeatable, and fact-based process required to reveal true (and often unarticulated) customer needs.

Even a project that is perfectly aligned with corporate strategy may not provide customer value. Emotions, pet projects, exciting ideas that cannot be commercialized, and technological wonders cannot substitute for the facts established with the adoption of a rigorous customer requirements process. A method such as the Market-Driven Product Definition (MDPD®) process developed by Product Development Consulting, Inc. and implemented in more than 40 companies is one example of a robust, fact-based way to clearly identify both expressed and latent customer needs. The advantage of such a system is that it provides the insight necessary to evaluate projects. Further, it provides a common unambiguous language to discuss projects with product development teams. Instead of arguing over unreliable financials or engaging in political one-upsmanship, teams can focus on getting done what's needed to meet customer needs.

Ideally, it should do both. In reality, it often achieves only the latter. For example, in an effort to reduce cost and improve customer service, a company decides to outsource call center operations. Customers who call for support will now hear "All operators are busy with other customers, but your call is very important to us . . . " Or they may hear someone speaking their language with a hard-to-understand accent, or interact with someone who doesn't understand the cultural context of their question. If a well-intentioned desire to improve customer service annoys rather than delights the customer, the company has simply reduced its costs *at the expense of value to the customer.* The memory of the unpleasant service experience will certainly return when the customer contemplates his or her next purchase.

Somehow, best-in-class or near best-in-class companies manage to avoid cost reductions that also reduce customer value. FedEx and UPS are examples of companies that have created value for their customers with package tracking via the Internet. Both companies were established during a time when the U.S. Postal Service provided a less costly though slower alternative. By determining that customers valued—and were willing to pay for—speed of delivery, FedEx and UPS created a customer value space in the air/ground package delivery market, which was not served prior to their emergence.

While DHL Worldwide Networks, traditionally a long-distance package carrier, has joined the fray in the United States with its acquisition of Airborne, it did not create any new or greater customer value. It is simply trying to take a larger slice of the market through acquisition, pressuring operating margins, and pushing toward commoditization in the process—hardly a formula for the kind of innovation that creates customer value and differentiates the product/service offering to the marketplace.

Remember that we are not advocating throwing the baby out with the bathwater or throwing away all financial measures after bathing the customer value baby. The financial measures, like the towel and the baby powder, come later. The company should review the business case (return on investment, assets, or equity, for example) only *after* it has determined, at *an executive level* and by examining facts rather than projections, that the project or program will achieve a value creation goal and fill a customer value space synergistic with company strategy. As Tony Frencham, business director for new business development at Dow Chemical explains, "We do not include financial measures in the first look of a project, assuming that it's exploration or early stage . . . at that point you know the very least about the project and so any NPV is based on such a large number of assumptions that it's almost meaningless."

THE RISK OF MANAGING YOUR PRODUCT PORTFOLIO LIKE A MONEY MANAGER

In the Introduction, we defined a portfolio as items to which a company must decide whether to allocate resources and differentiated between a product and a financial portfolio. Wikipedia, the free online encyclopedia, offers several articles on the term portfolio.[7] The first two read, in part, as follows (emphasis ours):

> ***Main article—Portfolio (finance)***
> In finance, a portfolio is a collection of investments held by an institution or a private individual. *Holding a portfolio is part of an investment and risk-limiting strategy called diversification.* By owning several assets, certain types of risk (in particular specific risk) can be reduced.
>
> ***Management, Marketing***
> In strategic management and marketing, a portfolio is a collection of products, services, or brands that are offered for sale by a company . . . *Typically a company tries to achieve both diversification and balance in their portfolio* of product offerings.

Notably, in both the finance and management contexts, these definitions concern themselves with the concepts of diversification and balance or risk reduction. Indeed, many companies behave as if the financial portfolio and the product portfolio operated according to the same rules. By now it should be abundantly clear that we believe the management/marketing definition above is a prescription for poor product portfolio performance. But ought a company to completely jettison the ideas of diversification, balance, and risk management when moving to a VIP approach to portfolio management?

In managing a portfolio of products, diversification may not always be the best antidote for risk, as there is more than one kind of risk. The mind-set that goes along with managing a product portfolio ought to be quite different than the mind-set around investment portfolio management. This is because the marketplace performance of financial investments falls largely outside of the money manager's control. The stocks, bonds, and other portfolio components are subject to outside economic forces such as inflation, rising and falling currency rates, and fluctuating interest rates, as well as the decisions of the management of the companies and institutions in the portfolio. Money managers may have the *illusion* of control, but because financial investments are almost exclusively *passive holdings*, most are a gamble.

Given this, managers of financial portfolios have developed strategies to *mitigate or hedge the risk of the gamble.* Top among these is diversification: the idea that owning many different types of investments buffers the portfolio against adverse events affecting one particular segment. Indeed, the usefulness of diversification as a hedge against risk helps explain the popularity of stock market index funds and balanced funds that purchase both stocks and bonds. Investors may not beat the market or take advantage of soaring stock prices, but they are protected from the down side.

Approaching a product portfolio in the same way may seem sensible on the surface. After all, if you don't know exactly which products will be successful, it makes sense to invest in many to spread the risk around. The flaw in this approach to the product portfolio is exactly its strength when applied to an investment portfolio. A diversified investment portfolio protects investors from losing everything, but it also prevents them from becoming wildly rich. Companies that spread portfolio risk in this way dilute development resources. They spread time and talent over too many projects and risk disappointing customers with mediocre offerings.

Remember the key difference between an investment portfolio and a product portfolio. Your product portfolio is a direct intervention in the marketplace and so *the market performance of your product portfolio is—or should be—directly under your control.* You are not gambling on how uncertain market forces will drive your *passive* investments. Instead, you are actively intervening in the marketplace with products that customers will value and purchase. This means a company can take the approach outlined in Chapters 2 through 5 so that it *knows* before embarking on a new product for the portfolio exactly why it will be successful and what steps to take to enhance that success. It's okay to put all your eggs in one basket when you know exactly what kinds of eggs your customers have been craving. Instead of mitigating risk by diversification, companies can put money where the success will be.

BETTING YOUR BOTTOM DOLLAR

The primary question senior executives must answer when deciding how to manage the portfolio is this: "Does this product or project result in increased or decrease the value to our customers?"

The balance of this book presents the evidence to support the adoption of a VIP approach to portfolio management and abandonment of a traditional financially based model to manage the company portfolio. We often ask our clients, "If you had to bet your salary three years from now on the success and accuracy of your portfolio decisions today, which would you choose: those products selected using today's financial projections or those products selected using today's highest customer value?"

We invite you to read the rest of the book and then decide on your answer.

NOTES

1. PDMA, "NPD Best Practices Study: The PDMA Foundation's 2004 Comparative Performance Assessment Study (CPAS)" (Oak Ridge, NC: PDMA Foundation, 2004).
2. Respondents came from diverse industry categories: Fast Moving Consumer Goods, Capital Goods, Consumer Services and Industrial Services, Materials, Chemicals, Healthcare, Technology Hardware, Software and Services.
3. Defined as (1) those companies in the top third in their industry for NPD success, (2) above the mean in NPD success, and (3) above the mean in sales-profit success from NPD.
4. PDMA, "NPD Best Practices Study: The PDMA Foundation's 2004 Comparative Performance Assessment Study (CPAS)."
5. Using the process documented in our previous book *Customer-Centric Product Definition* (PDC Professional Publishing, 2003), PDC has helped hundreds of companies launch successful new products.
6. Peter Burrows, "Steve Jobs's Tiny but Sure Bet," *BusinessWeek Online*, September 9, 2005.
7. Wikipedia is an open-source encyclopedia updated and maintained by the people who use it. Other, more traditional dictionaries and encyclopedias provide similar definitions, including *Wall Street Words: An A to Z Guide to Investment Terms for Today's Investor* by David L. Scott (Houghton Mifflin, 2003) and *The American Heritage Dictionary*.

2

UNDERSTANDING THE ROLE OF INNOVATION: THE RELEVANT PORTFOLIO

> "Anything that won't sell, I don't want to invent. Its sale is proof of utility, and utility is success."
> — *Thomas Edison*

Innovation is a hot topic. There are innovation Weblogs, books published by the hundreds each year, countless articles in business journals, and a separate section of BusinessWeek Online devoted solely to innovation.

What makes innovation the focus of so much attention? Most executives feel at a gut level that innovation somehow connects integrally with their companies' ability to excel in a chosen market and that selecting the most innovative products for their portfolios will bring success. Yet some companies encourage innovation so vigorously that they find themselves in the technology-in-search-of-a-customer quagmire: creating bell-and-whistle technologies without discerning whether the technologies solve a problem. They push innovation, but can't answer the question *What is innovation?* or the follow-up, *What does it have to do with success?*

What makes an idea—a moment of cognition in a human being's mind—worth pursuing as an innovation? Many senior executives will tell you they suffer no shortage of ideas. (Tom Luin, business transformation architect at IBM, told us: "Facetiously, I'll say, 'We've got too many ideas.' And then I'll come back and I'll say, not facetiously, very emphatically, 'We have too many ideas.'") What companies often lack is the ability to tell which ideas will become profitable new enterprises. An idea, even a fantastic, completely original, earth-shatteringly brilliant one, becomes a candidate for innovation only when it becomes an attractive opportunity—that is, when it delivers a solution to customers who place value on it for the problem that it solves. At one level, innovation is no more complicated than this.

More complicated is the process that transforms an idea into an attractive opportunity. This chapter is about setting the context for defining and executing that process. How do you select an idea that the marketplace ultimately will value as a solution to a problem it wants solved? Perhaps more challenging, how do you select a technology innovation that may solve a problem that the marketplace is unaware even exists? We look at the role of innovation in the portfolio, at whether innovation is always necessary, and if it is, at how it can be transformed through the process of commercialization into something that delivers value to customers.

WHAT IS INNOVATION?

Innovation is defined as the act of introducing something new.[1] Innovation for a business enterprise is the introduction of new products, services, or practices that yield commercial success in the marketplace. The criteria that determine whether an innovation is successful depend upon the organization. Success may be growth in a specific market, acquisition of market share, preventing entry of competitors into the market, increased revenue, a better return to the stakeholders, or recognition as a global leader. In this context, success is the achievement of the objective that the innovation enabled. (Note that we confine our discussion of innovation to the corporate world. We are not speaking of innovation in academia or a pure research environment.)

Innovation is hot because it allows a company to *differentiate* and *disrupt* the marketplace. The stronger the impact on the marketplace, the more sustainable the resulting competitive advantage. The U.K. company

NaturalMotion introduced its PC-based 3-D animation software *endorphin*, which integrates artificial intelligence and biomechanics to simulate human figures without the need for expensive motion capture equipment and the human labor to perform stunts and actions. The simulation of realistic human movement removes major obstacles for special effects in movies, computer games, and film animation.[2] Animators using endorphin save time and money in the construction of animated sequences while also improving realism and believability. This gives NaturalMotion a strong competitive advantage. The company is changing the approach to how moviemakers design, build, and reuse animation assets.

Innovations that confer competitive advantage are not confined to new industries or new companies. In 2001, Steelcase, the office furniture company founded in 1912 as The Metal Office Furniture Company, introduced RoomWizard. This conference room and resource-scheduling product further advances Steelcase's integration of the office space marketplace. The product improves communication and maximizes room use for events scheduling with wall-mounted displays outside conference rooms, helping Steelcase win business from competing office furniture companies.

While some innovations are logical extrapolations of existing products, Ford's Model T and Apple's Macintosh are classic examples of disruptive innovations. Disruptive innovation may introduce new technologies, which in turn spawn new products, services, and methods in the marketplace. Digital photography, container ships to modularly transport cargo, vertically integrated steel mills, and RFID (radio frequency identification) for remotely retrieving data (an Internet of things)[3] are examples of ideas that grew into innovations and fundamentally altered the markets that spawned them.

WHAT MAKES INNOVATION SUCCESSFUL?

The road to deliver innovation to the marketplace has traditionally been a rocky one. For every successful disruptive innovation, thousands never see the light of day. Many a product manager and executive have been burned by projects that consumed investment dollars but were never released, or if they were, quickly fizzled. The closets of corporations are filled with the proverbial skeletons that sit on shelves for years until someone at last takes them out, dusts them off, and turns them into an innovation, as was the case with 3M Post-it Notes.

What makes some innovations into market dominators while others are relegated to the dustbin of business history? As we stated earlier, an idea becomes an attractive opportunity only *when it delivers a solution to customers who place value on it for the problem that it solves.* So how do you select an idea that the marketplace ultimately will value? Even more challenging, how do you select an idea about a new technology *for a problem of which the market is as yet unaware?* (Ken Olsen of Digital Equipment Corporation is reported to have said in 1977, "There is no reason anyone would want a computer in their home"[4]—only a few years before the personal computer radically altered what people were able to do in their homes.)

The success of an innovation lies with the customer, the final judge and jury of the marketplace. Don DeLauder, director of product innovation and advanced development at medical imaging company Medrad, says his company pays a lot of attention to incorporating customer input into the innovation stages of portfolio planning. "We've got processes—mind mapping and brainstorming and so on—that operate at a very high degree of sophistication within the company in each of the business units. There's a lot of innovative capacity naturally built into our processes." The company's innovations group is responsible for trying to think beyond and outside of existing business areas. "We've got a lot of processes in place for making sure that people think innovatively . . . ethnographic work is very useful for figuring out what a product wants to be and not just assuming that we know. We're not just listening to a customer tell us 'okay, this is what we want.'"

REALMS OF INNOVATION

An innovation may take many strategic forms, from a *simple product or service* to a *complex business model* (see Figure 2.1). It may span a spectrum from *new and evolutionary to revolutionary and disruptive.* Whatever the route, a company must fully understand the realms of innovation, so it can present its case to the marketplace for approval by the jury of customers.

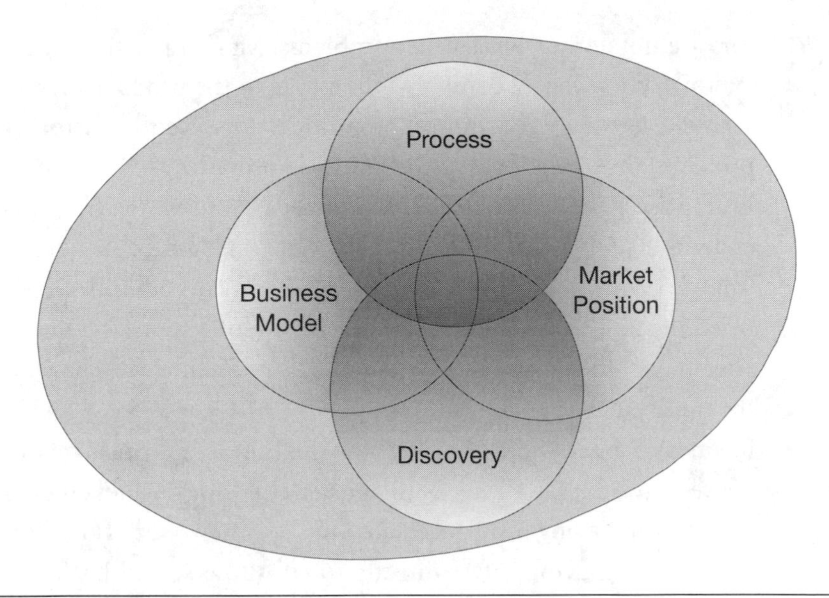

Figure 2.1 The realms of innovation.

Traditionally, innovation in business referred to a discovery that involved a flash of creative insight or an *aha!* moment. This definition is only one of several dimensions along which organizations now innovate:

1. **Process.** Altering the methods for delivering goods and services. Federal Express exemplified this with its 1986 introduction of SuperTracker, a handheld bar code scanner system to capture detailed package information and the ability to track packages from pick-up to delivery.[5] In 1990, SuperTracker won the prestigious Malcolm Baldrige National Quality Award for technical excellence, and in 2003 FedEx introduced handheld and wireless systems that further improved delivery times and tracking updates.
2. **Market position.** Changing the way the product is marketed. A company weaves its product/market segment fabric by matching the solutions it offers to customer problems in that market segment. The stronger the linkage between the solution and the problem, the tighter the weave in the product/market segment fabric. Holes in the fabric occur when a business or its competi-

tors are not addressing market problems. Market position innovation occurs when a company fills a hole in the product/market segment fabric by redefining the product to solve the customer problem, thus creating a new mainstream market. For example, Enterprise Rent-A-Car[6] became number one in worldwide revenue in 2005 by identifying in 2001 that some customers didn't want to go to an airport to rent a car. When competitors recognized the niche market for neighborhood rental spots as a mainstream one, they made moves to expand their rental sites beyond the traditional airport locations.

3. **Business model.** Modifying the way the business is organized to deliver a product. Dell Inc. is the poster child for business model innovation, having introduced a completely new way of marketing and selling computers directly to consumers. Dell has since expanded its low-cost, high-quality standardization and optimization model from PCs to servers to storage and networking products. Says Kevin Rollins, Dell's CEO, "We're very encouraged about the potential to grow into a broadly based and broadly acknowledged IT company."[7] At the close of 2005, well ahead of schedule, Dell had nearly reached its 2003 goal of doubling current revenue to $60 billion within five years.

   Another example is Starbucks Corporation, which bases its business model on selling a cup of coffee for a price two to four times what its competitors charge, but doing so in an appealing environment. Starbucks has built its retail business on a highly disruptive model, opening a new innovative retail store near an older one and cannibalizing the older Starbuck's business, only to shortly reopen the older location with yet another innovation. This distinct model has grown the operation in 2003 to more than 4,700 U.S. store locations.[8] Dunkin' Donuts is now copying the Starbucks formula—introducing high-end coffee and reconfiguring stores.

4. **Discovery.** Finding a radically new way of doing something by a process either managed or accidental. 3M did this in 1980 when

> it introduced Post-it Notes nearly 15 years after Spence Silver discovered an adhesive substance that didn't stick permanently and several years after Arthur Fry, Silver's colleague, had an *aha* moment while singing in the church choir. Fry realized a little adhesive on the bookmarks he used for marking the place in Sunday's hymnal would prevent them from falling out during a critical moment.[9] A second example of innovation discovery is the introduction of a novel chemical compound, phosphodiesterase 5 enzyme (sildenafil), commercially known as Viagra, for which the Pfizer research team won the prestigious *French Prix Galien.*[10] Yet in 1989 the original goal of the research team was not to cure erectile dysfunction but to find a treatment for angina by preventing the formation of blood clots, reducing the injurious action of platelets, and enhancing blood flow by relaxing the walls of arteries and veins. It was during clinical trials that some men reported having an erection as a side effect. The side effect became the discovery.[11]

These new realms bring new opportunity but also expand the complexity of innovation as it relates to a company's portfolio of products or services. At the most basic level, a company must somehow determine what realm is the most appropriate for innovation. A company must then effectively manage the accidents of discovery that occur during product development. Senior executives must examine the effect of innovation on the strategic alternatives available to introduce products to market. They must determine the right levels of investment and make decisions (using specific criteria) to bring an innovation into, maintain it within, or remove it from the portfolio. How does a company bring all this together to manage the path forward?

This question is easier to answer if you recognize that *innovation is the output of the portfolio*—what is introduced to the marketplace. In other words, the company's product portfolio is the container that holds all the types of *potential* innovations. Taking this perspective, the focus shifts to what you can do to recognize the potential and optimize the introduction of innovations to the marketplace. As we discuss in Chapter 4, part of managing innovation is applying a filtering process to determine which ideas are the most strategically relevant and the most valuable to customers.

RAISING THE BAR: MEETING THE CRITERIA FOR INNOVATION

Potential products must possess certain characteristics to fall within one of the realms of innovation. You can't build a competitive advantage simply making linear or incremental improvements unless these improvements differentiate you in the marketplace, because being better has become part of the mainstream. Starting in the 1970s, the quality movement initiated in Japan made products more reliable. This led to the Six Sigma method, introduced by Motorola, to eliminate defects. Quality, once a defined discipline within manufacturing, now is an accepted tool that permeates all parts of product development. Industrial design, like quality, is also now an expected item in the product design toolkit.

Albert Einstein is purported to have said, "We can't solve problems with the same thinking we used to create them." In the same way, a company can't innovate without thinking differently. And this new way of thinking extends beyond the company to affect external behaviors. Before the introduction of the Sony Walkman, for example, it was cool to blast music on a boom box. The Walkman completely changed expectations and behavior, creating a new market for personal sound/information devices and paving the way for such products as MP3 players and Apple's iPod. Today, music listeners make a statement silently with wires hanging from their ears.

Just as incrementally improving on a product without adding additional customer value is no longer sufficient, innovation for its own sake (in a business context) is inadequate. Innovation, including incremental improvements, must be done for a reason, and that reason must be to meet a need—either recognized or unrecognized—on the part of the customer. When customer value becomes the criteria for raising the bar, innovation shifts from being a pursuit that companies carry on because they think they should to a vital component of a company's continued success. Pure innovation (pie-in-the-sky, wild ideas) is transformed into *customer value innovation.* Two approaches—understanding the parameters of innovation and thinking outside the corporation—will allow your company to innovate with a purpose: to provide value to the customer.

The Parameters of Innovation

Understanding the parameters of innovation and seeing where it can be applied are as important as the ability to innovate. While rigid organizations that are unable to think outside their own walls may be unable to see innovations that are essentially in front of the corporate nose, wild creativity without parameters can lead to innovations with no market relevance. One of the ways to avoid this problem is to innovate *after* identifying a customer problem, validating that the problem is relevant, and confirming that its solution will be valuable. This is one of the two approaches we advocate with the VIP. The other more traditional approach is to use ideas created by the organization independent of any knowledge about specific customer problems. In the later case, you need to filter these ideas through customer value criteria before they become candidates for the VIP.

Much has been written about the voice of the customer and listening to customer needs. However, what passes for listening to the customer at many companies does not yield the kind of information companies need to adequately understand innovation parameters. Companies need to understand, at a deep level, the *experience of the customer*—what problems afflict their daily business activities or lifestyles in ways that create sufficient urgency to prompt them to attach value to a solution. They can do this only with rigorous methods for gathering and analyzing customer data, which we describe in Chapter 5. Medical technology company Becton, Dickinson and Company weaves customer input into its innovation process by doing focused voice-of-the-customer research within market segments. Steve Sichak, president of BD Diagnostics-Preanalytical Systems, gives an example: "We've got one particular segment, which we call microcollection, where we consciously said, 'There's many possible solutions here. Let's go out and find out what the customer's biggest problem is.' From there, we will develop solutions that, of course, will look innovative, but will in fact be intended and designed to address the customer need . . . it's almost—I don't want to call it forced innovation—but driven innovation as compared to the classic idea of the brilliant idea, the brilliant technology, the brilliant insight. It's little bit more methodical and, I think, a lot more successful."

A New Way of Thinking Outside the Box: Thinking Outside the Corporation

For years, the idea of thinking outside the box has been in vogue in creative circles. This certainly is a common-sense idea for generating innovations, but, like so many widely adopted new business practices, it has outlived its usefulness because it has become part of the mainstream. Thinking *outside the corporation*—thinking differently about the customer value space by combining out-of-the-box thinking with an in-depth understanding of customer problems—focuses the firm on where value resides, not just on getting beyond business-as-usual solutions.

Simply breaking the rules is not sufficient. Many innovators broke rules but got nowhere until focus shifted from the innovation to the customer. For example, Douglas Engelbart and a group of researchers at the Stanford Research Institute developed the NLS computer system in the early 1960s. NLS was the first system to present a user interface organized into separate regions of the screen, allowing users to navigate the regions with a computer mouse invented for the purpose by Engelbart. More than 10 years later in 1979, Apple cofounder Steven Jobs learned about graphical user interfaces (GUIs) at Xerox PARC, where a group of Engelbart's researchers had developed an interface of overlapping windows. Jobs' innovation was not the GUI, but the transformation of the technical innovation of the GUI into a customer-oriented improvement—the desktop metaphor—that made computers easier to use for everyone. Apple Computer then applied the desktop metaphor to the Lisa and later to the Macintosh. We will never know how many companies miss equal opportunities to create market-disrupting products, but the lesson is clear: If you want to reorder the world, you need to focus on the world, not on you!

INNOVATION ITERATIONS AT PITNEY BOWES

To develop the idea for a hospital application, a team from office technology company Pitney Bowes spent several months on-site in hospitals. The team collaborated with nurses, doctors, and hospital administrators to identify dozens of potential needs and built scores of prototypes to validate those needs. This work led to the identification of a real issue for hospitals: Weak documentation meant they were leaving money on the table. Knowing this, the team looked at several ideas that came from the prototypes it had developed. The first implementation of the idea had technical limitations, but the backup idea worked.

James Euchner, vice president, advanced technology at Pitney Bowes, comments on this experience: "I have a belief set that innovation flows easily once you understand [customer] needs. Obviously you need smart, creative technical and other talent. But the challenge is not just one of generating the brilliant idea. Great ideas don't just appear, and then go to product. The innovation process involves a lot of morphing of ideas. A lot of people have the notion that the key is to find the brilliant idea—go get a lot of ideas, and then pick the best ones, and then those are the ones that'll become your product. I've never seen that happen."

"What I see happening is this: ideas germinate—most often from real world experiences that people have, and then they morph. There's almost always something wrong with [the ideas]: they are too expensive, or they only meet part of a need, or they're clumsy to use, or they require integration. Or you understood the need, sort of, but you didn't really understand the need in essence. [Or] you understood it in essence, but to really create the innovation you have to approach it differently. And then you might have an innovation, but not a business model that will work for it . . . So there's a constant evolution, combining, morphing, dropping, simplifying, revising of concepts until you're able to create a value proposition. [T]he innovation comes from that cauldron . . . "

"[O]bviously, there're different types of innovation. There's innovation that is technology-driven and can create whole new possibilities. [There's] also innovation associated with driving costs, making things faster, better, cheaper than they already are. And then there's customer-centered innovation, which is driven by customer needs. This is a foundation of what we do—we focus on really understanding customer needs, then invent into them.

* * * *

Resolution	Evolution	Revolution	Disruption
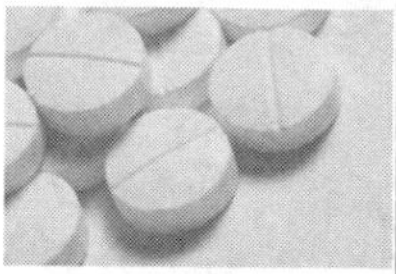			
Johnson & Johnson pulls product from store shelves due to poisoning; introduces tamperproof packaging to restore the brand	P&G introduces bleach into its standard detergent, which is safe for colors	University of Florida assistant football coach and a medical physician discover that replacing electrolytes of sweating athletes improves performance; launch the sports drink industry	Kelvinator introduces the commercial refrigerator, which allows the preservation of food; this changes society and civilization

Figure 2.2 The spectrum of customer value innovation.

THE SPECTRUM OF CUSTOMER VALUE INNOVATION

Customer value innovation seeks to improve the customer experience by coming up with a new solution to a customer problem or a new ending to an old and tired customer story. The spectrum of customer value innovation spans four perspectives: resolution, evolution, revolution, and disruption,[12] as shown in Figure 2.2.

- **Resolution.** *The customer values the solution because it eliminates an irritation.* This is the lowest common denominator of innovation. Without the innovation, the product or service is potentially unusable or so unappealing that customers choose other solutions. For example, a medical device may require modification to prevent serious injury or a call center may need to change its procedures to handle critical issues in a timely way. In this case, the customer values the fact that the product or service doesn't do what it did before, resolving a potentially crippling issue.

- **Evolution.** *The customer perceives an improvement in existing or familiar environments or circumstances.* It might be as simple as a mere extension of the current feature set, such as a laundry detergent including fabric softener to eliminate the extra step in the cleaning process of adding another ingredient. Or it might be as complex as changing a sophisticated algorithm to prevent the duplication of software or data stored on a DVD.
- **Revolution.** *Transforms the application for the customer by expanding its utility or merit.* In sports medicine, heat packs and cold packs provide not only relief but also more value to the user by being instantly available when most needed, at the moment of injury. Most people are familiar with the way the innovation of the Sony CD Walkman provided portable quality digital sound and eliminated bulky cassette tapes, but they may not recognize as revolutionary the napkin dispenser at a fast-food chain, which reduces costs and environmental impact by limiting the number of napkins per customer.
- **Disruption.** *The customer recognizes the innovation as a solution to a problem that they did not necessarily know they had.* Disruptive innovation creates a new paradigm. The customer's reaction to the value of a disruption can be summarized as: "I didn't know I needed it, but now I love it and couldn't get by without it." One example is the cell phone, which fundamentally changed how people communicate and their ability to remain connected. Another is the car door lock/unlock remote. This device eliminates the need for fiddling with keys, but more importantly it provides security by reducing the time and number of actions to open the driver's door, enter the car, and relock the door—especially valuable if you're getting into your car alone in an unsafe area. A disruption also may be valuable to customers indirectly. For example, the solid-state transistor, while an internal electrical component, started a consumer electronics paradigm highly valued by consumers for its attributes of miniaturization, reliability, and energy efficiency. The paradigm has extended to the present day with integrated circuits,

microprocessors, and very-large-scale-integration (VLSI) computer chips, enabling ubiquitous products that seem to morph almost daily.

THE INNOVATOR'S ATTITUDE

Pursuing customer value innovation means that organizations and individuals must acquire the skills and competencies to do things differently. Corporations must shed behaviors and attitudes that handicap their actions, such as risk aversion, inward egocentricity, lack of cross-functional diversity and integration, hierarchical and stratified approval processes, and layers of decision making. The elements of corporate and organizational behavior that foster innovation and the creation of a VIP portfolio are the antithesis of these handicapping behaviors and attitudes.

A new product or direction, like a new venture, is uncertain; the outcome is unknown. Like an entrepreneur—a person who organizes, operates, and assumes the risk for a business venture[13]—an executive who seeks to foster innovation must be comfortable with ambiguity. Senior executives must be comfortable living with the uncertainty inherent in defining the customer space. While they must spend time and resources to acquire information by gathering and validating customer data, they must be willing to act on partial data until more is validated. Sometimes they have to be comfortable with being wrong. Further, they must be willing to admit mistakes while moving the organization along an alternate path. Tweaking decisions as new evidence becomes available is the rule, not the exception. Senior managers who accept failure, and then push past it, increase the chances for success. They must develop leaders who are willing to do the same, no matter their discipline, level in the organization, or assigned role.

These individuals—business entrepreneurs—are found in all types of firms, from start-ups to Fortune 500 companies. As a manager, it's your job to identify these people and move them into positions where they can thrive and inspire their colleagues not only to think differently but also to act differently. The business entrepreneur may become your portfolio champion, touting a different approach to creating and managing the product portfolio and promulgating it throughout the company. Those with the innovator's attitude travel nontraditional paths and can think outside the corporation.

The skills and abilities that contribute to this type of performance may be innate or learned. Business innovators don't focus on superior functionality or price (being incrementally better, however that is defined). They don't think about form, fit, or function. They don't spend time determining the set point where the price beats the competition. Rather, they focus on determining where the value to the customer exceeds the cost by an acceptable margin. Entrepreneurial thinkers will harness all product strategies (branding, market growth, the capabilities of R&D, and global impact) and jettison all burdens (such as an industrial mind-set that clings stubbornly to outdated ideas) to create value for the customer. They are involved with customers and pursue innovation for the customers' sake.

REQUIRED COMPETENCIES FOR CUSTOMER VALUE INNOVATION

The competencies necessary to provide customer value innovation are the same as those required to transform traditional markets into new ones or create emerging markets where none existed before.

Recognizing Early Signs of Change

An important skill among the executive management team is the ability to recognize early warning signs that indicate the beginnings of a market change. In the late 1970s, neither Wang Corporation management nor managers at Digital Equipment Corporation foresaw the changes on the horizon for their markets. The personal computer toppled these two giants of word processing and minicomputing, respectively. This shift was so profound that it affected even those who might not have seen any relationship between their businesses and personal computing, such as typewriter maker Smith-Corona, whose management likely never imagined that its product, the quintessential tool of secretaries and students, would go the way of the dinosaur by the mid-1980s. Even the telephone and health care industries—which contribute billions to

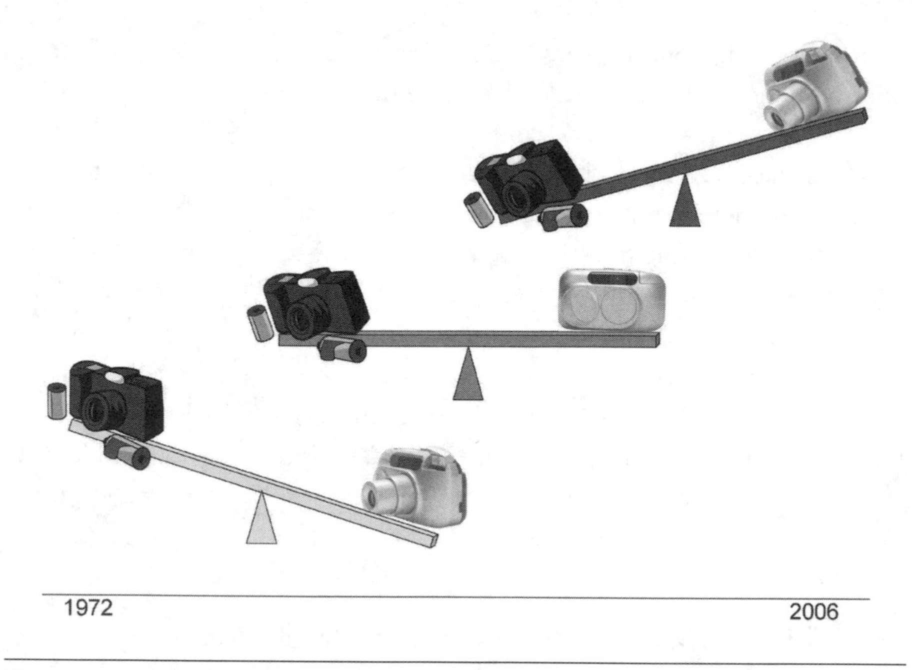

Figure 2.3 Market disruption occurring over time.

the U.S. gross national product—did not fully understand the implications of personal computing for their domains.

Knowing When to Act and When to Be Still

Another competency necessary for customer value innovation is knowing what *not* to do and when *not* to do it, how to make the decision to *stop* doing it, and how to lead initiatives to bridge the chasm often created by disruptive innovation. Nikon, one of the early entrants into the field of digital photography, was the first to stop producing film cameras.[14] One week after the Nikon announcement, competitor Konica announced it would phase out most of its film and camera business and market only digital cameras.[15] These moves represent only the latest in a market trend begun in the early 1970s in response to the ascendancy of digital photography (see Figure 2.3).

Chip maker Intel Corporation provides another example of knowing when to stop doing something, in this case as a result of seeing early signs of change. At the beginning of 2006 (and after 30 years of market success), Intel's

Chief Marketing Officer Eric B. Kim and Intel's new CEO Paul S. Otellini dumped the "Intel Inside" initiative, the first market branding of a microprocessor. The new "Intel Leap ahead" logo is one of the first public signs that an industry transformation is underway. Even retired Intel founder Andy Grove, who acts in a senior advisory capacity, agreed with the move, demonstrating that the changes go beyond the company's branding efforts. Intel realized—very early—that cell phones and handhelds are replacing PCs as the devices that provide greatest customer value. Otellini and Kim are reinventing their company to move beyond supplying chips to computer makers. They are positioning Intel to play a critical role in consumer electronics, wireless communications, health care, and other technology-based customer markets. Time is of the essence. Intel must complete its transformation into a supplier to these emerging markets before PC margins drop to unsustainably low levels.[16]

Trends, Time, and Innovation

Intel's transformation demonstrates a further competency that is important: time management. As we describe in Chapter 4 in relation to portfolio development, customer value does not stand still but shifts according to the standards set by currently available technologies. Value in the personal stereo market has evolved through a series of innovations beginning with cassettes and CDs and progressing through shock and vibration skip prevention, small headphones, MP3 format, longer battery life, and music sticks for the Apple iPod. The evolution of online mapping, shown in Figure 2.4, has followed a similar path. Map usage is down due to easy access to online directions and GPS technology. The dynamic nature of disruptive innovation is forcing MapQuest, Yahoo, Google, MSN, and others to redefine themselves in this space.

The transformation of industries occurs continually, albeit more noticeably and quickly in some than others. No matter what the rate of change *within* an industry, companies also must recognize that changes *outside* their industries may radically affect their businesses. For example, changes in computer storage technologies have changed the entertainment industry. Competition to movie theaters in the last several years has expanded beyond

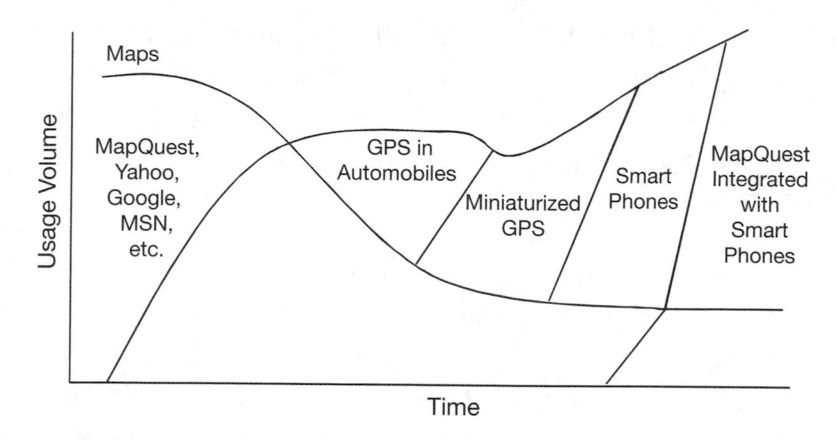

Figure 2.4 Evolutions of revolutions. (*Source:* Francica, Joe, and Schutzberg, Adena, "MapQuest Reinvented," Directions Magazine, October 7, 2005.)

the local DVD movie rental stores and on-demand cable companies to include the DVD-by-mail Netflix and Blockbuster.

Finally, changes in one industry may affect another, which in turn may impact yet another. Senior executives must be vigilant for this domino effect, since the early signs may come from an industry they are not necessarily following. For example, the transformation in entertainment affects consumers not only as theatergoers but also as electronics purchasers. This transformation has not gone unnoticed by Sir Howard Stringer, chairman of Sony Corporation. He has stated in private briefings quoted in the *Financial Times* that Sony decided to focus on so-called champion products, which he defined as having content that pulls them into the marketplace, rather than relying on marketing push. This customer value approach allows Sony to "concentrate on products that would give consumers more freedom to enjoy entertainment content wherever they were and whenever they wanted to."[17] Trends in consumer value affect even world-class multinational corporations. In changing the contents of its portfolio, Sony is demonstrating the sensitivity to larger market trends that positions it to remain competitive in the future.

Senior Managers Must Drive the Quest for Customer Value Innovation

Like portfolio management, raising the bar through innovation is an activity that senior managers should own. It is not the domain of middle management, but rather a strategic undertaking that involves recognizing how to create value for customers from the myriad of innovation possibilities. To do this, senior leaders may have to reinvent the organization—not in the traditional sense of calling for new tools, new processes, or new skills, but by completely changing a company's approach to customer data acquisition (making it continuously available) and communication (sharing data quickly throughout the organization), clearly formulating customer-focused objectives and actions, and making the decisions necessary to move forward. It is about getting the data to the right people who can analyze it, synthesize it, evaluate it, and make decisions about it.

Deirdra Dougherty, director of global marketing communications and analysis at clinical diagnostics company Dade Behring, works directly with the company's strategic decision makers "to bring the voice of the customer into deciding which products should be developed." Cheryl Perkins, senior vice president and chief innovation officer at consumer products company Kimberly-Clark, agrees that senior management's role is critical. "That is the value senior leaders bring—to be able to identify the right sources of data, extract the insight, and take action. There's still a lot of people involvement and business judgment required . . . you can't just put it in a tool and say, 'here's the magic answer.' It is taking the right data, looking at the business strategies, and understanding the challenges and the opportunities to define the best solutions."

While senior management drives and owns customer value innovation, its execution is not limited to the upper echelons of companies. The competencies and actions necessary to raise the bar in a meaningful way are *holistic* and must permeate all parts of the corporation, from the boardroom to the loading dock, and extend beyond all functions to suppliers and partners. Small competencies combined through cross-functional efforts and leadership will yield a large competitive advantage. Innovating in a way that's meaningful to customers is not internal to the firm. It is about thinking outside the corporation, starting with what the customer values, then using the power of the firm to transform the marketplace by the delivering the innovation.

DEVELOPING A SCIENCE OF INNOVATION

Innovation used to be an intuitive undertaking (and still is, in some circles). But we believe that innovation is a science, not an art, as does Peter Drucker, one of the most influential business thinkers of recent history, who said, "Innovation is the specific tool . . . the means by which you exploit change as an opportunity for a different business or a different service. It is capable of being presented as a discipline, capable of being learned, capable of being practiced."[18] We believe the process of innovation can be learned, integrated into a company, and used to deliver solutions that eliminate problems and change how people behave.

If you conceive of innovation as solving customer problems, then you can agree with G. Polya, who said, "Solving problems is a practical skill like . . . swimming. We acquire any practical skill by imitating and practice."[19] You can transform innovation from art to science. While artistic beauty may be in the eye of the beholder, science operates on methodology, not intuition. Science is measurable, repeatable, and traceable and can be documented. Therefore, a business's innovation process must be measurable, must lead to the same conclusions each time, and must be based on data.

The problem-solving (read: *innovation*) process has four elements: *understand, plan, execute,* and *evaluate.* The process of introducing an innovation to the marketplace combines these elements into a broader method encompassing multiple perspectives—for instance, customer, industry, related markets, and technology—that help a company discern the shortest path forward. We have identified a set of steps, outlined below and summarized in Figure 2.5, that can form the basis for a measurable methodology, increasing a firm's ability to successfully innovate. Success derives not from executing particular activities, but from bringing together tens or hundreds of resources, skills, and competencies. It is about motivating people to follow a process, making them comfortable with navigating the unknown, and inspiring them to help convince nonbelievers that customers desire the innovation.

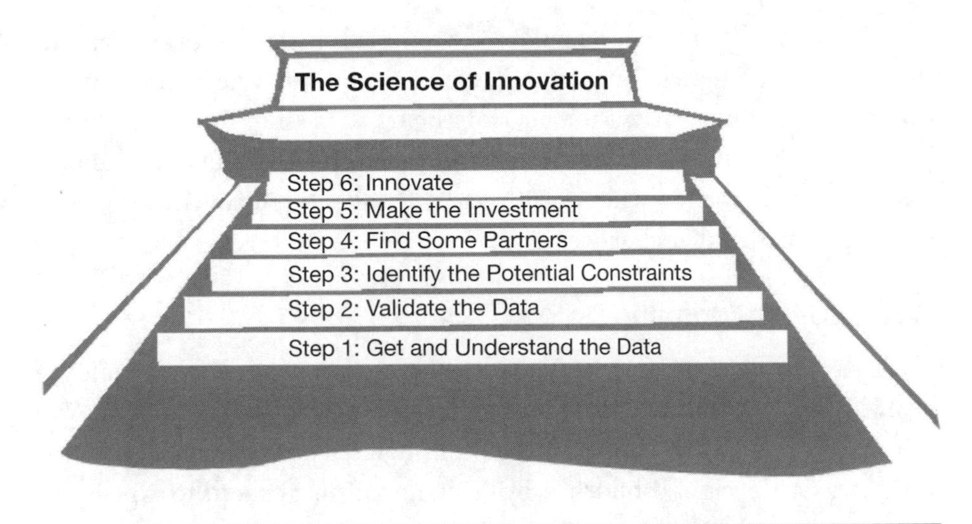

Figure 2.5 A set of definable, repeatable steps compose the *science of innovation*.

Step One—Get (and Understand) the Data

Companies often kill a project when managers suddenly realize it won't succeed, or neglect to kill a failing project that has acquired its own momentum, letting it consume precious resources while it dies a lingering death. These actions result from lack of clarity: The strategic or portfolio direction is unclear, or teams lack information required to make critical decisions about balancing priorities, making time and budget trade-offs, or responding to market changes. Worse, companies simply lack data about the customer problem.

A scientific approach relies on data. Yet as we explain in Chapter 5, the typical processes used to gather customer data don't always capture unspoken or as-yet-unknown needs, leaving the front end of the portfolio process ambiguous or fuzzy (as in the "fuzzy front end"). Yet it is precisely in the area of unarticulated needs where innovation will be most fruitful. When you choose a research method that enables customers and potential customers to clearly articulate problems, paint a picture of the world in which they live or work, and articulate why the problems are so painful, *you will have a chance to introduce a customer value innovation.* The fuzzy front end can become crystal clear if you understand not only the ecosystem and its attributes and parameters—where customers operate and spend time—but where the problem lives and how it prevents customers from being successful. Your understanding of these three things feeds the innovation process. As a result of this understanding, you may change not only the product but also the way you create it, package it, market it, and deliver it.

Step Two—Validate the Data

If you're committed to a scientific approach to innovation, once you define the problem you need to validate it—prove that it's real and worth solving. You can achieve this in any number of ways: through scientific methods that provide statistical levels of confidence, by bringing together experts to explain the significance of the problem, or by creating a prototype of the product or service to help clarify conclusions from the data.

Scientific methods may include using surveys to reach more people than you can with one-on-one interviews, increasing sample size. You may also further refine your conclusions about what customers value using statistical surveys such as the Kano survey described in Chapter 5, which uses pairs of questions to evaluate the customer's level of satisfaction with proposed solutions. Another approach is to assemble experts to review and challenge the conclusions from the data by performing an audit. Experts have skills, knowledge, and experience those inside the company might not possess, as well as objectivity. Such an outside view not only enhances the organization's capability to innovate, but it can also save time and money and possibly prevent disaster.

Step Three—Identify the Potential Constraints

Once you identify and validate the customer problem, you then must examine the potential constraints on your company's ability to provide a solution. Constraints come in two flavors: external and internal.

External constraints come in many forms and vary across industries and countries. Medical device makers must have their innovations approved in the United States by the Food and Drug Administration (FDA) after lengthy clinical trials. The FDA's regulatory approval requirements vary depending upon

SCRUTINIZE THE AFFORDABILITY CONSTRAINT

One of the constraints teams almost invariably always identify during portfolio planning is the amount of money available to spend on a portfolio initiative and in particular the amount that can be spent in particular areas. The business community typically calls this constraint *affordability*, defined as the ability to buy something or the ability to meet the cost of something without unacceptable difficulty (according to MSN's Encarta dictionary).

Looking at affordability as a constraint is eminently reasonable. A company's supply of dollars is not unconstrained and consequently the development organization needs guidance on appropriate spending boundaries. The challenge comes in putting the concept into practice. Too often, basic decisions about the *right* amount of money to spend in a given area (i.e., what is affordable) are based on organizational assumptions that may not be valid for the portfolio options at hand. In many cases, investing in targeted areas at levels that may seem out of line against standard operating limits can be the path to winning. (See Chapter 8 for a discussion of the DuPont Certified Stainmaster Carpet story, where the decision about what an affordable consumer advertising campaign looked like differed dramatically from carpet industry standards at the time). Leadership teams that want to include affordability as a constraint should do so in the context of a thoughtful exploration of the assumptions underlying the specific constraints proposed.

* * * *

the type of product or service, where and how it is used, and the distribution channel. Approvals and regulations for health and safety, electronic emissions, and connection to the power grid or the telecommunications network vary from nation to nation. Nokia, for example, uses a staged approach to introducing cell phone innovations, phasing the innovations into procurement and manufacturing as the company acquires approvals.

Identifying internal constraints (such as whether the company possesses the right skills and resources to create a solution) demands both guts and honesty—a willingness to hold a mirror up to the company and acknowledge its potential weaknesses and constraints. While budget and schedule limitations may be readily apparent, lack of skills and abilities may not be. Employees may possess theoretical knowledge of a subject but may be unable to perform at the necessary level. This resource deficit or lack of mapping to a core competency may not become evident until well into the development process. Other constraints include technical or market risk, product or service costs, capital costs, and risks in manufacturing or parts sourcing. The radar chart in Chapter 4 provides a way to evaluate these constraints and their impact on the portfolio.

Step Four—Find Some Partners

Being human, most of us would like to avoid revealing our weaknesses. However, the most valuable outcome of a constraint audit is a determination of what the company *cannot* do. Recognizing these limitations is not a reason to come to a hard stop or to kill an innovation project. Instead, it provides an opportunity for the firm to focus on its core competencies and reach out to partners to help fill in the gaps. Working with a partner—in any of the ways we describe in Chapter 3—may actually eliminate more than one deficiency in the company's arsenal of resources, reducing risk and enabling the company to get to market faster.

Step Five—Make the Investment

Increasingly, creating competitive advantage depends on a firm's innovation capabilities—the ability to exploit new assets by transforming knowledge and intellectual property into valued solutions. Often the biggest challenge comes in deciding which knowledge set or intellectual property presents the greatest opportunity. A recent study of technology companies found that executives at these companies feel that they lack an effective set of processes to select and manage their investments in innovation.[20] Further, they identify investment in innovation as the most critical competitive factor, not just as a component of success but also as its driver.

These issues, while particularly evident in fast-paced technology companies, are present in all industries. The forces that stymie investment decision making are such competing interests as short-term versus long-term investment horizons, the attractiveness of an opportunity versus the risk of pursuing it, and the need for open-ended creativity versus financial control. Executives seek a means of balancing these forces while carrying out the day-to-day operations that gets the company from where it is to where it needs to go.

Companies often oversimplify innovation investment decision making, reducing it to answering a single question: How big is the R&D cost? In an attempt to bring more richness to the decision-making process, companies may then expand their consciousness to include stockholders, which shifts the focus to maximizing future earnings rather than limiting R&D spending. With this broader approach, companies can move beyond purely financial considerations to examine how they can enhance the entire value chain—which may come in any of the innovation realms we outlined earlier in the chapter.

But what investment decisions really come down to is balancing investment intensity (a concept we introduce in Chapter 3 and expand on later in the book) with considerations of strategic value and customer value. In a world where the business climate changes hourly and where any business decision is influenced by potentially hundreds of considerations from cycle time and life expectancy to marketplace attributes and the skills of the workforce, there is still one critical decision point: Which projects demonstrate that their value to the customer exceeds their cost by an acceptable margin? Chapters 4 and 8 explore this question in depth.

Step Six—Innovate!

Once you have gathered and validated data, overcome constraints, selected partners, articulated the customer value, determined investment intensity, and aligned investment intensity with the strategic objectives of the firm, your only job is to get out of the way and let the innovations happen.

MAKING INNOVATION RELEVANT

This chapter looked at the innovation component of the VIP. A VIP approach, as we discussed, takes the fuzziness out of the front end of portfolio development because it insists that innovation be rooted in a real, documented customer problem. As you manage the VIP, whether for a brand-new company and product or as part of overseeing an ongoing product pipeline, you examine all your decisions in the context of real, validated customer data. Only with absolute clarity about the value customers place on the solutions to their problems can you make innovation decisions that keep the product portfolio and its management relevant.

As we describe in more detail in the next two chapters, portfolio management is really about strategic decision making. It's about not only the decisions you make today and how you're going to innovate, but also about what's going to happen in the future. The VIP approach to portfolio management is more about resource choreography (defined as the carefully planned or executed organization of resources across the organization, or the maneuvering of people or things) than resource allocation. We turn next to the process of creating the musical score that will guide that choreography: the creation and iteration of corporate strategy.

NOTES

1. *The American Heritage Dictionary of the English Language*, 4th ed. (Boston: Houghton Mifflin Company, 2000).
2. NaturalMotion Web site, www.naturalmotion.com.
3. Wikipedia, en.wikipedia.org/wiki/Disruptive_technology.
4. Kevin Maney, "Cyberspeak" column, *USA Today*, July 5, 2005.
5. "Itronix Delivers the Goods with FedEx," corporate press release, December 5, 2000, and "Consignment Tracking: Courier Companies Leverage the Net," *Financial Times*, May 7, 2003.
6. Laura Mazur, "How to Innovate through Scaling Up a Niche Idea," *Marketing*, December 11, 2003, p. 16.
7. Darell Dunn, "Dell Sees Future Growth Outside the PC Market," *Computing*, February 17, 2005, p. 14.
8. Dina El Boghdady, "The Starbucks Strategy? Locations, Locations, Locations," *The Washington Post*, August 25, 2002, p. H01.
9. P. R. Nayak and J. Ketteringham, "3M's Post-it Notes: A Managed or Accidental Innovation?" in *The Human Side of Managing Technological Innovation*. Ralph Katz, ed. (New York: Oxford University Press, 1997), pp. 367–377.

10. "Pfizer Scientists Receive Prix Galien Award for Discovery of Viagra," *PR Newswire*, November 27, 2000.
11. Rosie Mestel, "Sexual Chemistry: Discovery of Viagra," *Discover* 20, no. 1 (January 1999), 32.
12. A customer solution that does not require any innovation is not considered part of the spectrum.
13. *The American Heritage Dictionary of the English Language*, 4th ed. (Boston: Houghton Mifflin Company, 2000).
14. Mike Musgrove, "Nikon Says It's Leaving Film-Camera Business," *The Washington Post*, January 12, 2006.
15. Yuki Noguchi, "Konica Minolta Plans to Drop Sales of Film, Digital Cameras," *The Washington Post*, January 20, 2006.
16. "Inside Intel: Paul Otellini's Plan Will Send the Chipmaker into Uncharted Territory," *BusinessWeek Online*, cover story, January 9, 2006.
17. Michiyo Nakamoto and Paul Taylor, "From Push to Pull: Sony's Digital Vision," *Financial Times* (London), January 7, 2006, p. 19.
18. Peter F. Drucker, *Innovation and Entrepreneurship: Practice and Principles* (New York: HarperCollins, 1985)
19. G. Polya, *How to Solve It* (Princeton, NJ: Princeton University Press, 1945).
20. Study by Ernst & Young cited on Ernst & Young corporate Web site: "Technology Companies Require Better Disciplines to Manage Innovation Investments, According to New Global Study by Ernst & Young; Executives Say Technology Innovation More Important than Ever, Worry about Lack of Best Practices to Manage Risk and Deliver Results," September 19, 2005.

3

VISION, MISSION, STRATEGY, AND VALUE: THE INTENTIONAL PORTFOLIO

> "Good business leaders create a vision, articulate the vision, passionately own the vision, and relentlessly drive it to completion."
> —*Jack Welch, former chairman and CEO of GE*

Most businesses (approximately 80 percent[1]) have mission and vision statements. Recognizing that it's hard to get somewhere if you don't know where you're going, companies now treat these as a standard part of corporate operations. In theory, vision, mission, and strategy are pretty straightforward: Each is a way station along the continuum of knowing where you want to end up and creating the means to get there. In practice, choosing a vision and consistently linking it to mission and strategy are challenging tasks—never mind the further requirement of linking those to customer value!

When vision, mission, and strategy are aligned, unambiguous, and set a clear direction, they keep the business on course. This chapter reviews our definitions of these common business terms and explores the idea of what strategic value means in the context of a customer value-driven portfolio. We urge you to look at vision, mission, strategy, and customer value as a continuing information loop with each part influenced by the others. Once you do, you will need to consider the important question of balance—not balance as usually defined in the context of a portfolio as simply risk/reward or investment/return on two sides of a scale, *but balance in terms of bringing into equilibrium the various strategic purposes of the products you decide to finance.* The question of balance may also include outsourcing, a business practice that, when elevated to a strategic level, can have a profound impact on the direction of portfolio decisions.

It can be all too easy to succumb to paralysis when confronting strategy development and its integration with customer value concerns. A circle or loop, after all, is a metaphor for a process without beginning or end. But therein lies its beauty: You can begin anywhere. And, when you do, you will begin to gain control over the interplay among business strategy, customer value, and portfolio creation. When that happens, your portfolio ceases to be accidental and becomes an intentional part of your company's course.

DEFINING VISION, MISSION, AND STRATEGY

Sports analogies, like war analogies, are often useful in understanding business issues. (The origins of many approaches to business strategy can be traced to Sun Tzu's *The Art of War*, a Chinese text dating back thousands of years.) To use a sports metaphor, suppose you're the owner of a football team whose *vision* is to make your team into a football dynasty. Your *mission* (how you get there) might be to win the Super Bowl this year. Your *strategy* is made up of a judicious combination of all the alternatives at your disposal to fulfill your mission. You might, for example, concentrate on strengthening your defensive line so as to minimize points scored by your opposition. You might instead, or in addition, focus on increasing the effectiveness of your offense.

Once you have settled on a strategy, you select the tactics that help you realize the strategy: running, passing, kicking. Your strategy helps define your activities as a team—whom you should draft, what coaches to replace, what plays to develop, what free agents to go after and which to ignore, and which players to let go and which to offer new contracts. Your coaches make play-by-play decisions that are in keeping with the overall team strategy.

Table 3.1 Common Terminology Regarding Vision, Mission, and Strategy

Term	Alternative Terms	Definition
Vision	Purpose	Where the company wants to end up and its reason for being
Mission	Goal, objective	What a company will do to realize its vision
Strategy	Blueprint, game plan	The activities a company will undertake in the next year or two to achieve its mission

Whether called *vision*, *purpose*, or something else, a company's *vision* is just that: a picture of what the company can become when it follows its mission. (Table 3.1 presents some common business vision and strategy terms.) *Strategy* defines how a company will achieve its mission in the next year or two—or longer, depending on the length of a typical product development cycle in your industry—and provides a comprehensive framework for action. The process of developing a strategy

- Identifies potential business opportunities
- Analyzes company strengths and weakness
- Establishes priorities, policies, and short- and long-term objectives
- Apportions resources by category
- Monitors performance
- Plans for contingencies

A product portfolio is one of the tangible outcomes of executing corporate, divisional, or business unit strategy, just as drafting a top offensive lineman to strengthen its offense or a halfback to enhance its running game are tangible *outcomes* of a football team's strategy for winning the Super Bowl.

The mission statement, whether at a corporate or divisional level, defines the company business and objectives and the approach to achieving those objectives. While senior management creates the company's overall vision and mission, divisions or business units may write individual statements for their particular parts of the company. The decisions made at each level mean that the Value Innovation Portfolio exists at both the corporate level *and* the business unit or divisional level. At the corporate level, portfolio decisions revolve around what lines of business the corporation should include. Within divisions, VIP decisions relate to selecting opportunities in the market space the division is targeting.

CREATING THE STRATEGY/PORTFOLIO LOOP

Our purpose in this chapter is not to assist with the formulation of a corporate strategy. Scores of other books and articles are available on that subject and there are many approaches to doing so. In general, however, developing a strategy involves some combination of setting objectives, analyzing corporate strengths and weaknesses, analyzing the market and competitive landscape, formulating the strategy, and implementing and assessing the strategy.[3]

A company's starting point necessarily determines how it goes about creating a vision, mission, and strategy. Is the company just forming, or does it have 50 years of accumulated history, 20 years of a successful brand, and products on the shelves? No matter what the starting point, defining the market space in which the company plays and envisioning where it wants to go in the future are understood to be executive-level undertakings. The key—and often missing—step is to make customer value part of the process by elevating it to an executive-level concern. We like to think of strategy and customer value as part of a continuous loop, as shown in Figure 3.1, rather than as a linear process. When customer value considerations become part of the process of strategy development, the company can begin to create an intentional portfolio that delivers value to the customer *while also supporting the company's strategy and, indirectly, its mission and vision.* The portfolio has a reason for existing beyond meeting sales targets or capitalizing on a company's core competencies.

David Miller, vice president and general manager for DuPont Electronic Technologies, describes how strategy has influenced the portfolio—and vice versa—in his business: "You take a step back and say, 'Wow, semiconductors drive electronics. We really need to be in semiconductors if we're going to be relevant to electronics long term.' We had very little in semiconductor fabrication materials." The company had to decide how to best enter the semi-

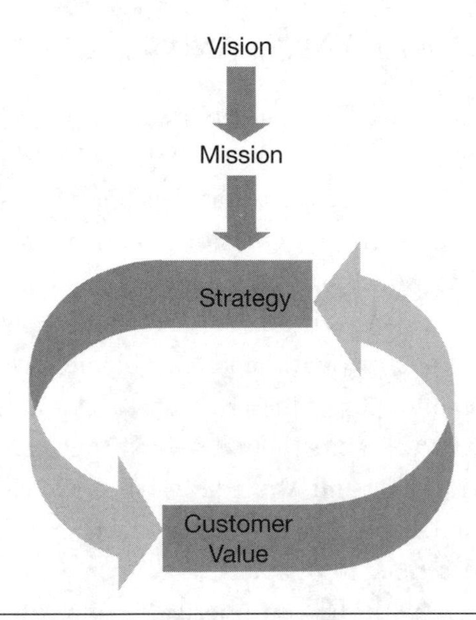

Figure 3.1 Mission and vision feed the strategy, which influences a company's pursuit of customer value. This pursuit in turn influences the strategy.

conductor fabrication market. "We had a lot of technology that we thought we could apply, but it was longer term. We ended up acquiring a company called Chemfirst that was already in semiconductor fabrication materials and used them as a route to the market." Once DuPont entered the market with the acquisition of Chemfirst, it used its enhanced understanding of the market to leverage the capabilities it already possessed.

Miller continues, "Strategically we say, where do we need to be? And then how do we get into that space? First you'll try to develop a product, then you might license it, then you might acquire, then you might do a joint venture, depending on what you're trying to get done strategically. That's a high-level portfolio decision. Once you decide you're going to be in semiconductor fabrication materials, you've got to look at a more detailed map . . . and figure out how you're going to do it. You may still may want to acquire, license, develop yourself, or do a joint venture."

STRATEGY, CUSTOMER VALUE, AND INNOVATION

Instead of leading you to a defined end point, the results of initial strategy creation help define both an *innovation space* that provides direction to the company's innovators and a market space that puts boundaries on which markets to explore. Strategy suggests what kinds of customers to talk to and in what areas you need to gather information. (This is how you know if you are making computer components or surfboards.) Companies then conduct systematic research of customers, prospects, and technologies *in this innovation space* and build a portfolio of opportunities, a database or storeroom, if you like, of problems from which they can draw to develop products.

The customer research and strategic work don't stop there, however. Sometimes, after conducting the exploratory research necessary to ascertain customer value, as described in Chapter 5, a company discovers that its initial strategy is inconsistent with the customer value opportunities it has uncovered. Further iterations with customer data help you evaluate these opportunities based on how well they fit customer needs and may nudge corporate strategy in one direction or another. You may expand your strategy to neighboring market spaces or drop an area that seemed enticing if the data indicates that a market for the new product doesn't exist.

Conversely, without adequate customer research, companies may make strategic decisions that lead them astray, breaking the customer need/portfolio/strategy loop and leading to decisions that serve neither the customer nor the strategy. For example, while the TiVo entertainment system is one of the best-selling products at retailer Best Buy, it also is among the most returned—many customers just can't seem to get it to work properly.[2] According to an e-mail from TiVo, one of its proposed product enhancements is aimed at physicians: "If you are a physician and have a TiVo Series2 box connected to your home network, then you can participate in testing a new feature that allows you to download physician-oriented programs to your TiVo box over your broadband Internet connection." Expanding its offerings to appeal to doctors may seem like a good idea for a company seeking to reach a wider market. However, unless TiVo makes the strategic decision to use voice-of-the-customer data to drive solutions to existing problems, doctors will presumably have the same challenges getting their system to work.

Medical imaging company Medrad began exploring a new product for its portfolio that would have involved expanding on some of its current technology for delivering fluid into patients. As it began developing ideas and talking with thought leaders, there seemed to be considerable excitement about the product's potential. However, as Medrad continued pursuing its research, it discovered that while customers found the product useful and interesting, the clinicians who used it would do so infrequently and would receive only about $100 per procedure in reimbursement. Based on those reimbursement numbers, Medrad decided the product did not have anywhere near the revenue potential to justify the cost of developing it and decided not to pursue it.

THE CHALLENGE OF ALIGNING STRATEGY, CUSTOMER VALUE, AND PORTFOLIO PLANNING

Strategy directly influences which customers you research and the type of information you gather. Medical equipment manufacturer Dade Behring tightly couples its strategy, research on customer value, and portfolio definition. "We have a highly rigorous, very sophisticated five-year strategic planning process that is annual in nature, and has qualitative and quantitative aspects to it," says Deirdra Dougherty, director of global marketing communications and analysis. "The qualitative aspects look at market analysis, both from a syndicated, secondary point of view as well as primary data collection through [a customer-centric product definition] process." From these, corporate leaders make decisions about company direction, and research moves into a more quantitative phase, looking at how to allocate the dollars across all the potential products. "What works extremely well is that Dade Behring has a clear strategy and follows it. They do all of this work, they develop the strategy, and we truly follow our strategy . . . It's calendarized, so it's happening every year."

Properly aligning the company portfolio with the vision, mission, and strategy of the organization is not easy or simple. For many organizations, it requires a complete transformation of company organization and culture. As we discussed in Chapter 1, The Clorox Company has effected such a transformation. It has managed to align its portfolio with its vision (to make people's lives easier, healthier, and better), its mission (to achieve number one or strong number two market position for every Clorox business and brand), and its strategy (focus on the three C's: consumers, customers, and cost). As Gerald Johnston, former Clorox chairman and chief executive officer, succinctly summarized in the 2005 Clorox annual report, "Clorox begins and ends with the consumer. That is our purpose, and nothing is more important . . . The strategy choice is about building world-class consumer insights capability and applying it to our innovation work and to our integrated brand-building activities."[4] The company's clear alignment of its strategy with its mission and vision signals middle managers and product developers to stay the course based on the stated mission. The business focus as manifested in Clorox's strategy does not have to tie to specific actions regarding the portfolio, but the focus must clearly be on delivering customer value.

Clorox operates in attractive niche categories where it can win market dominance. Its strategy is to stay away from the laundry detergent market, choosing not to venture into head-to-head competition with Tide detergent and concentrating instead on bleach and specialized laundry products such as stain removers. It owns the charcoal market with Kingsford charcoal but leaves the barbecues and grills to others. In Clorox's case, corporate strategy becomes a filter for product portfolio decisions.

Drug company Penwest Pharmaceuticals, Inc. provides an example of the alignment of a product portfolio with corporate strategy. In his 2004 letter to shareholders, Robert Hennessey, Penwest's president and CEO, described how the company set its future direction as a specialty pharmaceutical company by focusing its product portfolio on therapeutic treatments. "Through market analysis completed in early 2004, we identified the most promising market segments to potentially enter . . . As a result of this process, we began developing products during the year to treat chronic diseases of the central nervous system (CNS), including epilepsy, depression, pain and schizophrenia." In Penwest's case, its strategy clearly guided it to a particular market in which to conduct further customer research and from there to a product portfolio.

STRATEGIC BALANCING

Your mother may have said "You are what you eat," but as a corporate entity, you are what you fund. The USDA's food pyramid doesn't tell you whether to eat cheese and crackers or a slice of pizza or a bowl of applesauce. It does, however, provide guidelines for how much of your daily intake should be from grains and how much from dairy products and fruits. Similarly, while strategy formulation should not tell you whether to fund a particular product, your strategy should address generally where and when you will invest resources, since projects and products you support with investment today define where your company will be two or three years from now. Achieving strategic balance within a portfolio means deciding at a strategic level how much to invest in various types of development projects, just as eating a balanced diet means deciding what proportion of your nourishment should come from each food group.

There are several kinds of strategic portfolio balancing. We discuss two in the next several pages: balancing *types of products* and balancing *internal and external resources* (outsourcing).

Balancing Product Types

Defining the amount of resources to allocate for each *type* of project is an integral part of a business's strategy. Each of the three broad categories of products—new-to-the world, incremental, and platform—can fulfill a strategic role in a product portfolio.

The Stanley Works made an explicit decision to use new products (innovation) as part of its growth strategy. Beginning in the late 1990s, The Stanley Works' vision was to deliver incremental, profitable growth through innovative products that raise customer expectations and industry standards. Its strategy was to deliver incremental growth at twice the industry average. As William Hill, former VP of engineering and technology, put it, "We started with a vision, which was: deliver incremental profitable growth through innovative products that raise customer expectations and industry standards . . . we wanted [new] products to [account for] greater than 10 percent of sales . . . Then we wanted 25 percent of sales from products new in the last thee years." According to Hill, the company exceeded its goals, achieving 12 percent on the

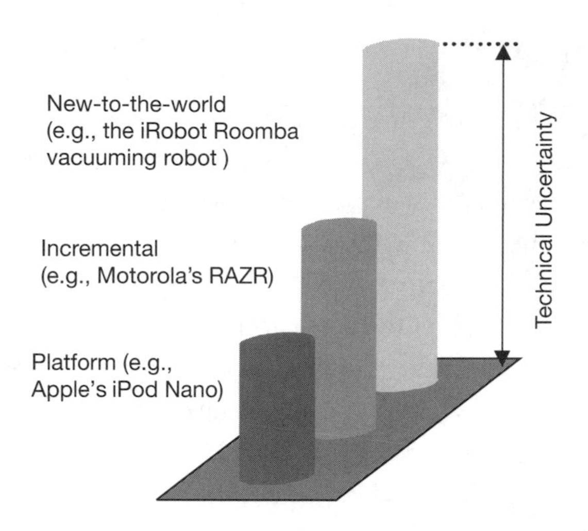

Figure 3.2 Different types of projects come with varying levels of technical uncertainty.

annual measure and 30 percent on the three-year measure, which enabled it to survive the downturn of 2000.

New-to-the-world products are the truly innovative, category-defining products that customers may not even have known they wanted. These can open up new markets and confer competitive advantage. They will, however, require significant investments of time and money and tend to present higher risk. Incremental products enhance existing products or categories of products with new features or functionality. These new features may be valuable to customers, but they do not redefine value in the way that true innovations do, although often they cost less to develop and can be brought to market more quickly. Platform projects provide a new set of capabilities on which the company can build future products—for example, a new software architecture or a new drug delivery mechanism. Platform programs often are an engineering organization's way of starting with a clean slate. However, if the resultant platform does not create value, these projects can be a huge investment that contributes little or nothing to the bottom line. (Note that value in the case of platform projects may be indirect—customers may ultimately benefit from better support if you redesign the help desk software platform to provide speedier responses to calls.)

Development Project Type	1990	2004	% Change from 1990
New-to-world (true innovations)	20.4%	11.5%	43.7% decrease
New product lines to the company	38.8%	27.1%	30.1% decrease
Additions to existing product line in company	20.4%	26.7%	20.8% increase
Improvements and modifications to existing company products	20.4%	36.7%	80.1% increase
Total	100.0%	100.0%	

Figure 3.3 Breakdown of the portfolio by project types, 1990 to 2004. (*Source*: APQC 2004 study cited in R. G. Cooper's "Results are Down! Your NPD Portfolio May Be Harmful to Our Business Health," PDMA *Visions*, April 2005.)

Figure 3.2 shows the level of technical uncertainty in each type of undertaking. You could do the same analysis with market uncertainty, organization uncertainty, or other unknowns. The point is that the strategy should set some targets for the distribution of uncertainty in the portfolio. You then use the radar chart in balancing the portfolio, as discussed in the next chapter.

We often see companies letting internally driven product roadmaps or platform strategies influence fundamental business decisions, essentially letting tactics drive strategy, when considering the issue of time to market. PDC discovered in a 1999 study of the printer industry that getting to market rapidly may become a goal in itself, whether because of quarter-to-quarter financial pressures or intensified competition. This in turn biases the company to undertake incremental product development projects, which are an easy way to reduce time to market. Such a trend seemed to be happening in the years between 1990 and 2004, when as Figure 3.3 shows, there was a 43.7 percent decrease in investment in new-to-the-world products.

However, getting to market quickly does not necessarily create the greatest customer value, and it is customer value, not time to market, that ultimately drives profit and shortens payback time. Figure 3.4 demonstrates that projects with a medium cycle time, those of around 70 weeks, had by far the fastest payback. These products typically take longer to develop than incremental products because they can offer more than the incremental value of a

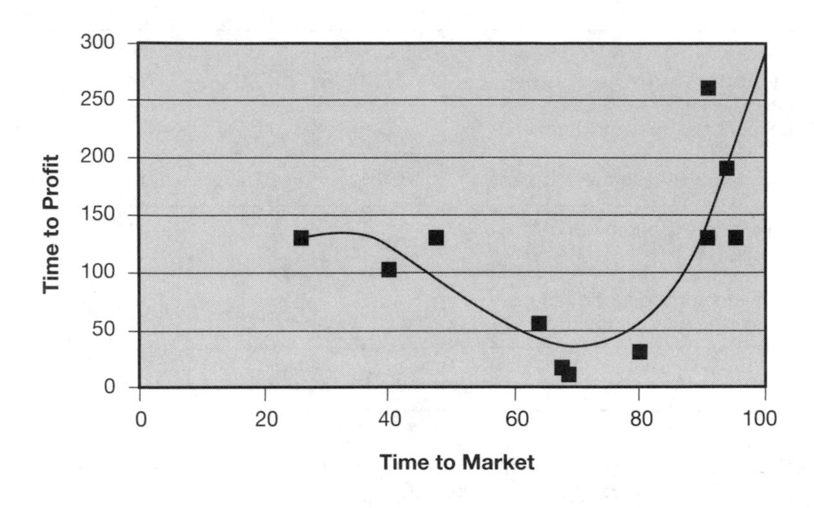

Figure 3.4 Cycle time and project payback.

new feature or two added to an already extensive feature list; it takes creativity and time to create this value. Platform programs, which can take 100 weeks or more to develop, often take a significantly greater time to pay back—if they ever do.

The message to take away from the PDC study and Figure 3.3 is to ensure that your strategy is accomplishing what you want. If your strategy is to focus on shorter time to market, you may actually increase time to profit, since such a strategy will drive you to create incremental products. Thus you may remain in a commodity market with more competitive pricing while avoiding the longer time-to-market products, which may represent the breakthroughs that open new market opportunities to provide higher margins and increase market share.

Platform projects are not always bottomless pits for money and resources. One case of a very successful platform project comes from Johnson Controls, Inc., a major supplier of systems and controls to the automotive industry. As part of the Core Product Portfolio (CPP) process it introduced in 2002, the company unveiled a customizable platform that allows its customers (automobile manufacturers) to adapt automobile seats to satisfy the needs of *their* customers (automobile consumers). In this case, the platform itself became a part of a strategy to offer additional customer value. As Jeff Edwards, group vice president, product and business development for Johnson Controls, said in a corporate press release, "With our CPP process, we put consumers back in the driver's seat, so to speak . . . By shifting the development focus from the base structure that consumers don't care about, and moving it to the area they see and touch, we can help automakers reduce development costs and drive value-added activity to the surface of the product." As people spend more and more time in their cars, Johnson Controls has become expert at measuring consumer comfort and improving comfort for drivers and passengers. Automobile manufacturers value Johnson Controls' solutions as a means of offering more and better choices to their customers.

Balancing Outsourcing: The Impact of Outsourcing Strategy on the Portfolio

Another dimension of strategic balance is the company's approach to outsourcing, which also affects the types of projects selected for the portfolio. Some companies choose to include in their portfolios only products that map to their core competencies, while others decide that some level of outsourcing or partnering is appropriate to achieve their missions. Figure 3.5 shows how three different products map to a company's core competencies.

Companies may use outsourcing to reduce risk, lower their initial investment, or accomplish something they couldn't do on their own. "If there are areas that we determine are gaps in the portfolio . . . we might look at alternative sources of getting those technologies, mainly from the outside, buying them," says Anthony Carter, senior director, new business development for Motorola, Inc. "Of course, that links it to strategy—trying to determine make vs. buy. Is it a core competency or should it be?" Customers, of course, don't care about your efforts to leverage core competencies, decrease time to market, or increase productivity. So companies can create customer value most effectively by shifting development to the most appropriate players, either internal or external. This shifting is the basis of strategic design outsourcing.

In our experience, design outsourcing has become a successful strategy at many companies because customer perception of product and service value now changes so rapidly. Consider personal computer DVD disc drives. Just a few years ago, customers perceived that these devices added a great deal of dif-

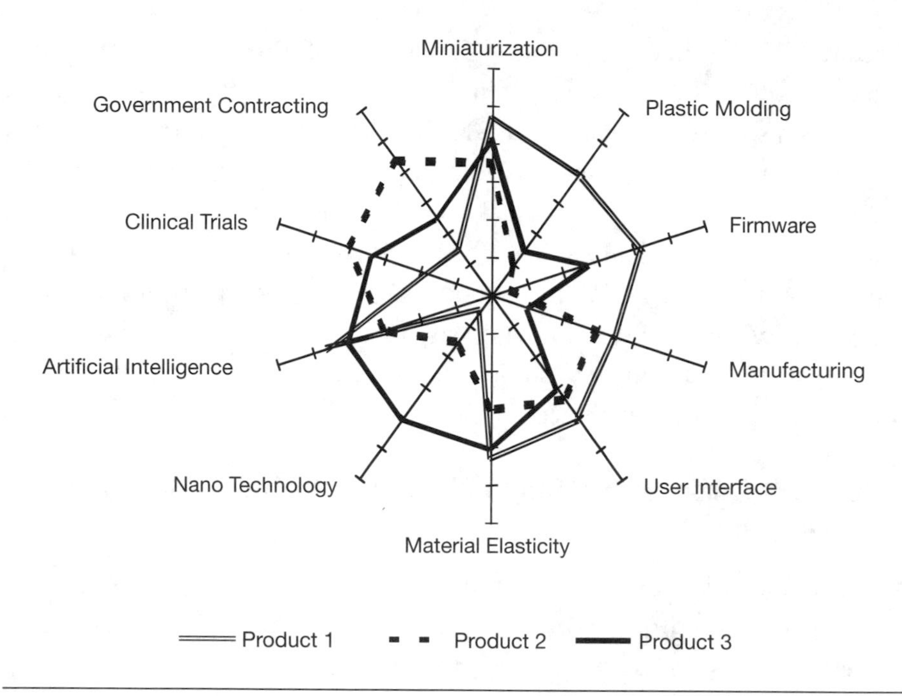

Figure 3.5 How products map to core competencies.

ferentiation. Now such equipment is standard and expected. When the perceived value of your products is temporary, you risk losing your market position to a new competitor unless you constantly realign internal and external development activities to create new customer value. Faced with a choice between keeping up with rapid advances in DVD technology via internal development or outsourcing DVD design, most computer companies chose the latter.

Strategic design outsourcing also works because modern communications tools and the Internet have obviated the need for product design partners to be physically close, so you can shop the world to find the best partners. Partners need not be exclusive (dedicated to your product only), but they must possess unquestionable ethics and irrefutable integrity.

The ultimate expression of strategic design outsourcing is a value broker: a company that outsources most or all of the design and manufacturing of its products. A storage drive company, for example, strategically outsources design and production for the majority of its products. In turn, the storage

ASSESSING DESIGN OUTSOURCING MATURITY

PDC has found that companies generally fall into one of the following four categories with regard to outsourcing. Knowing where your company fits can help you create an effective outsourcing strategy.

Vertically Integrated Company

A vertically integrated company typically does almost all design work in-house. Its suppliers are not involved in the concept phase of design. Few professional staff people are involved with partner, supplier, or subcontractor relationships. The company meets with suppliers only when problems arise. Few partners are connected via ERP (enterprise resource planning), supply chain APO (advanced planning and optimization), or PDM (product data management) software. The company assumes all risks and claims all profits, merely paying suppliers. Involvement of outside distributors, retailers, and customers in product design is minimal.

Selective Outsourcer

Selective outsourcers often pick partners to create components of their products, but don't farm out what might be considered the core of the business. There is no sharing of risks and rewards, although there may be delivery performance incentives and penalties.

Strategic Outsourcer

Companies that apply outsourcing strategically are willing to share the value of their products, the risks of development, and the profits with allies and partners. Further, they are constantly reassessing what customers value, then changing their outsourcing activities to reflect what customers will value in the future.

Value Broker

A value broker does little or no design or manufacturing in-house. Major suppliers are involved in the concept phase of a large percentage of designs. The average number of suppliers for each major purchased component is low. A large percentage of the company's professionals are responsible for partner and supplier relationships. Typically, the company has many professionals from its partners or suppliers working on site. It meets often to discuss performance metrics, and it is connected with partners via enabling IT infrastructure.

* * * *

company acts as a strategic outsourcing partner for most of the major computer manufacturers, essentially becoming a value broker.

Not all companies want to become value brokers, nor should they. But all companies do need to remain competitive and provide value to customers. Aligning outsourcing strategy with corporate strategy helps you provide this value. This is not to imply that your strategy should specify particular outsourcing partners, just which approach you expect to take. Tony Frencham, business director for new business development at Dow Chemical, describes why his company waits to choose a partner until more is known about a particular project, although it may know early on that a partner is required. "Our thinking now is that at the early stages of a project you know the very least about a project, [less] than you do at any other point in the project life cycle, so this is a time where it's not entirely clear who is going to be advantaged by your new development, who is going to be neutral, and who is going to be disadvantaged," Frencham says. "Clearly you would want to not work with someone who is going to be disadvantaged in the future, because they might become a very unhappy partner, or potentially a disabling partner. So [early in a project is] a bad time to pick a partner."

THE FINANCIAL COMPONENT OF STRATEGY

We can't conclude a chapter on strategy without mentioning the financial component. Every company has a budget limit for research and development and capital expenditures. Operating costs are part of the budget plan and therefore need to be addressed in the strategy. Operating costs will affect available resources and could have an impact on the outsourcing strategy, as discussed above. Chapter 4 discusses balancing the level of investment (investment intensity) for each product in the VIP and for advanced research (the R in R&D).

Regardless of the size, age, or market in which a company operates, the criteria for portfolio success are the same. A successful portfolio of products provides strategic and customer value, moves the organization closer to its vision, and can be accomplished within the investment capabilities of the organization. The next chapter looks at how you can find the sweet spot where customer value, corporate strategy, and investment intensity are all at optimal levels.

NOTES

1. PDMA, "NPD Best Practices Study: The PDMA Foundation's 2004 Comparative Performance Assessment Study (CPAS)" (Oak Ridge, NC: PDMA Foundation, 2004).
2. "Business Strategy Origins," published online by the IEE (Institution of Electrical Engineers) in its *Management Keys* series.
3. Martin J. Menard, director of platform capability at Intel Corporation, in a presentation at the IIR/PDMA best practices event, Strategic and Operational Portfolio Management Conference, February 27–March 1, 2006, Fort Lauderdale, FL.
4. Clorox 2005 Annual Report and IIR/PDMA Front End of Innovation Conference, May 2005, keynote address by Gerald Johnston.

4

AIMING FOR THE SWEET SPOT: THE OPTIMIZED PORTFOLIO

"You've got to be very careful if you don't know where you're going, because you might not get there."
—*Yogi Berra*

"To be defeated is pardonable, to be surprised—never!"
—*Napoleon Bonaparte*

Baseball players looking for hits or game-winning home runs aim to contact the ball on the bat's sweet spot. A hit on this spot makes balls sail farther because more of the force of the swing transfers to the ball. Executives looking for home run products for the company portfolio search for the sweet spot too: that figurative juncture where a variety of factors come together to produce favorable conditions for success.

Even the best ballplayers strike out more often than they get hits. In fact, one of the best hitters of all time, Ted Williams, managed a batting percentage over .400 only three years of his career (.406 in 1941, .400 in 1952, and .407 in 1953 with the Red Sox). While this may be an outstanding major league hitting statistic, it is not an acceptable success rate for the product portfolio. A

2005 study by AMR Research indicated that 52 percent of new product introductions resulted in failures.[1] Even a 5 out of 10 hit rate isn't acceptable by Wall Street standards. The primary reason for these failures, cited by AMR and confirmed by the PDMA CPAS study cited in Chapter 3, was that products missed customer needs.

Half the time, companies fail to either identify the market sweet spot or to conduct business in such a way as to create a portfolio that targets it. Why do companies continue to pour resources into projects that ultimately fail? Retailer John Wanamaker famously said of advertising effectiveness: "Half my advertising is wasted. I just don't know which half." Do companies take the same view of new products investments? Or are companies simply continuing to use familiar and comfortable approaches to portfolio selection and management that fail to improve their batting averages?

In this chapter, we look at what goes into determining the sweet spot for your portfolio and the challenging process of whittling down the number of potential projects to pursue. By ensuring that projects are in the sweet spot, then further filtering them based on criteria relevant to your company and market space, you can dramatically raise your portfolio batting average, spending precious resources on those projects destined to become market winners and killing early those that won't. We also take a fresh look at what it means to balance the portfolio.

TOO MUCH OF A GOOD THING

Companies usually generate far more ideas than they can afford to pursue. Motorola, for example, generates between 400 and 500 projects annually according to senior director of new business development Anthony Carter. In 2003, Motorola established an early stage accelerator (ESA) organization. The organization's responsibility, as part of the chief technology office at Motorola under ESA vice president Jim O'Connor, is to provide a first-level cut at distilling the hundreds of potential projects to a manageable 20 or 30. ESA's task is to identify the most significant projects or ideas from a number of perspectives, including the attractiveness of the solution, market disruption, competitive sustainability of the resultant product, competitiveness, strategic alignment, and portfolio synergy.

Whether a company generates 10 ideas a year, of which it can fund one, or 100, of which it can fund 10, some type of filtering must take place. As we discussed in Chapter 3, the first stage of filtering occurs at the strategy development level. Before doing anything else, you decide what business you're in and define the sandbox in which you'll play. You can reject any idea that doesn't fit in your sandbox. Of course, properly aligning the company portfolio with the strategy, mission, and vision of the organization—that is, playing in the appropriate sandbox—may not be a simple undertaking. The example of The Clorox Company, which we cited in Chapter 3, showed that sometimes achieving this alignment requires a complete overhaul of company culture.

The second filter should be whether a product falls in the sought-after sweet spot, defined as the simultaneous optimization of customer value, strategic value, and investment intensity. *Investment intensity* is more than just the total amount of resources—people, capital, material, and so forth—you need to invest to completely develop a product and fully support its commercialization. The concept also includes having the *right investment profile* so that you have the *right resources* invested at the *right time* focused in the *right areas* so you can fully and profitably deliver the promised customer value for the purchasing volume you expect. This includes all dimensions of resources: labor, capital, material expenses during development, manufacturing capital and expenses to prepare for volume shipping, IT investment (for ordering, Web customer interfaces, or computerized customized manufacturing), advertising, retraining the sales force, retooling and training technical and/or field support, as well as legal, regulatory, and clinical areas. You want to optimize investment intensity precisely because resources are limited and how you choreograph them is key.

For DuPont Electronic Technologies, the sweet spot is "the intersection between capabilities and opportunities," says David Miller, vice president and general manager. "If anywhere in DuPont we have capabilities that can be leveraged, for example photopolymers or fine particles, or whatever the technology may be, we map them against the opportunities in the electronics space. You'll end up with great opportunities and no capability or capability and no great opportunities—you don't really have much interest in either of those. Then you'll have some areas where you'll have capability and good opportunity, and you figure out how to leverage your technology, your capability into that space."

After making initial in-or-out decisions about projects based on strategic fit and sweet-spot targeting, you filter yet again based on balancing issues such as market and technology risk and type of project. You may reject some products that passed the initial sandbox test because they cause the portfolio to tilt, like an improperly ballasted ship, too much in one direction or the other. For example, you may decide that your portfolio can tolerate only a certain degree of market risk and so are not willing to enter a completely new market. Or you may choose to pursue more new-to-the-world products than incremental or platform products.

USING THE RADAR CHART

We have found the radar chart pictured in Figure 4.1 to be a useful tool both for identifying the sweet spot and for continuing the filtering process based on how you decide to balance the portfolio. Because it represents multiple attributes, it more richly represents the multitude of factors affecting portfolio decisions than many typically used tools such as a bubble diagram. The center of the radar chart represents a value of zero, with values increasing along each axis toward the circle's perimeter. You can rank a potential product for each attribute along the appropriate axis and compare the resultant plot with other projects under consideration. The relative importance of each attribute to the company determines which axes to include. You could remove or add to the axes pictured in Figure 4.1, although in our experience more than 10 becomes confusing.

The strategic alignment, customer value, and investment intensity axes along the top guide your assessment of where the sweet spot is. Company strategy drives selection of additional axes, which will be unique to a particular company. For example, a medical device company would certainly include such factors as regulatory approval risk, governmental regulations, or reimbursement risk, which may have a significant impact on its portfolio.

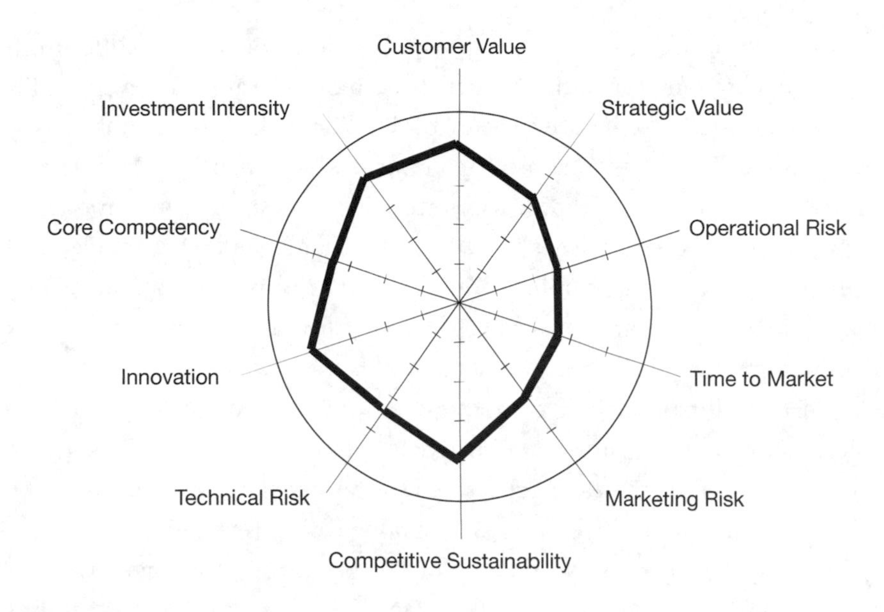

Figure 4.1 Single-product VIP radar chart.

All companies, however, need to identify relevant consent-to-operate issues—those legal, regulatory, or social issues that may stop the show for your proposed product. The BlackBerry handheld device (a successful product based on patent-infringing technology), a communications device based on an unavailable portion of the broadband spectrum, or a global agriculture company selling genetically modified seed to European countries that have rejected GMOs (genetically modified organisms) are examples of cases where consent-to-operate issues interfere with what might otherwise have been a successful idea.

Representing these important, high-level filters visually on a radar chart enables the executive team in charge of portfolio definition and management to objectively evaluate each project *before* considering the business case. Monetary concerns move off center stage and become one dimension of a multifaceted evaluation. Via its multiple spokes or axes, such a chart establishes, quickly and visually, the relative merits of each product concept. Each spoke represents a quantifiable value you can analyze and compare with other values.

As we mentioned earlier, the axes or spokes on the radar chart differ from company to company depending on which are most relevant. However, the filtering process—and the iterative nature of decision making—remains consistent. Consider The Dow Chemical Company, which manages its portfolio from its new business development group. The first test the group applies to any proposed product is what it calls SDS—Significant, Deliverable, and Sustainable. Is the idea *significant* enough to work on? Is it big enough? Does anyone care, internally and externally? Can we *deliver* it and get into the Dow system within our current business structure? Is it *sustainable*? Will it provide a long-term and maintainable competitive advantage through cost structure, intellectual property, or proprietary patents?

Putting ideas on the radar chart allows the first-level evaluation to be qualitative, not quantitative. Tony Frencham, Dow's business director for new business development, explains: "At the beginning, the answers to all those questions are qualitative, in that you don't have great numbers, but you do have a sense. So you can look at a new product, and look at the way we make the product, and have a sense of whether this should be cheaper than the way people are doing it today. That will give you a sense that you're going to have a cost competitive advantage." At this point, Frencham says, you don't exactly understand competitive cost, your cost, or the impact on customers' costs. "But you can have a sense. You can also have a sense about intellectual property."

It's the same, Frencham says, with whether a project is significant. "You can have a sense of, is this really, really big? Is this a mega-project? Or is this a relatively small project?" And significant can also be, is it relatively close to your corporate knitting? Is this something that the rest of the company is interested in, or is this something that's so wild and far from the rest of what the company's doing . . . [that it won't get] corporate support?"

The values at this point may be based on the executive team's best guesses. However, as you move along the path from defining the broad portfolio to the specifics of each project, you can plug in more specific values as part of the ongoing management of the portfolio (see Chapter 9). According to Frencham, "[A]s you progress the project through the portfolio, from early stage to late stage, these questions will become increasingly quantitative. We

BUBBLE DIAGRAMS

Many companies use bubble diagrams to evaluate proposed products. This popular portfolio management tool is a diagram consisting of two axes, with areas of intersection such as proven technology/current customers or long-term/new customers. Proposed projects are represented in these areas as bubbles, with the diameter of the bubbles corresponding to investment intensity—larger bubbles mean bigger investments. While bubble diagrams can be useful to determine the position of the products in a portfolio, they are limited by their two-dimensional nature. With only two axes, they are useful only to compare the risks versus rewards of the attribute being measured. This does not reflect the multifaceted nature of portfolio management, which must consider all the relevant factors influencing project/product selection.

* * * *

want to know what the numbers are and we want to see IP, we want to see the patents mapped out, we want to see who's who, and we want to see our cost, the competitive cost, the value pricing, the value chain. And so, it becomes more quantitative."

Dow's SDS model applies during the prevalidation stage. But once the project moves into the validation stage, the resource commitment becomes significant. Frencham explains: "The move into validation for us is a big one, because . . . [that's] when you really start to spend significant dollars." Dow has two definitions of success: (1) a project that is stopped prior to moving into validation and incurring additional costs and (2) a project that moves into validation and then achieves full commercialization. "For us, a failure is a project that moves into validation or beyond and then stops. As we move further through the process, we want to be able to quantify that in terms of what the customer would pay, what it means to them, how much more value will it deliver to them, and in turn, how much value do we think we can extract from bringing this opportunity to market."

EVALUATING MULTIPLE PROJECTS USING RADAR CHARTS

One of the most important things to keep in mind about the values on the radar chart is that deciding which to maximize and which to minimize is not always obvious. For example, it seems as if minimizing market risk would always be a good idea. However, in some cases a particular product may be so highly aligned with your strategy that you are willing to accept high market risk to realize that product.

In light of this, the radar chart becomes an even more powerful tool, providing the ability to quickly compare several proposed products on the same chart. Not only is this particularly useful when filtering dozens of products, but looking at products simultaneously also allows you to balance the portfolio in terms of *overall* values—how much risk will you accept in the *entire* portfolio? How innovative should the *entire* portfolio be? Evaluating potential projects in this way reveals another idea that should be obvious but often isn't: Not all products in the portfolio need to be new-to-the-world or out-of-the-park home runs. On the contrary, you may decide to balance a technically risky, highly innovative product with others that represent incremental improvements to an existing product line.

Figure 4.2 shows how you can simultaneously view the profiles of products A, B, and C. As the figure shows, Product A scores highly on all but the core competency axis. Product C scores highly on customer value with nearly the same investment intensity as A and B, but ranks lower for strategic alignment. Since Product C's customer value is at the upper range, it might be worthwhile to revisit and review the strategy, which in this case may now act as a constraint for the product. An example of this might be a product that will require additional manufacturing capacity, while company strategy calls for consolidation of manufacturing capacity. Product C has high ratings for customer value, competitive sustainability, and innovation, but it rates lower in technical and operational risk. Time-to-market and market risk values also are most favorable for this product.

You can even use radar charts to evaluate competitive offerings, if any, in the same market space. Comparing your product with the competition before product development even begins is certainly an advantage.

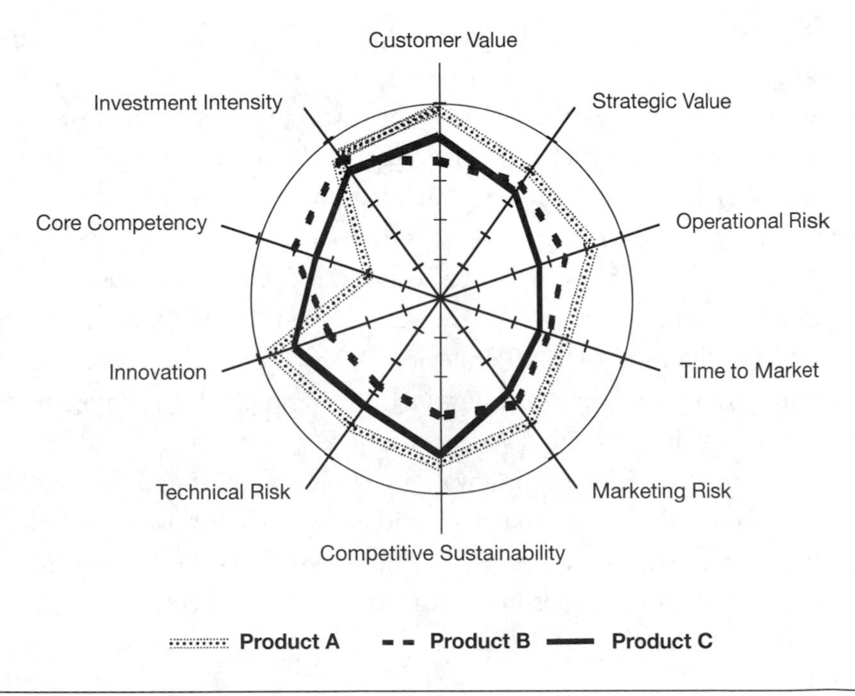

Figure 4.2 Multiple-products VIP radar chart.

MAKING TRADE-OFFS

Any discussion of achieving balance implies its prerequisite: making trade-offs. In a world of limited resources, each activity you take on and each attribute you maximize decreases resources available for other activities or attributes. Without a tool such as the radar chart, which seeks to bring together all significant criteria for evaluating potential projects, you may be back to the old methods of making trade-offs—listening to the most articulate division VP and green-lighting the projects with the rosiest spreadsheets.

What do some of the trade-offs look like in the context of a VIP approach to portfolio management? At Dow Chemical, for example, Tony Frencham's new business development group scrutinizes the size of various projects. Both large and small projects can be worthwhile. "A small project can be good if it easily bolts on to an existing business and it's an enhancement to that business, with an existing go-to market organization that would handle it," Frencham says. "But if it's a relatively small opportunity and you have to build an entirely new business to go deliver to market, it's probably not something you want to do."

Sometimes achieving balance may involve working with partners or other outside resources on codevelopment because a project doesn't fall within the core competency of the company but has other attributes that make it extremely attractive. Introducing an outside resource might increase investment intensity and technical risk due to the complexity of codevelopment; alternatively, partnering may be a way to reduce the investment intensity required. (See the discussion of strategic outsourcing in Chapter 3.) Going back to our example in Figure 4.2, Product B scores high in core competency with approximately the same investment intensity as Product A, but low in competitive sustainability and innovation. While technical and operational risks are reasonable, and time to market and market risk are favorable, it does not rank highly in strategic alignment (as indicated by its strategic value ranking). These analyses raise questions with which the management team must grapple.

IMPACT OF TECHNOLOGY AND MARKET TRENDS

In addition to balancing the portfolio on the several dimensions of your strategy, you need to consider technology and market trends when developing your portfolio. Customer requirements have different implications over time based on available technologies. For example, if you were in the personal stereo business before Sony introduced the Walkman, your customers might say they would be delighted if they could more easily listen to music while they walked down the street. At the time, that meant not having to carry around the mobile music technology of the day, a boom box. The Walkman disrupted the mobile music market and changed the consumer's expectations. It also created ancillary industries for cases and headphones.

As you can see in Figure 4.3, the evolution of the personal stereo changed the definition of mobility and raised expectations for sound quality. By viewing your customer requirements *over time in parallel with the changes you foresee in technology* (in the case of personal stereos, smaller footprint, longer-lasting batteries, greater storage capacity), you can establish research

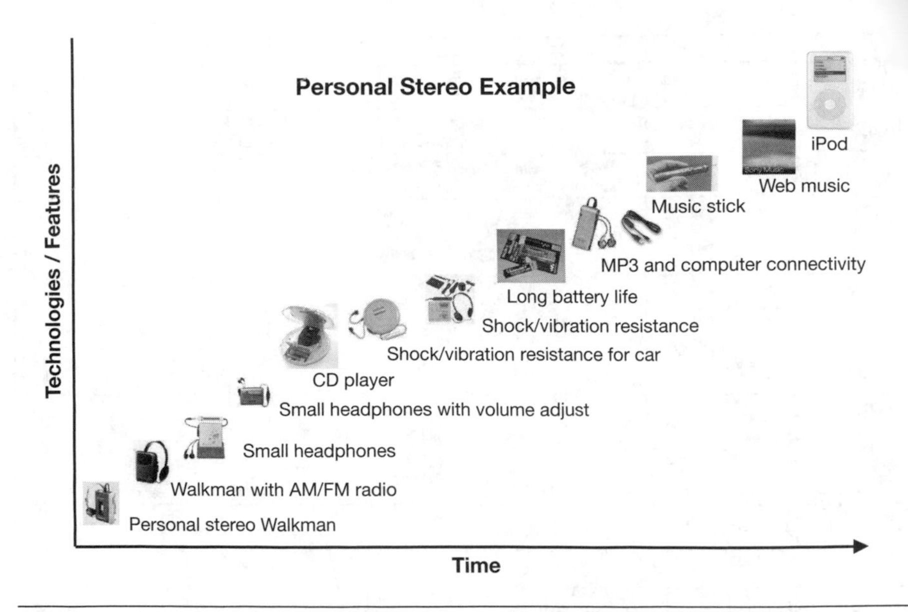

Figure 4.3 Market trends over time.

projects and partnerships that prepare your company to act when the trends become reality.

As you look at the portfolio over time, the important criteria illustrated by the radar chart still remain. For example, what happens when a competitor launches a product in your target market space? The new competitive offering may increase your market risk and interfere with competitive sustainability, not to mention increasing time to market and the need for innovation. Plotting the new data on your original radar chart may reveal a totally different picture that convinces you to alter or cancel the project. On the other hand, a competitive entry that does not target your identified sweet spot may signal a competitive advantage for your original project.

Motorola pays careful attention to technology and market trends as part of its portfolio planning. The company looks at its innovation portfolio "from a market perspective of customer and consumer needs for products and services and aligns these needs with our strategy," says Anthony Carter. "Further segmentation of the innovation portfolio is provided by looking at different technology sets or clusters and determining which innovation belongs in which set. For example, innovations could fit in mobile communication,

	2005	2006	2007	2008	2009
arket Trends	Example: Low Carbohydrates				
Regulatory Trends		Example: FDA Regulation Changes			
Customer Requirements	Example: Minimize Additives				
Technologies:					
Technology A — Maintain crunch without trans fats					
Technology B — Minimize heaviness of baked goods using whole-grain flour					
Technology C — Enhance vitamin content with new preservation methods					
Portfolio:					
Product Line 1 — Kids' cookies					
Product Line 2 — Packaged muffins					
Product Line 3 — Dried fruit snacks					
Competitive Sustainability					

Figure 4.4 Simple portfolio roadmap.

telematics, digital rights management, networking infrastructure, video services, and several others. We analyze these innovation clusters we create to determine what we think the market needs are going to be two to five years out and where our portfolio stands in meeting this need. Motorola has an organization that looks at trends across the technology space and makes predictions. The analysis of these trends is performed by internal experts, academia, consultants, and industry experts."

Carter is describing what we refer to as *roadmapping*. The output of the roadmapping process is a guide to identify and track technological trends, marketing trends, and resource requirements based on future projected needs. It offers a way of defining an end point for market needs, external forces, products, services, technologies, or resources and tracks alignment with the organization. As the former CEO of Motorola Bob Galvin puts it, "The fundamental purpose of the Technology Reviews and the Technology Roadmaps is to assure that we put in motion today what is necessary in order to have the right technology, processes, components and experience in place to meet the future needs for products and services."[2]

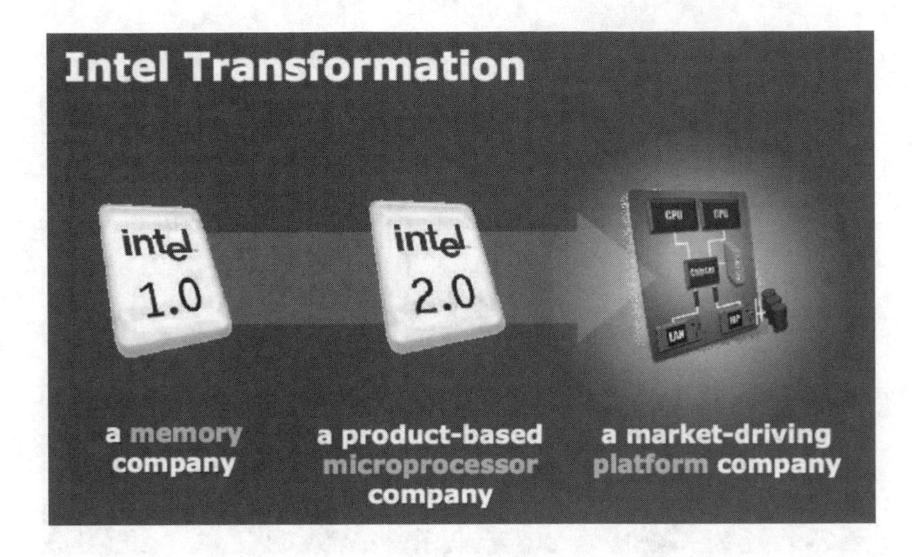

Figure 4.5 The platform plays a role in Intel's strategic transformation. (*Source*: Presentation by Martin J. Menard, director of platform capability, Intel Corporation, Information Services & Technology Group, at the IIR/PDMA best practices event, Strategic and Operational Portfolio Management Conference, February 27–March 1, 2006, Fort Lauderdale, FL.)

Figure 4.4 shows a simple roadmap for a hypothetical food company. The roadmap will help support critical planning and track progress against the organization's goals and objectives.

A roadmap also can provide a high-level, strategic picture of the relationship between a company's portfolio and the forces shaping the market. Intel Corporation, for example, takes two high-level approaches to roadmapping. The roadmap in Figure 4.5 looks at platform transformation, displaying the role of the platform in Intel's company strategy (from memory- to processor-based to market-driving). Figure 4.6 shows the role of Intel's platform organizations and the value added by each, offering another means of tying technology trends to marketing trends.

ASKING THE TOUGH QUESTIONS FROM THE TOP

"As a general manager, you're always dealing with the allocation of scarce resources," says Steve Sichak, president of medical device company BD

Figure 4.6 The role of Intel platform organizations. (*Source:* Presentation by Martin J. Menard, director of platform capability, Intel Corporation, Information Services & Technology Group at the IIR/PDMA best practices event, Strategic and Operational Portfolio Management Conference, February 27–March 1, 2006, Fort Lauderdale, FL.)

Diagnostics-Preanalytical Systems. "You have to make choices about what you're going to do with your resources. And the more complete an understanding you have of your customer, the more likely you are to allocate your resources to working on problems that are most important to them, which translate into larger revenue opportunities for us."

As we have argued from the beginning of this book, executive managers must be involved in the analysis of the portfolio and in making the trade-offs and decisions over time. Typically, senior managers develop the corporate vision, mission, and strategy. Senior operational managers then flesh out the strategy, conducting voice-of-the-customer research, creating the technical roadmap, and involving lead technical staff and product directors in defining product concepts.

But senior managers cannot simply set the strategy and then sit back while mid-level managers create the product portfolio. The portfolio itself, by virtue of how well it fits into the market sweet spot, both articulates and influences corporate strategy. So senior executives, from the CEO on down, must be involved in continuing to ask the tough questions. If the company has in place an organization such as a new business development group or a product review board, senior management should attend meetings of those groups to ask the following:

- What are the three to five highest priority customer requirements?
- What customer requirements will the portfolio address?
- Which customer requirements are not being addressed? Why?
- What is the product roadmap for addressing all requirements?
- How does the portfolio fit with our strategy?
- What customer requirements do competitive offerings address? How?
- What requirements do competitive offerings not address? Why?
- What innovations do we have that might map to customer requirements?
- What research work might we want to initiate that would create innovative products to meet some of the requirements?

These are hard fundamental questions that demand factual answers before management ever considers the business case for a portfolio. What's more, instituting an executive review based on adding customer value to the portfolio sends a loud and clear message to the development teams responsible for realizing new products. When a VP of development knows that any decision about future R&D spending, cost reduction, and incremental projects must first surmount the *customer value* hurdle, he or she will be sure to apply the VIP test *before* requesting company resources. This test involves ascertaining customer value by defining requirements and then collecting statistically significant data to validate, prioritize, and check segment differences, as described in Chapter 5. This should prevent projects with mediocre value from clogging the new product development pipeline. And redirecting resources from marginal or pet projects allows companies to focus limited resources on projects with the greatest probability of enhancing the portfolio—putting money into the half of the portfolio that will succeed, rather than tossing a coin.

The portfolio process at The Stanley Works, a producer of consumer and industrial tools, begins with total commitment of the management team from the CEO down through the organization. In fact, VP of Engineering and Technology Will Hill identifies management commitment as one of seven critical factors in portfolio success. Hill describes management involvement in one typical process at his company: "The CEO and all his staff sat through [three days of] meetings, where every business came in and presented." The presentations ranged from an hour for a business doing $100 million in revenue to a full day for a business in the billion-dollar range and covered the activities of each business unit. "It was a big deal," Hill says. "First off, everybody complained about how much work it took, but the really key thing was the analysis and thinking. That is the piece people tend to lose sight of as they get wrapped up in making PowerPoint slides and charts."

This process has led to many successful offerings. One of the most successful is the FatMax 1.25-inch-wide tape rule. "It's a phenomenally successful product in the marketplace," Hill says. "It's clearly one that everybody and his brother tried to copy . . . but our team did an awesome job on the intellectual property side. And, as far as I know . . . Stanley has fended off everybody who attempted to copy it."

The project had started, Hill says, as a "classic internally driven innovation, where a bunch of people sit around in a room and think of different things they can do with measuring tape rules. They came up with some unusual looking ideas." But Hill's group insisted that the team take training—which the company CEO promoted at a kickoff meeting—about how to research and evaluate and prioritize customer needs.

The team discovered that one of the big unmet needs for tape rules was standout. "If you ever have used a tape rule you know for the first twelve inches or so it's pretty rigid. As you pull it out further, at some point the thing collapses," says Hill. The value for the customer would be a tape rule that retained its rigidity as it was extended over longer distances. "The further it can stand out, the more jobs a carpenter can do by himself without needing a helper," says Hill. "The holy grail was eight feet, because, if you think about it, most [building] materials come in eight-foot lengths."

Once the team discovered the previously unmet customer need for standout, it did additional customer research. At the same time, the team was investigating the physics of tape rules, to understand how to achieve 8 feet of standout. While doing this, it occurred to team members that increasing the standout further—say, to 11 or 12 feet, the length of drywall and other materials—would yield an even greater competitive advantage.

Thus was born a proprietary manufacturing process that enables the FatMax tape rule to achieve 11 feet of standout. Its success, however, was due to more than just an idea with customer relevance. "Along with that was some very significant branding and industrial design. We had an awesome industrial design group and the marketing was world class. Obviously there was significant investment in machinery and manufacturing processes, but the rest is history," Hill says, in terms of the success of the product.

MAKING VIP MANAGEMENT WORK

In this chapter we discussed approaches to finding the sweet spot, where you're investing the right amount of resources into a product that aligns with your strategic goals and with the needs of the customer. This is an iterative process in which you start with products that provide customer value, then weed out the products that don't map to your strategic constraints. (See Figure 4.7.)

You then go back to examine the impact of market, technology, and competition and realign your portfolio to ensure that you have projects funded that map to future trends. This might require you to integrate technologies, partnerships, and other initiatives into the portfolio. Now you face what may be the most difficult part of portfolio definition: strategic balancing. In planning the proper investment intensity, you need to balance high-investment-intensity, high-risk, new-to-the-world projects that offer make-or-break potential with lower-risk and lower-investment-intensity projects that may move your company only minimally in the marketplace. You want to invest only as much in such areas as advertising, manufacturing, IT, distribution, sales realignment, and distributor networks as needed to yield the marketplace and business performance you seek. The strategy sets the direction, but ulti-

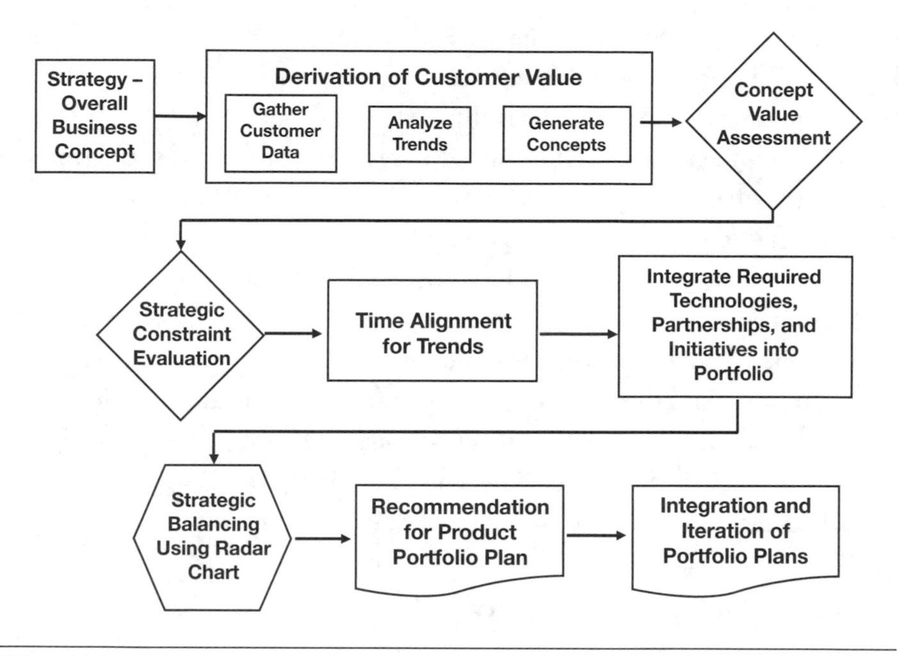

Figure 4.7 VIP management flow.

mately senior managers must make the hard choices based on the optimal level of investment intensity to achieve that strategy and ultimately provide customer value. (See Chapter 8 for an in-depth discussion of investment intensity and Appendix B for more on the investment intensity planning process.)

The VIP cube in Figure 4.8 is a means of viewing your portfolio after you have used the radar charts to balance it.

Each company develops a process for identifying the sweet spot that is unique to its culture, structure, and organization. However, we have observed that companies with successful portfolio management processes and robust product development processes exhibit the following:

- A commitment by the highest levels of corporate management to innovation and new product development
- The use of a qualitative filter process based on objectively determined customer value

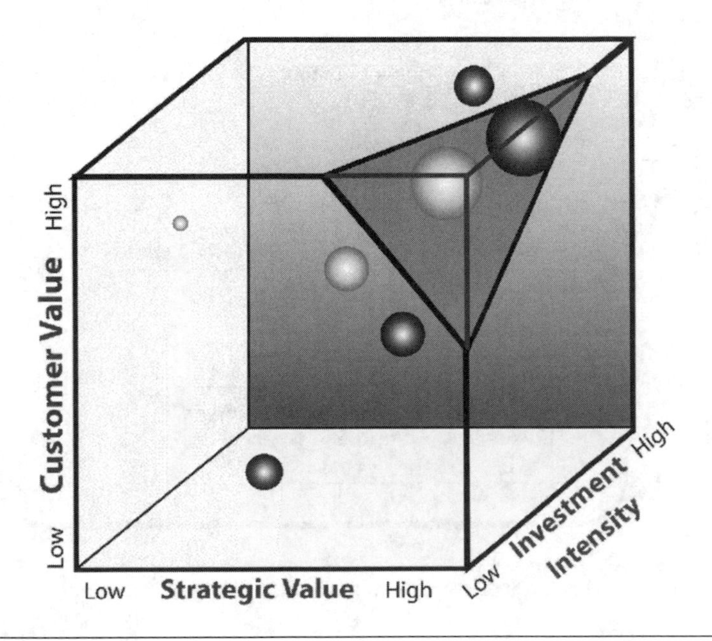

Figure 4.8 VIP sweet spot.

- An alignment with strategic values of the company, which identifies the axes of significance to further define the sweet spot
- A rigorous process for setting priorities to focus on the important projects
- A holistic approach to review and monitoring of portfolio management
- Evaluation of the business case *after* the other criteria have been satisfied

Figure 4.9 shows how the elements of the VIP management process would function in a typical organization. The linkage to other business processes clearly is driven through understanding and acting upon identifiable customer value.

Simply identifying the sweet spot and developing a better mousetrap does not ensure successful commercialization. In the next chapter we examine what's required to understand customer requirements in a quantifiable way. In subsequent chapters we define the necessary investments in marketing, distribution, manufacturing, and personnel, examine the elements that compose

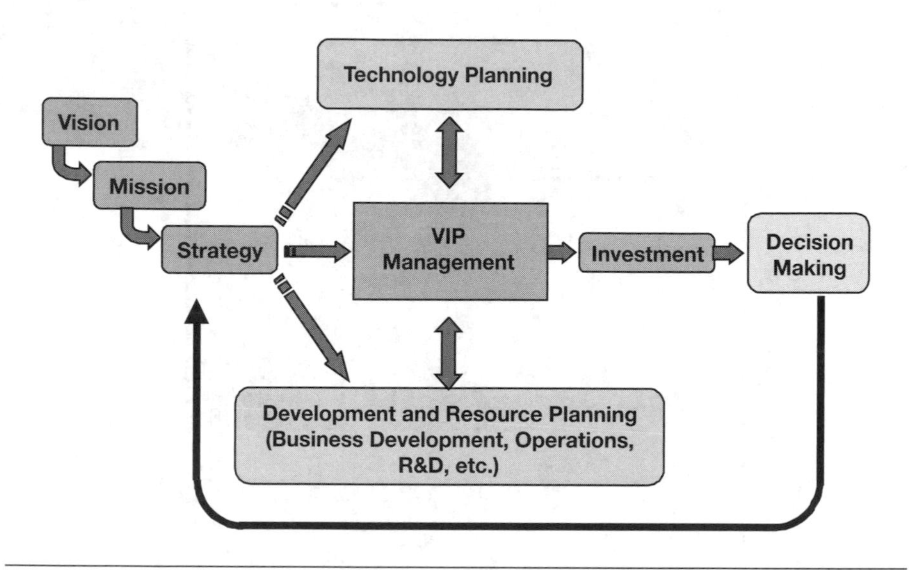

Figure 4.9 VIP management and business process linkages.

investment intensity, and begin to quantify the business case as additional components of VIP management.

NOTES

1. Michael Burkett, vice president of AMR Research, Inc., in a presentation, "Product Portfolio Management: Is It Critical to a High-Tech Company's Growth?" delivered in an IDE Webinar, December 14, 2005.
2. As quoted by Ed Crowley, founder of Photizo Group LLC, in a presentation titled "Winning Road Maps."

5

ACCURATE CUSTOMER VALUE DATA: THE MEASURED PORTFOLIO

"I'll tell you a story. My mother is 91 years old. She's a dear old lady. Now, your mother is someone you've known all your life. My relationship with my mother has become fixed over time, so I'll hear certain things said and just put it aside—heard that before. Recently my youngest brother, his wife, and I accompanied my mother to Scotland. So here we were, all four of us traveling together, and I consciously started to use interview techniques I've learned as part of customer-driven product development—open-ended questions, asking for explanations and expansions on specific statements, peeling away the layers of the onion. It's quite eye-opening! Because when you get down to it, a lot of things that you assumed, things you were conditioned to think, don't turn out like that at all, even with your own mother! It's only taken 60 years to get here. If you want to understand better, then pay attention to how you approach gathering all the information that you need to understand."

—John Fowler, marketing process development director of CNH, in an interview about his company's portfolio process

As any professional painter can tell you, most of the work in a paint job is preparation. You need to remove old wall coverings, fill holes, smooth the surface, and apply a primer. If you don't, your gorgeous new paint job won't last.

Preparation is a huge part of creating the Value Innovation Portfolio described in this book, and a big part of that preparation is, in John Fowler's words, "gathering all the information that you need to understand." That's why we devote this chapter to the framework and tools for obtaining accurate customer data. While you may be itching to choose the color and begin rolling on the paint, collecting and verifying customer data is the essential foundation of the VIP. Without such a foundation, your portfolio, like a slapdash paint job, won't have staying power. This chapter provides an overview of the process by which companies can prep for the job by gathering quantifiable, reliable data on what customers value.

PORTFOLIO SELECTION IS NOT A BEAUTY CONTEST

As we indicated in Chapter 4, the most-often-cited reason for product development failure is that companies don't understand customers and what they value.[1] More importantly, when companies attempt to innovate, the failures are staggering. "Despite spending huge sums on R&D, most corporations have dismally low levels of innovation productivity. The brutal truth is that 96 percent of all new projects fail to meet or beat their targets for return on investment."[2]

If failure to understand the customer accounts for most product failures, it follows that the opposite is true—understanding what customers value leads to success. We have proposed from the beginning of this book that companies must make portfolio decisions on the basis of value to the customer, not on the financial projections for individual projects. This reflects our belief that financial tools, especially when introduced early in the process, can be manipulated, misleading, and irrelevant as a foundation for deciding which ideas or projects receive funding from the company resource pool to become part of the company's portfolio of product offerings.

The Dow Chemical Company's approach to portfolio selection is successful precisely because it does not rely on financial data until later in the process.

Tony Frencham, Dow's business director for new business development, sees that at many companies "project selection comes down to, unfortunately, what I'd call a bit of a beauty contest . . . whichever project has the best PowerPoint presentation and the highest NPV [net present value] wins the competition and gets selected." For this reason, Dow does not include financial measures in its "first look" at a project in the exploration or early analysis stage. This is because at that stage, NPV is based on such a large number of assumptions as to be, says Frencham, "almost meaningless."

Although the financial data in the early stages can be of questionable integrity or simply meaningless, companies continue to use it for lack of an objective or believable alternative. Executives might argue that using customer value as the criterion for selection is subject to the same types of manipulation and is equally as misleading. The difference is that financial tools are based on *assumptions* regarding market and market growth *estimates*; *projected* market share, pricing, development, and manufacturing costs; and *potential* technical and commercial risks and capital costs. Companies use these assumptions, estimates, and projections to make evaluations based on return on investment (ROI), payback, or discounted cash flows.

By contrast, customer value is *identifiable, quantifiable, fact-based, objectively determined, derived through consensus*, and *repeatable*. For example, the manufacturer of a next-generation, industry-standard computing platform for service providers and corporate data centers discovered that two of the driving requirements for its new product were (1) enabling technicians to get their systems up and running as quickly as possible and (2) letting system managers sustain their computing environments with minimal disruptions. More specifically, a high percentage of technicians indicated that they would be delighted if they could configure their systems in less time than they could today, but expected configuration to take no longer than it does today. With this data in hand, the manufacturer can measure how long its next-generation platform takes to configure, making this aspect of customer value quantifiable. The company knows, with a 95 percent level of confidence, the exact percentage of technicians who want the system to perform better than it does today. The company can objectively measure existing solutions technicians use and set a target for its new product development—with the consensus of the team—because it has the necessary facts. The company can continue using the metric developed during the customer research phase for this requirement throughout product development to make sure the requirement meets its target as the team makes technology and architecture decisions.

When this team began its customer research, it thought customers were totally satisfied with the product's configuration time, because this aspect of the product represented an improvement over the previous system. But now, armed with data derived from actual customer voices translated into customer requirements and quantifiably verified and prioritized, the team can determine what functionality the new platform must have. Team members can depend on *the data* instead of wondering if they made the right assumptions. If changes in market dynamics affecting customer value occur, as they occasionally do, the company can quickly verify them during the product development phase before product development begins, to mitigate and minimize risk.

A common response to assessing what customers value is to look at a company's portfolio of products in light of the competition. How does our widget compare to Company X's widget? Worse yet is a comparison of features and benefits: Is our widget's torque greater or less than Company X's? In either case, the discussion of value is occurring at too low—and too literal—a level. Analysis of customer value as it relates to portfolio management must occur at a higher level of abstraction.

Office technology provider Pitney Bowes uses specific data on customer value to evaluate potential projects while at the same time elevating the analysis far above the level of product features. James Euchner, who manages the Advanced Technology group at Pitney Bowes, describes his company's approach to customer-centered innovation, shown in Figure 5.1. A key step in this process is validating the value delivered to the customer. "We had a hypothesis that if we implemented a certain system [in a hospital], it would change an index that was important to the hospital and very tightly tied to revenue. We did a baseline analysis before we implemented it, then measured the change. We also captured data that affected the index so that we could validate it from another angle." Pitney Bowes is now working on trial of another system, which offers a way to reduce undeliverable-as-addressed mail. "We will measure how much undeliverable-as-addressed mail [the customer has],

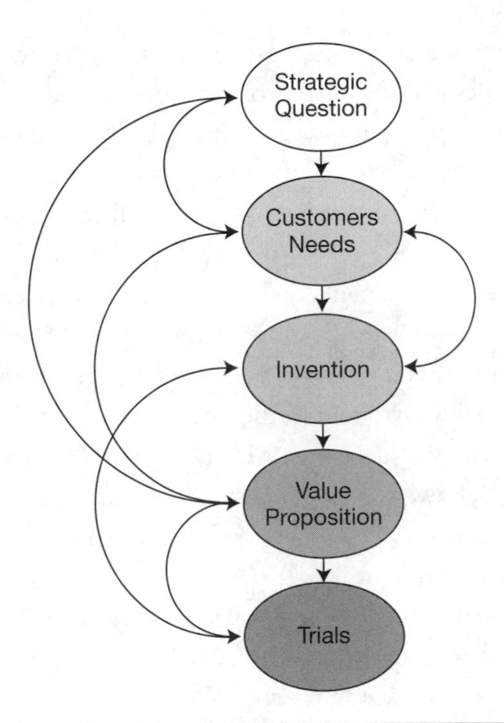

Figure 5.1 Pitney Bowes customer-centered innovation process. (*Source*: © Pitney Bowes, Inc.; used with permission.)

what the use of our application does to reduce undeliverable-as-addressed mail, and the cost associated with achieving that value." Euchner concludes, "If you understand your value proposition, then you're able to say, 'Here's why someone would buy it.' That's what we try to measure."

UNEARTHING WHAT CUSTOMERS VALUE BEGINS WITH RIGOROUS RESEARCH

Unfortunately, many approaches to gathering customer data—even ones that have been part of the marketer's arsenal for years such as surveys and focus groups—are not necessarily exacting. The constraints of the survey format leave little room for deep understanding of the customer. The data returned often bears a striking correlation to the questions asked; rather than getting at customer needs, the questions are based on the surveyor's assumptions. Focus groups bring customers and prospects together in an artificial environment that does not resemble their everyday work surroundings. These data-gathering methods *do* have a place in capturing market information—just not in uncovering customer needs, particularly unexpressed ones.

John Fowler, marketing process development director at CNH (parent company of the agricultural and construction equipment brands Case-IH, Case, and New Holland), comments on his company's experience introducing a customer-driven process for product definition: "[T]he big eye-opening part about our experience with [customer-driven product definition] is the process of going and completely separately finding out what the questions are to be asked before conducting [a survey] . . . That was, for us, the novelty of that process. Sure, we *thought* we went out and talked to customers and all the rest of it and knew the customer and understood it, but whenever that's based on your own questions, it's not true."

Fowler continues, "One of the impressive consequences of applying a customer-requirement-driven definition process has been the elimination of internal experts who are replaced by a cross-functional group who have actually been out and encountered customers in their own circumstances and brought back information and interview transcripts, which form the basis of being able to identify what it is that the customers need and what the customers ultimately require and being able to validate that."

The same eye-opening results obtained by CNH for defining individual products await companies that use this approach for portfolio definition. The process used to gather information about what customers value must be based on contextual interviews, quantitative surveys, and in-depth data analysis and must begin with a plan in preparation for customer visits. An ad hoc approach will result in exactly the type of unverifiable estimates you seek to avoid. In this initial phase, having or developing a clear and articulated business strategy, as discussed in Chapter 3, ensures clear direction and consistent understanding of the mission and scope of the portfolio project by all players. Essentially, you need to get everyone on the same page from the start.[3]

Doing this type of research, Fowler contends, "changes completely the internal dynamics of how products get defined. No longer is it just analysis of competitive gaps, technology gaps, what this market says it wants, what that

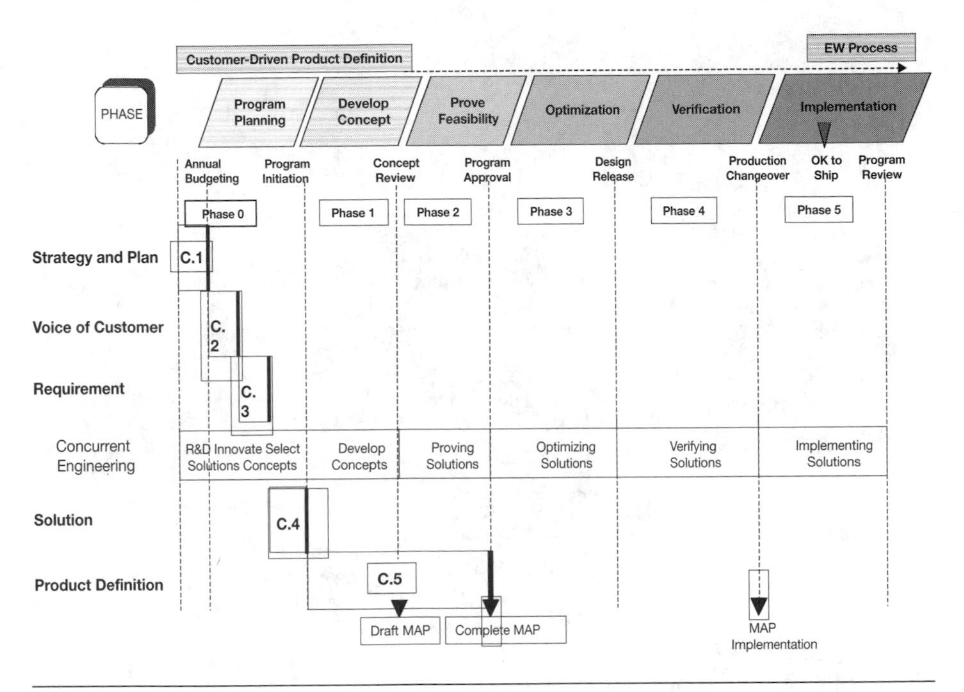

Figure 5.2 CNH's CDPD integrated into global product development (*Source*: Used with permission.)

market says it wants. It becomes a much more structured discussion led by a statement of what the customer requires. From that, where does the competition stand? Where do we stand? And what should we do about what we see? . . . [I]f you can do that for product definition, I fully believe you can do the same for portfolio management . . . at a higher level . . . within the organization."

To accomplish what John Fowler discusses, you need to integrate a robust product definition process like the one shown in Figure 5.2. CNH uses a market-driven product definition approach it calls CDPD (for customer-driven product definition, based on PDC's MDPD, or Market-Driven Product Definition).

Companies often lament, "We talked to our customers extensively but still missed the mark with our product." They therefore conclude that gathering data from customers is not particularly helpful in creating a successful portfolio of products. The problem, however, lies not with the idea of gathering customer data, but with the methods used to collect, analyze, and disseminate it—the when, where, and how of gathering data.

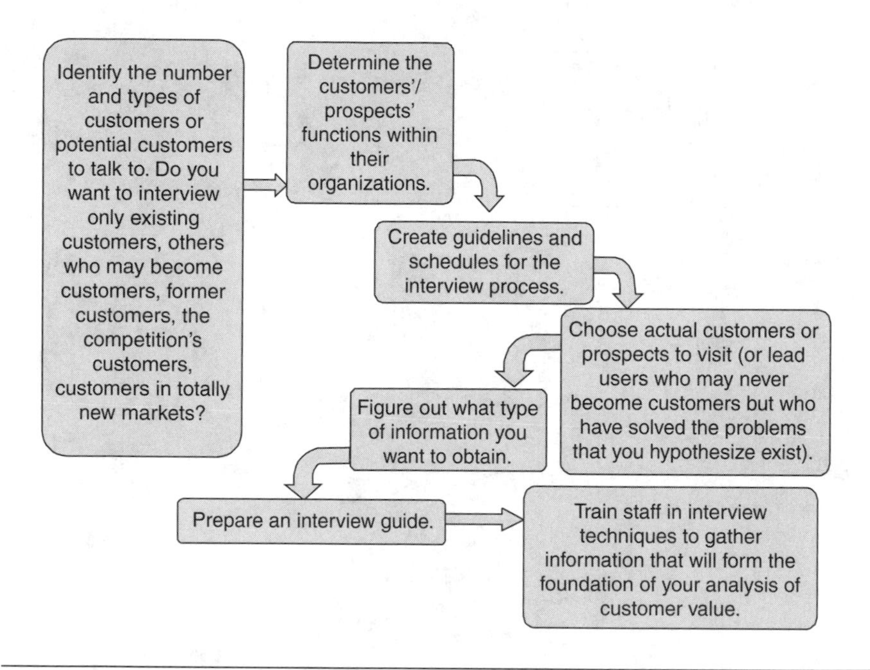

Figure 5.3 Customer interview prep work.

The traditional customer visit process accounts for much of the failure of customer data in directing the portfolio. Too often, these visits occur on the spur of the moment and are not directed at obtaining the valuable insights required in this phase of investigation. In this part of the process, preparation is again the key. Figure 5.3 shows seven steps a company needs to take before ever venturing into a customer's office to ask questions.

Trade shows, conferences, occasional lunch meetings, or customer relationship management systems are not the venues in which to obtain deep and meaningful customer insights. The interviews must occur *at the customer site* so you can observe customers in their own environments.

IN SEARCH OF THE PEA UNDER THE MATTRESS

Other naysayers dismiss customer-value-driven approaches to portfolio management with the criticism that such approaches lead only to development of incremental products, not products that define new market spaces. This indeed may occur if interviewers question customers about existing or proposed new products, or even ask such seemingly open-ended questions as "If you could design the best widget in the world, what would it look like?" The problem with such questions is that they have already put constraints on the possible problem space to be addressed. They assume that the answer to the problem is some type of widget—maybe a better, easier-to-use widget, but a widget nonetheless.

Done right, customer research visits can unlock entire new markets. Asking truly open-ended, probing questions—and listening carefully to customers' answers—lets you identify problems your company can potentially solve using an approach as yet unimagined by competitors. Tony Frencham describes how Dow Chemical tries, whenever possible, to interview customers in person, using Dow staff people. "We will occasionally want to protect our identity and in those sort of cases, we sometimes will just talk with consultants, rather than with active members of the industry . . . But generally we prefer to be face to face. We prefer to see the body feedback and to get the sort of human interaction that goes on there." The key to a question that asks for the ideal product is to focus more on asking interviewees about the ideal *processes* for doing their jobs and following any answer with the question: "What problems would that solve?" This approach yields the richness of the interview results.

What senior executives really need to find out as a result of these visits is what drives customers crazy. These findings may come from what customers *say*, but they just as often come from what customers *do*. Remember the children's tale of the princess and the pea? When asked about her problem, the princess didn't complain about the pea under her mattress. All she knew was that she had spent a sleepless night in an uncomfortable bed. The job of the collector of customer data is to observe what gets in the way of customers' lives (in the princess's case, a rotten night's sleep) and use that knowledge to solve their problems (get rid of the pea).

Suppose, for example, your company manufactures hand tools for professional carpenters. If you simply survey customers by phone or e-mail, you may get feedback about your hand sander such as "make it quieter" or "make it easier to change the paper." During interviews conducted at a job site, however, you have the opportunity to gather data that may lead to the development of an extremely valuable solution. You may observe carpenters attempting to prevent the sawdust raised by sanding from settling on recently varnished cabinets at another part of the site. They may lose time moving cabinetry around or waiting for it to dry before starting sanding work. You may then come up with the idea of a self-vacuuming hand sander—a completely new product that solves a problem your prospects may never have articulated in an interview. Had you simply focused on getting feedback on your existing product line, you would have missed a new opportunity and joined the ranks of those who believe that gathering data from customers leads only to development of incremental products.

Of course, this type of observational process for data collection can take a tremendous amount of time. Unless you spend weeks at a customer site, you won't see all the different situations customers may face. That's why you also need to use interviewing techniques that get at examples of all different types of problems—another method of uncovering the pea.

Pitney Bowes treats the process of interviewing customers as a type of ethnographic research, as shown in Figure 5.4. "We'll start with a strategic question," says James Euchner. "This generally defines a reasonably broad but clear opportunity area. So it may be, for example, document management opportunities in law firms. Or it may be opportunities to provide mailing solutions to people who currently use stamps. And we use anthropology—or ethnography, which is borrowed from the field of anthropology—to go out and understand emerging customer needs from the perspective of the users. When we went into hospitals, for example, we spent a lot of time doing comparative ethnographies of different hospitals to try to understand their document management needs. During this part of the overall process, the focus is really on uncovering and understanding customer needs." By being at the customer site and taking an ethnographic approach, the Pitney Bowes method of combining observation with on-site customer exploration uncovered some surprises about how customers viewed documents and record-keeping that wouldn't have been identified in a focus group or phone survey.

Figure 5.4 Pitney Bowes hospital medical records example (*Source*: © Pitney Bowes, Inc. Courtesy of Jill Lawrence; used with permission.)

CUSTOMER PROBLEMS AS STORIES

The next step is just as crucial as data collection and just as often left to imprecise methods. Customer visits yield stacks of interview transcripts and seemingly random observations. What's needed is a way to refine the raw customer data and integrate it with results from ethnographic observations (the observation of the carpenters struggling with dust or the princess tossing and turning on her mattress). We use a method called *image mapping* or *image diagramming* to identify key images and achieve consensus with the portfolio team on a consolidated image. This method works as a means of prioritizing requirements from the customers' perspective.

The result is creation of a clear image that identifies a scene, a story, or event from the customer's perspective. This is where the customer's pain becomes real, tangible, and memorable. Because it derives directly from experience with a customer in his or her own environment, the image map carries both quantifiable information and emotional weight. For example, one PDC client interviewing customers about medical diagnostics equipment observed a large yellow Post-it Note taped to the existing diagnostic system stating: "Push here *twice* to start." That image was clearly etched in the minds of the team members conducting the interview in a way that would never have been conveyed through a phone interview or focus group. When translated into a requirement, that image became the basis for solving the customer's problem: remembering how to start the system.

The purpose of conducting interviews and gathering images is to define the customers' expressed problems in getting their jobs/goals accomplished and, more importantly, problems *not explicitly stated* but implied or latent. The next step, translating the customer's voice into customer requirements, allows the team to reach consensus on the key requirements the development team will address. The word *requirement* in this case does not refer to a statement of product features such as "padded sides" or "minimal footprint." Instead, requirement in the context of portfolio definition refers to attributes that customers value. In the golf example described in the sidebar, the images centered on the golfers' frustrations that the golf bag got in their way instead of being an asset. Golfers desire the removal of all obstacles to playing better golf. A requirement for a golf bag, then, would be this: *Golfers have a bag that stays in the position they put it under a maximum number of conditions.* Clearly, this is a different kind of requirement than *The golf bag has to have soft sides and a rigid bottom.*

Clear requirements definitions lead to clear metrics for each requirement that reveal quantitatively whether the portfolio meets customer requirements, as we will discuss in Chapter 9. Armed with fact-based criteria with which to evaluate changes that may occur during the life of the portfolio, the portfolio team can quickly and confidently evaluate trade-offs against specific customer needs. The resulting balance helps ensure that the portfolio meets customer requirements even within the constraints of the real world, where resources are finite and compromise is a reality.

WHAT GOLFERS WANT: USING IMAGE MAPPING TO UNCOVER CUSTOMER VALUE

To give an idea of how observations can become customer images that in turn become portfolio requirements, we offer the analysis we conducted to provide portfolio insights for the hypothetical maker of golf equipment. Though the company is imaginary, the potential customers, surveys, and process of gathering and analyzing data are all very real (although we didn't scientifically validate the study results, since they were intended merely to provide a roadmap through the process).

Our first step was to develop a representative sample of potential customers. We constructed the customer matrix to include a geographically diverse cross section of participants: lead users, users with low to high golf handicaps, both sexes, various ages, and various income levels. We did not consider frequency of play because differences in use did not surface between recreational golfers and avid ones.

Next we interviewed the golfers, in their own environment—on and near the golf course. This was the fun part! When new information stopped appearing, we stopped interviewing. We collected hundreds of images and concepts from the transcripts of these interviews. Here are a few examples:

"When we played in Silverado, I retrieved my golf glove. It was soaking wet from the previous day. It was very uncomfortable and cold."

"I lost my shoes when I was playing golf last year at a resort. There was no special place for the shoes and so I just left them with the attendant and they were not there the next day."

"I was walking the course and going down a hill to get to the next hole when my bag and cart took off and rolled all the way down and everything fell out. What a mess!"

"The bag has so many compartments that I never know where I put the chocolate candy drops that I want."

We extracted the images from the transcripts and narrowed them to the vital few, then combined these vital few to create an image diagram—essentially, a document containing descriptions of the key images, logically grouped (see Figure 5.5).

We then reviewed the customer transcripts a second time to ensure we had extracted all the themes and problems the interviewees identified. By taking the voices from the transcripts and superimposing them onto the customer image

Continued on p. 125

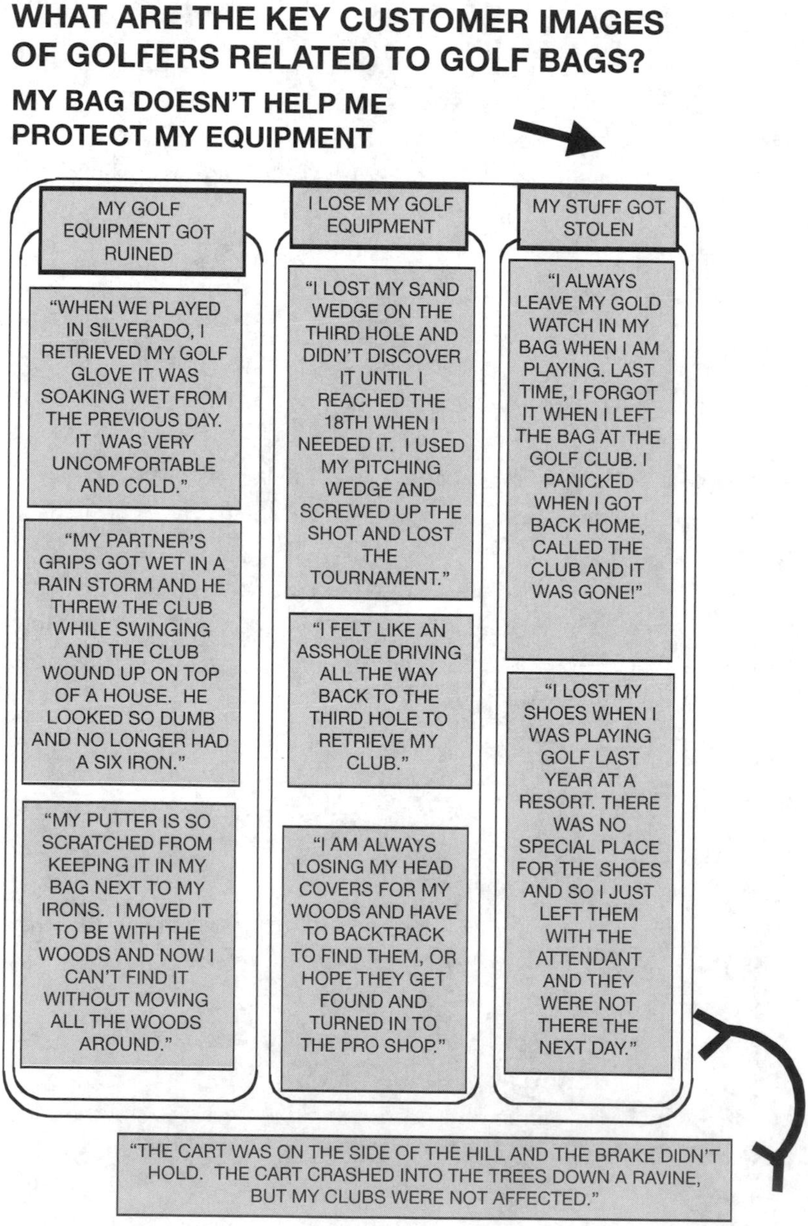

WHAT ARE THE KEY CUSTOMER IMAGES OF GOLFERS RELATED TO GOLF BAGS?

MY BAG DOESN'T HELP ME PROTECT MY EQUIPMENT

MY GOLF EQUIPMENT GOT RUINED

"WHEN WE PLAYED IN SILVERADO, I RETRIEVED MY GOLF GLOVE IT WAS SOAKING WET FROM THE PREVIOUS DAY. IT WAS VERY UNCOMFORTABLE AND COLD."

"MY PARTNER'S GRIPS GOT WET IN A RAIN STORM AND HE THREW THE CLUB WHILE SWINGING AND THE CLUB WOUND UP ON TOP OF A HOUSE. HE LOOKED SO DUMB AND NO LONGER HAD A SIX IRON."

"MY PUTTER IS SO SCRATCHED FROM KEEPING IT IN MY BAG NEXT TO MY IRONS. I MOVED IT TO BE WITH THE WOODS AND NOW I CAN'T FIND IT WITHOUT MOVING ALL THE WOODS AROUND."

I LOSE MY GOLF EQUIPMENT

"I LOST MY SAND WEDGE ON THE THIRD HOLE AND DIDN'T DISCOVER IT UNTIL I REACHED THE 18TH WHEN I NEEDED IT. I USED MY PITCHING WEDGE AND SCREWED UP THE SHOT AND LOST THE TOURNAMENT."

"I FELT LIKE AN ASSHOLE DRIVING ALL THE WAY BACK TO THE THIRD HOLE TO RETRIEVE MY CLUB."

"I AM ALWAYS LOSING MY HEAD COVERS FOR MY WOODS AND HAVE TO BACKTRACK TO FIND THEM, OR HOPE THEY GET FOUND AND TURNED IN TO THE PRO SHOP."

MY STUFF GOT STOLEN

"I ALWAYS LEAVE MY GOLD WATCH IN MY BAG WHEN I AM PLAYING. LAST TIME, I FORGOT IT WHEN I LEFT THE BAG AT THE GOLF CLUB. I PANICKED WHEN I GOT BACK HOME, CALLED THE CLUB AND IT WAS GONE!"

"I LOST MY SHOES WHEN I WAS PLAYING GOLF LAST YEAR AT A RESORT. THERE WAS NO SPECIAL PLACE FOR THE SHOES AND SO I JUST LEFT THEM WITH THE ATTENDANT AND THEY WERE NOT THERE THE NEXT DAY."

"THE CART WAS ON THE SIDE OF THE HILL AND THE BRAKE DIDN'T HOLD. THE CART CRASHED INTO THE TREES DOWN A RAVINE, BUT MY CLUBS WERE NOT AFFECTED."

Figure 5.5 Image diagram from golf bag example.

MY BAG IS A PAIN IN THE BUTT

"IT STARTED TO RAIN AND MY BAG FILLED UP WITH WATER. CAN YOU IMAGINE HAVING TO DUMP EVERYTHING OUT TO DRAIN THE WATER?" "I LOST A BALL IN THE WATER AND RAN BACK TO MY BAG TO GET MY BALL RETRIEVER. I LOOKED EVERYWHERE AND COULDN'T FIND THE DAMN THING. WOULD YOU BELIEVE IT HAD FALLEN ALL THE WAY DOWN AND WAS IMPOSSIBLE TO GET OUT?"

MY BAG GETS IN MY WAY

"I WAS WALKING THE COURSE AND GOING DOWN A HILL TO GET TO THE NEXT HOLE WHEN MY BAG AND CART TOOK OFF AND ROLLED ALL THE WAY DOWN AND EVERYTHING FELL OUT. WHAT A MESS!"

"WE WERE LEAVING THE AIRPORT WITH OUR LUGGAGE AND OUR GOLF BAGS AND MY HUSBAND'S BAG KEPT FALLING OFF THE CART AND SOMEONE TRIPPED ON IT."

"I DRIVE A MIATA AND HAVE TO PUT THE TOP DOWN IN ORDER TO CARRY MY WIFE'S AND MY GOLF BAGS. IT STARTED TO RAIN AND WE HAD TO PUT THE CLUBS IN THE CAR AND GET OUT OURSELVES. BOY, DID WE LOOK STUPID STANDING ON THE SIDE OF THE ROAD NEXT TO OUR CAR."

"MY BAG IS MY BEST FRIEND. I HAVE HAD IT FOR 20 YEARS AND IT IS JUST ME."

GOLF IS BOTH TOUGH AND FRUSTRATING SO GOLFERS NEED ALL THE HELP THEY CAN GET

I AM CONFUSED

"I MISTAKENLY TOOK A SIX IRON FOR A NINE IRON ON A 110-YARD PAR THREE AND I HIT THE SIX IRON 60 YARDS PAST THE PIN, INTO THE WOODS AND DOWN A HILL. I WAS OUT OF BOUNDS!"

"I CANNOT FIND WHAT I AM LOOKING FOR WITHOUT CHECKING SEVERAL POCKETS."

MY BAG IS CONFUSING

"I WAS RETURNING MY BUNCH OF CLUBS THAT I HAD JUST USED INTO THE BAG WHEN MY HUSBAND YELLED HURRY UP, WE ARE HOLDING UP EVERYBODY. IT WAS SO EMBARRASSING TO BE YELLED AT ON THE COURSE."

"WHEN I GO SEARCHING FOR BALL MARKERS, TEES, AND REPAIR TOOLS AND ALL THE OTHER ACCESSORIES, THEY ARE ALL IN THE BOTTOM OF THE BAG AND I HAVE TO DIG A WHOLE HANDFUL OF STUFF OUT TO FIND WHAT I AM LOOKING FOR."

" BAG HAS SO MANY COMPARTMENTS THAT I NEVER KNOW WHERE I PUT THE CHOCOLATE CANDY DROPS THAT I WANT."

Figure 5.5 (Continued) Image diagram from golf bag example.

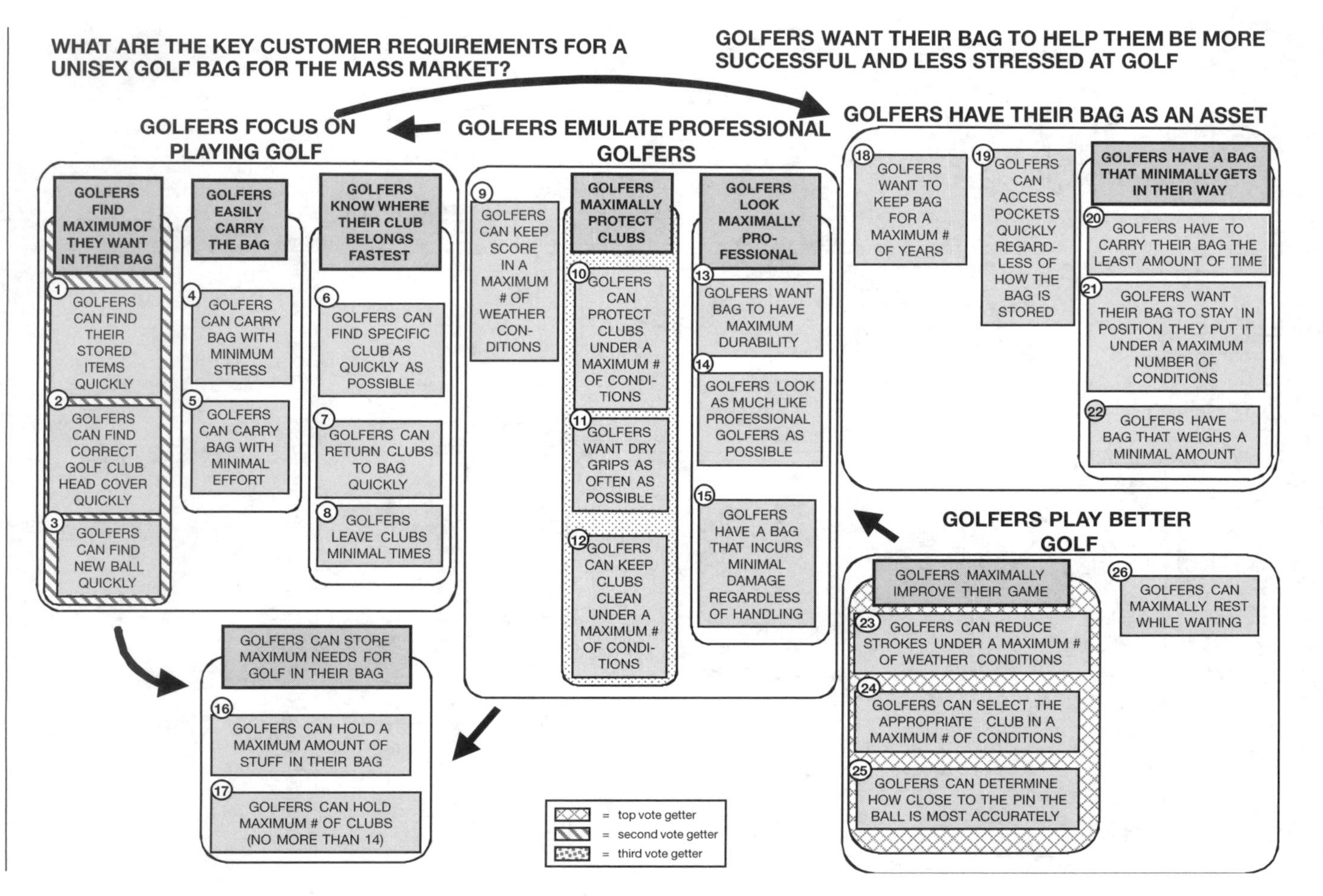

Figure 5.6 Requirements diagram from golf bag example.

WHAT GOLFERS WANT: USING IMAGE MAPPING TO UNCOVER CUSTOMER VALUE (Continued)

developed in the image mapping, we were able to develop customer requirements that extended well beyond what the customer had stated—revealing the latent or unstated requirements that are key to going beyond the perspective of an individual customer.

Hundreds of requirements were extracted, and the key requirements were selected and organized to ensure that no key requirements are missing. From this bottom-up approach of asking open-ended questions, synthesizing the responses, and revisiting the responses in light of the synthesis, a picture emerged of what dedicated golfers value. As the requirements diagram in Figure 5.6 shows, they want to focus on playing golf rather than worrying about their equipment. They want to emulate professional golfers. They want their golf bags to be assets in helping them play better golf.

* * * *

GENERATING AND EVALUATING POTENTIAL SOLUTIONS

There's more than one way to skin a cat, as the old saying goes, and there may be tens or even hundreds of different solutions to the needs identified through gathering customer data. After conducting initial customer surveys, you do solution brainstorming. Generating potential solutions involves defining solutions, whether new-to-the-world or incremental. This is the point at which your organization's creativity comes into play, where you have the opportunity to differentiate your company from others. You should involve your organization's top talent to define the best way to meet a customer's requirements based on the decisions you make from your quantitative research.

Executives charged with defining the portfolio also need to be concerned with cat-skinning. Which requirements will the solution address, and why? It's important to recognize that this is a portfolio issue, not simply a product issue. Your research may uncover many opportunities to create value for customers. You don't have to address all customer requirements in a single product, but you may decide to address some by enhancing existing products and others by developing a new technology.

All requirements aren't created equal, so you need a way to decide which requirements are most important. In the absence of a rigorous method for doing this, executives involved in portfolio planning are vulnerable to the beauty contest problem we identified earlier: the prettiest PowerPoint presentation and the most persuasive VP get the nod. Using surveys to determine the importance of requirements provides results with a level of statistical significance that circumvents the beauty contest problem.

The Kano method (based on the method of questioning developed by Dr. Noriaki Kano of Japan's Tokyo Riko University) is one approach to validating and prioritizing requirements. The Kano method ranks each requirement according to the level of customer satisfaction or dissatisfaction elicited by solving it and the degree to which its solution contributes the customer's perception of value. We've all experienced the make-or-break feature—one that absolutely *must* be in a product or we won't buy it, the feature that is so attractive it induces us to buy the product in the first place, or the feature that would affect our purchase decision only if it were missing completely.

Kano rankings capture these customer responses in a quantitative way that lets the portfolio team evaluate requirements against the solutions under consideration (Figure 5.7). As an added bonus, you can use Kano analysis not only to evaluate your own proposed solutions but also to evaluate how *competitive* offerings address each of the stated and unstated requirements. And here the true power of this kind of slogging-through-the-mud customer research becomes evident. *Now you can mold your market offering to address the requirements the competition is ignoring.* You have moved beyond the incremental to the breakthrough.

As the final step in solution evaluation, you examine alternative solutions based on whether they meet customer requirements (as defined by the survey results) and targets set from your evaluation of the competition. Finally, you look at potential solutions in light the constraints discussed in Chapter 4.

MAXIMIZING YOUR INVESTMENT IN CUSTOMER RESEARCH

The organizational and operational issues involved in doing good customer research prove challenging for some companies. As we touched on in Chapter 1,

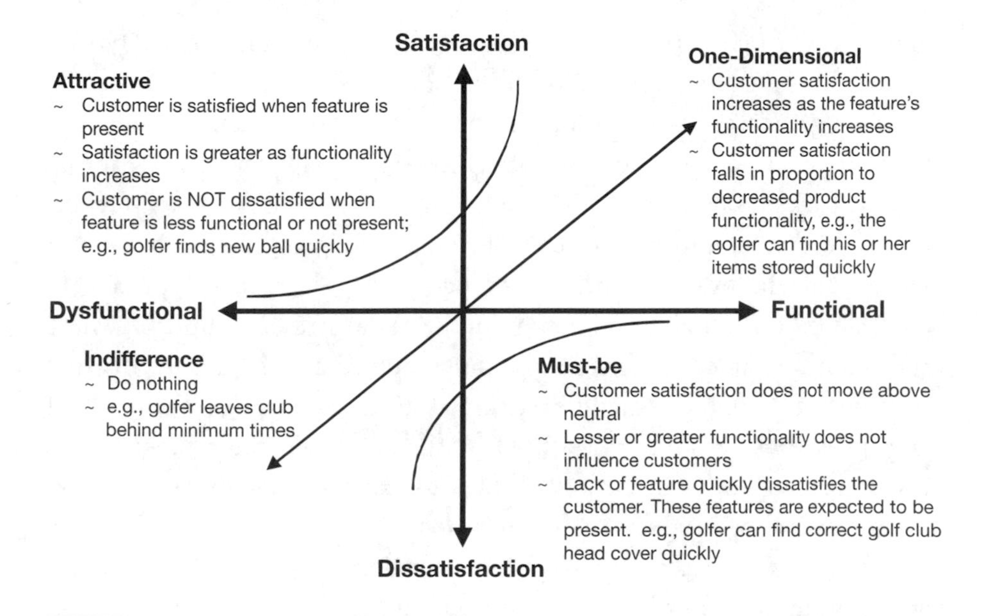

Figure 5.7 The Kano diagram plots levels of customer satisfaction against requirements.

telecommunications company Avaya pulled back from doing customer research during tough economic times, potentially crippling its ability to deeply understand the market and generate ideas that offer customer value.

Other companies, despite being large organizations with numerous business units and product lines, have developed strategies to leverage every cent they spend on customer research. For example, if you conduct voice-of-the-customer research for each business unit as part of portfolio development, all projects in that business unit could take advantage of that data. At medical diagnostics company Dade Behring, customer data drives the corporate culture, which means that individual business units are always collecting this data. "I would say virtually every single presentation has customer data in it. Every single one. How does it happen that they get it? It's just part of our culture, now. We have a very data-driven decision-making approach," says Dade Behring's Deirdra Dougherty, director of global marketing communications and analysis. The company achieves additional efficiencies by centralizing storage of customer data. "From a functional perspective, I'm the central source. If people have questions or are looking for something, either they come to me or I go to them and say, 'I really think you could use this type of information. Are you interested in getting it?'"

Leverage comes as well from making the most of the information you already have. For one segment of its business, Dougherty says, Dade Behring is "going back and pulling all of the data from the previous five years [for] . . . any product development project that's related to drugs, highlighting that data, and then innovating or brainstorming—not on the specs of a product to be developed but on how you communicate about it. What's unique, what's important to people, where are those differentiated areas? [You might] find out that even though you might have some features in previous products that really meet those customer needs, you just never highlighted them. That's been a big focus for us in the past year . . . to really leverage the data that we have for selling the products that we have today."

Hewlett-Packard, an even larger organization than Dade Behring, also benefits from a customer-research-based culture—reinforced by its customer visit centers, where customers come specifically to interact with potential products and provide feedback—as well as a centralized system for disseminating customer data. "We're constantly doing research to understand customer needs," says Deborah Nelson, vice president of marketing and alliances for HP's Technology Solutions Group. "All of that data is available to everyone. So, for instance, if someone in a product group has done a bunch of research, it's probably going to help the services people who have to help maintain that product . . . [W]e have a research portal and all of the marketing teams have access to it so that we can better share information." As they use the data, various groups also may contribute to it. "One group may look at all that data, and use it, and not have to do any additional research. Other groups may decide that gave them a great foundation but they still have six questions they need to go out and do research on . . . then that research becomes available to the other teams so that we can share and build up the understanding of what is required."

Companies that spend a lot of money on R&D could achieve an enormous payback by allocating even a small portion of that investment to good VOC research.

CROSSING THE LINE: CUSTOMER DATA FOR PRODUCT DEVELOPMENT

This chapter discussed the process and customer data required for *portfolio definition*. But customer research doesn't stop once you have identified a portfolio of products to meet identified customer needs. The product definition phase—figuring out what the product should look like, what features should be included, and how your solution will address requirements—necessitates *more* customer research. This deep-dive customer work, conducted by the teams charged with developing specific products, while beyond the scope of this book, is what allows you to turn the potential of the portfolio into the reality of a collection of products. Appendix A offers a taste of the market-driven product definition process, and our previous book, *Customer-Centric Product Definition* (PDC Professional Publishing, 2003), covers the topic in depth.

EXECUTIVES IN THE HOT SEAT

None of the benefits of conducting the quantitative, directed, and strategically aligned customer research we have outlined in this chapter will occur unless those running the company—presidents, CEOs, COOs, CFOs—believe in this approach. They will set the tone by their directives and their actions. If they themselves are not champions of the VIP approach, then at the very least the company needs a management-level champion who can promote customer research to executives as an equal of business-unit leaders.

In keeping with the higher level of this assessment, executives charged with running the business must become involved and active participants in brainstorming as well as generating, evaluating, and selecting solutions. Their involvement keeps these decisions consistent with the vision, mission, and strategy for the business. The output from this initial customer research, data analysis, and solution generation is the VIP roadmap—the final, actionable end product that propagates the vision for providing customer value through the company.

The overview of requirements gathering in this chapter is necessarily a cursory one. The customer research process takes at least several weeks—and more often months—for a cross-functional team to complete properly. Our intention was not to provide a step-by-step guide, but rather to light the fire under senior managers to prompt them to make sure customer input—*the right kind of customer input, done the right way*—is part of the portfolio decision-making process. This chapter has given you new management tools and language to encourage your teams to do some hard prep work before making the case for a new product to add to the portfolio. Much more is required, however, to inculcate the VIP approach throughout the organization. In the next chapter we address another essential element: orchestrating the deployment and communication of the VIP.

NOTES

1. PDMA. "NPD Best Practices Study: The PDMA Foundation's 2004 Comparative Performance Assessment Study (CPAS)" (Oak Ridge, NC: PDMA Foundation, 2004).
2. Bruce Nussbaum, "How to Build Innovative Companies," *Business Week* special report, August 1, 2005.
3. The market-driven portfolio selection (MDPS) process is designed to gather customer requirements and thus identify solutions that customers do and do not value. MDPS is not the only process available for researching customer needs, but it has proven effective and successful with many companies of various types and in various industries.

6

ALIGNING THE ORGANIZATION: THE SUPPORTED PORTFOLIO

"Where there is unity there is always victory."
—Publilius Syrus, Roman philosopher and author, ~100 B.C.

If you have ever observed a half-time show at a football game, you know it can involve many individuals, each performing a different activity. However, when seen from afar by the audience, the individuals become much more than just a tuba player making a 90-degree turn or a gymnast doing three handsprings. The audience sees a flag unfolding, a flower blooming, or a star forming. The job of the show's choreographer is not only to design what the audience will see but also to figure out what each of the individuals will do to create the desired end result, and then communicate that to the bandleader who will manage the whole process. While the tuba player can't see the flower blooming, he or she knows that marching in the right place and turning at the right time will contribute to the overall picture.

At the moment of creation, the newly conceived portfolio may be a company's best-kept secret—like the half-time show that is still a sketch in the choreographer's notebook. Only a handful of people outside of the management team that spearheaded the effort may know anything about it. The senior manager who carried the torch as the portfolio champion to unite the company's vision, mission, and strategy with customer needs now must effectively communicate the portfolio—and the customer needs that spawned the portfolio—to the rest of the company. Each person, like the members of the half-time team, must understand specifically what he or she needs to do to make the portfolio a reality.

The fact that the rest of the company consists of many individuals with very different jobs can make communication a challenge. Just as the half-time choreographer communicates differently with a tuba player than with a gymnast, senior managers need to communicate appropriately with each constituency in the organization. This chapter offers a way of simultaneously deploying and communicating the portfolio using the *deployment tree*, a method PDC has created for translating corporate strategy into relevant action. Only when the actions of everyone in the company are fully aligned to support the portfolio can the VIP come to life.

A MATTER OF PERSPECTIVE

What would you picture if you heard the following three descriptions?

> "It's mazelike, with many long corridors, lots of pipes, and doors leading to electrical service rooms."
>
> "There's lots of wood paneling and thick beige carpeting. There are huge plate glass windows; I can see the whole city."
>
> "The sun is reflecting off the windows. I can see clouds floating past in the sky behind it."

All three, as dissimilar as they may sound, actually describe the same skyscraper: one from the perspective of the basement, one from the top floor, and one from outside. In the same way, how you view the product portfolio depends on where you are, which, in turn, depends on *who* you are. To the CEO, a new product line is part of the strategy for expanding market share and increasing shareholder value. To the marketing VP, it's an expression of the corporate brand. To the customer, it's a much-anticipated solution to a nagging problem. All of these views are correct; the portfolio naturally means different things to each constituency. The challenge is to integrate and connect the views so that everyone is working toward a common purpose.

WHY THE *WHY* IS SO IMPORTANT

When a company embarks on a customer value-driven strategy, company culture and strategic direction must change accordingly. Employees must buy in to the new approach. Project managers, designers, architects, software engineers, customer service reps, and even building maintenance staff all should understand how their roles fit into meeting customer needs—not simply the what but the why of their activities.

Managers may fear that sharing too much with staff about why a particular product was chosen for the portfolio will distract people from their jobs. After all, they reason, it's *management's* job to figure out why we're doing things, and staff people's job to make things happen. Yet we believe it's crucial for everyone in the company to understand the customer needs that influence decisions about which products will be developed.

Many people simply don't connect with their jobs unless they have a sense of how those jobs fit into a larger context. In our half-time show example, the tuba player may not want to put up with marching around in circles getting dizzy unless he knows that he's part of an enormous flag waving impressively on the field. Beyond that, working without knowledge of the big picture can cause all kinds of problems, from unmotivated employees to poor decision making.

Even if we could all work in a perfect world, one without the inevitable last-minute changes and frequent disruptions to the flow of product development, we would never have sufficient time to document everything that everyone in the organization must consider in their everyday tasks. The best output of professionals in most functions always results more from mastering their creative crafts than from following directives captured in specifications or drawings. Specs and drawings are important in setting up the big picture and choreography, but it's up to the professionals to execute the steps at game time.

Jane Mockford, former R&D director of chemical company Uniqema, describes the unquantifiable element of the portfolio management process this way: "I think it's probably stating the obvious, the fact that it's important to have rules . . . [Y]ou have to be quite hard nosed about it, but if you combine that with a good knowledge and understanding of the business, then . . . it's intuitive, there's a hard and a soft element to it. [Applying] the rules to the exclusion of everything else is not what it's about either. Everybody could quote an example of a fantastic business opportunity that would not have gotten through the rules."

Further, when we fully engage our professional employees, they will put much more effort and pride into their work. An old business cliché—the 20 percent rule—comes to mind here: If you let staff people run with their own ideas that are 20 percent worse than the ideas you might dictate to them, people will work 50 percent harder to make the ideas a success. When the output of an employee's endeavors bears the stamp of his or her own design, the employee not only knows what the product does and why but also has the experience of working through what might go wrong and learning how to prevent it. The resulting robust design is much better suited to the real world than a design born of documenting every nuance of an inherently creative process.

Having that full picture of why a product was chosen for the portfolio and how the product contributes to creating customer value gives staff members all the information they need for decision making. Product designers will be able to make better design trade-offs. Line managers in manufacturing will be motivated to help speed production. Tech support will understand why 24-7 uptime is crucial to the firm's customers and won't be tempted to provide a quick fix for a problem in one area that jeopardizes continuous uptime.

John Fowler, marketing process development director at equipment manufacturer CNH, describes how a poorly developed communications process hindered his company. "There was no structured communication program. It was just messages carried back to individual product/projects . . . they might be told that the budget you've put in for based on the strategic plan has been cut by 40 percent; now tell us what you're going to do." Further, there was little communication among groups. "Marketing [staff] were not given a clear view of what happens. When the budgeting process goes into operation, they just heard bits and pieces— isolated, fractured, dislocated pieces of information." No company wants to operate using isolated, fractured, or dislocated information. Communicating the portfolio throughout the organization *in a meaningful way* removes obstacles to getting things done.

THE COMMON LANGUAGE OF CUSTOMER VALUE

Too many executives rely on the language of finance, which doesn't translate well to other functions, to communicate strategy and corporate goals to the rest of the company. A designer's eyes may glaze over when you begin talking about hurdle rates and accounts receivable turnover. By moving daily discussions of tasks and evaluation of success out of the realm of financials, you create a communication flow-down mechanism that's simpler and more relevant to everyone in the organization.

You might argue that *all* employees should care about revenue growth, market position, and share or shareholder value. In truth, these topics, which may interest a mid-level or senior executive, would put a front-line worker or supervisor to sleep. Although employees at every level should be concerned with these topics, it's often difficult for employees to make the topics germane to their own actions.

Senior management's job is to make these topics relevant to everyone. When managers begin to speak in the language of customer needs and customer value, they have introduced a shared language that people can talk in manufacturing, engineering, and purchasing. Then, when the purchasing department has trouble obtaining a part or getting a supplier to conform to standards, the purchasing team understands how these failures will affect the company based on meeting customer needs. Decisions at all levels of the organization then become context-rich, rather than context-free. Executives concerned with stovepipes or silos, where communication occurs within but not between departments, will discover that this common language dissolves some of the walls between groups within the company.

Tony Frencham of Dow Chemical comments on the challenges of communicating throughout the organization in a language everyone can comprehend: "Within NBD [new business development], within our internal organization, [communication is] relatively easy. We chart where the projects are relative to the various stage-gate stages, and track them by how big they are and by how much resource we're spending on them. Communicating those to the rest of the Dow organization is a little more problematic because not everybody else gets it, or at least [understands] the sort of measure we use. The measures they would use are a little different than the ones we would use so there's a little bit of, constructive conflict I'll call it, about how people would like to see them measured."

When employees speak a language that is not only applicable to their jobs but also understood outside their departments, they minimize conflict about how to pursue common goals. They also have the ability to communicate *back up the organization.* The common language of functionality and customer need spans all levels of the company, from application people up to executives. This means faster communication—and sometimes communication where none existed before—eliminating the unpleasant surprises that, in the absence of two-way communication, often come to light only near the end of a project when communication back up the organization is difficult.

At Dade Behring, "There's a higher corporate strategy—all of the individual strategies fall underneath it. It ties very well together, and we execute on it. So you get input from all your different points," says Deirdra Dougherty, director of global marketing communications and analysis. The company is working on improving communication flow from its 6,000 or so employees, half of which are in front of customers every day. "How do we continually get a flow of information from the people in the field to better inform our decision?"

TRANSFORMING STRATEGY INTO ACTION USING THE DEPLOYMENT TREE

As we mentioned earlier, at this point, the product portfolio has not yet been born. The portfolio champion has worked on selecting potential ideas, perhaps from the company's innovation group, based on strategic alignment, customer value, and the amount of investment intensity required. Small groups may have conducted further customer research to validate and flesh out a particular proposed solution. Senior managers may have a great blueprint for success, a roadmap to create the products and services defined in the portfolio. Now they need a way to make it happen.

Let's begin by debunking the myth some companies seem to operate under that a wisely chosen portfolio will sell itself to the employees charged with making it a reality. Unlike many exciting and lifestyle-altering innovations, the company's new product portfolio usually doesn't spread virally within the company. While people may gather around the watercooler to chat about a new electronic gadget, they're unlikely to stop a coworker in the hallway to extol the virtues of the newly announced portfolio direction. In fact, without proper communication, some people may actively resist the portfolio's implementation. It will require some straightforward hard work to get everyone behind it.

Deploying the portfolio requires work, but this work need not be complicated. In fact, the inverse is most often true. *Simple* tools, used consistently and effectively, will always beat complex approaches with spotty application. A good gauge for evaluating complexity is the amount of training required for your staff to understand the portfolio decisions. If the amount of training is zero, you're on the right track. Expending all your deployment efforts on communicating broadly and none on figuring out the tools used to communicate will allow your teams to use their brainpower to begin implementing their work instead of fighting the new system. When it comes to deployment tools, less is more.

Even companies that do a good job on the strategic planning side may run into trouble when they reach the deployment stage—transforming strategic direction into tangible activities. At most companies, people don't come to work each morning thinking about how they can carry out the corporate strategy. They look at the day's tasks and plan ways to execute these tasks that will generate rewards and recognition for themselves. Companies sometimes seek to raise employees' awareness of larger corporate issues through management initiatives—going on group retreats, employing a walk-the-halls management style, delivering a consistent strategy message to everyone in the company at the annual company meeting. There's nothing wrong with retreats, a hands-on management style, or consistent messages. But these methods don't specifically relate corporate goals to each individual's daily work, and those don't address the core issue of how to infuse the corporate mission and strategy into the daily actions that result in the creation of a product or service.

The way to ensure that mission, strategy, and the resulting product portfolio are married to the daily actions of every individual is to organize the company and its actions in such a way that top-level strategy flows meaningfully down to each level of the organization in understandable words tied directly to goals and performance. The *deployment tree* provides one *simple* tool to do this.

The deployment tree is built on the straightforward idea we introduced in the beginning of this chapter: Corporate objectives look different depending on who and where you are in the company. This means that the CEO has different goals than the assembly-line manager—*but individual goals all support a common corporate goal, and each individual goal can be linked, via action, to goals directly above it.*

The deployment tree is generated by first setting goals at an appropriate level. For example, you wouldn't ask the CEO to worry about drill press tolerances or the drill press operator to be concerned with stock price. The question to ask, beginning at the highest level of the organization, is this: *What business or customer goal are we trying to achieve through our portfolio?* This ties back to the vision/mission/strategy flowdown discussed in Chapter 3. The top-level goal should encapsulate corporate strategy (e.g., we want to become the number one supplier of medical imaging devices to hospitals in the United States). Then, individuals responsible for achieving the goals ask of every goal, *What **actions** will **cause** me to reach this goal?* Asking this question at every level generates a so-called tree of causal actions extending through all levels of the organization. Beginning with the top-most organizational goals, usually defined by the CEO, each causal action becomes the goal of the next level, as shown in Figure 6.1.

Now, here's the kicker. Once the goal is defined—*forget about it.* Shift focus away from the goal and focus instead on the causal actions: what it takes to make the goal happen. This shift is essential, but often counterintuitive. Take the example of dieting. Most people diet with the goal of losing weight and therefore approach weight loss by focusing on the number shown on the

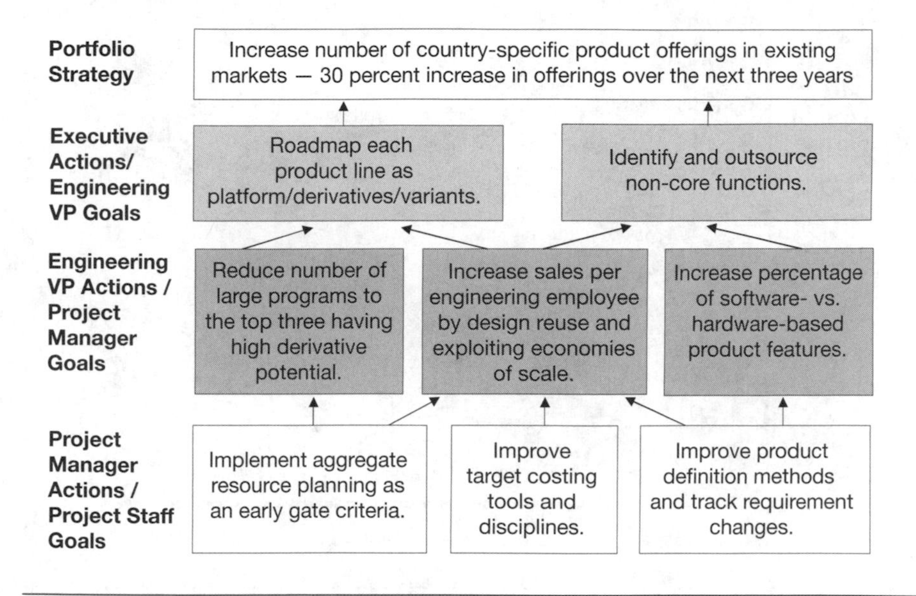

Figure 6.1 The deployment tree links the goals of each organizational level with the ones above and below.

scale. We contend that this focus is wrong, and won't, in fact, contribute efficiently to losing weight. Why? Because the *action* that causes weight loss is not measuring weight but rather engaging in exercise or reducing caloric intake. So, to lose weight, a dieter sets a *goal* (lose 10 pounds), identifies the *action* to achieve that goal (eat 10 percent fewer calories each day), and then stops focusing on weight and focuses instead on the action of eating less.

Focusing on causal actions results in measures of success that are predictive in nature and can give early, regular feedback about progress toward a goal. (See Figure 6.2.) In the dieting example, knowing that each unnecessary 350 calories consumed turns into a pound of fat helps the dieter assess progress toward losing 10 pounds. Individuals involved in carrying out the daily activities that make the portfolio happen will receive almost continuous feedback in a meaningful, relevant form.

Using the deployment tree solves another potential problem that can sideline even the most promising new initiatives, programs, or product portfolios: lack of ownership and buy-in. When goals are handed down from on high, staff members feel no sense of ownership and may not care about their

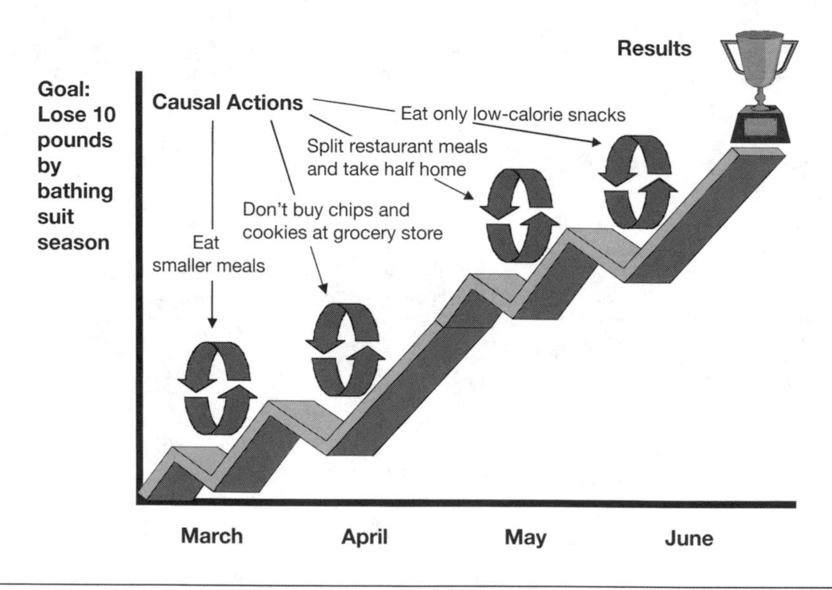

Figure 6.2 Shift focus from goals to causal actions.

performance (remember the 20 percent rule). Since the deployment tree requires goal setting at each level *by the people who are actually doing the work*, it promotes buy-in for corporate strategy at every level. When everybody works on goal setting with an understanding of how their individual goals relate to their division's goals and how their division's goals relate to the company's, there is automatic buy-in for the larger goals of the organization. While the entire organization may be working on hundreds or even thousands of goals, each individual is concerned only with the critical few that relate to his or her job.

Involving the individuals closest to the required actions also makes judgments more sound and responses more accurate. If individuals are divorced from the everyday real world of making the goal happen, they can only guess about what factors determine success or failure. Another common mistake management teams make in deployment is to assume that since they used a particular process or approach many years ago to reach a similar goal, the same approach will apply today. Advances in technology, changes in regulatory requirements, and process improvements, among other factors, often

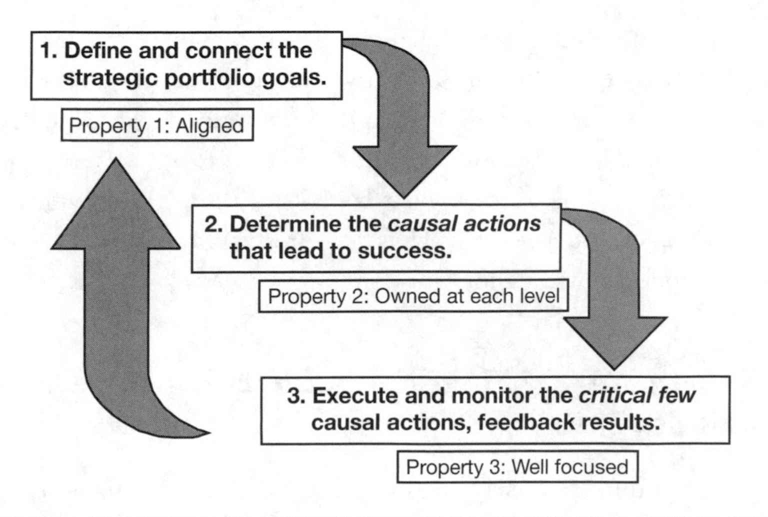

Figure 6.3 Closed-loop deployment at each level.

render past skills obsolete. To fully leverage the experience of the staff, you simply must involve those members of the staff who are closest to the action.

Going back to the half-time marching band example, the choreographer's goal is to create an exciting show for the half-time audience that keeps them entertained and in their seats. The choreographer then takes *actions* to accomplish this: making sketches and trying out songs in combination with various movements. These *actions* become the goals of the bandleader: produce harmonious music and movement based on the choreographer's instructions. To do this, the bandleader passes out sheet music and holds rehearsals. Finally, individual band members have their goals, flowing directly from the actions of the bandleader: learn the music and movements in time for the big game.

As you can see in Figure 6.3, the deployment tree is bidirectional. Information flows both *down* from management to staff and back *up* from staff to management. The people who are working on projects have particular insight into how things are going. They know what's easy to develop and what's challenging because they are trying to make things work in the real world. They know the shortcuts and the possibilities allowed by new technology. They read technical journals, order the latest tools, and use the newest software compilers. They have insights that can affect investment intensity decisions (how hard or easy it will be to create something) and often can tell where investments will be most beneficial. The deployment tree takes advantage of this by encouraging small, iterative communications loops that bring critical information about the portfolio back up to executives who use these insights to make decisions about current projects.

As you can see, one of the biggest benefits of using a deployment tree is *automatic strategy deployment*, which is a by-product of the way the tree is created and propagated throughout the company.

A DIFFERENT WAY OF STARTING, A DIFFERENT WAY OF COMMUNICATING

Effective communication is a two-way process of transmitting and receiving information, which implies both speaking and listening. Unfortunately, most of us don't really know how to listen. Even when people believe they are actively listening, they forget from one-half to one-third of what was said within eight hours.[1] We speak at a rate of 100 to 200 words per minute, but *think* three to four times as fast. The lag time between rates of speech and rates of thought allows the listener to form opinions and responses while the speaker is still talking. This process impairs our ability to focus completely on what's being said and to fully receive and understand a message. Clearly, given the challenges inherent in even the simplest forms of communication, companies need to devote considerable energy to the strategy and process of communicating the portfolio.

An effective communications strategy and program is a necessary prerequisite to successfully implementing a VIP approach. The communications strategy, like the VIP approach itself, must be led from the top of the organization by those who have both understanding of and influence over corporate strategy. Executives such as GE's former CEO Jack Welch play a major role not only in setting strategy but also in communicating that strategy to employees and stakeholders. The deployment tree discussed in this chapter shows that communicating does not mean telling people what to do. Rather, it means communicating what needs to get done and inviting staff members to participate in figuring out how to do it.

In contrast to traditional portfolio management methods, the VIP approach looks different from the beginning. There's more input and participation from every level of the organization. Instead of just announcing a new product in the portfolio, a company committed to the VIP approach will kick off the project by discussing the overall goals with everyone in the company. Each individual will participate in setting his or her own goals for the tasks that support the corporate goals.

Creating a deployment tree may sound like a complicated undertaking, but the VIP approach actually simplifies the communication of the portfolio. It can help harness individual enthusiasm by explicitly explaining each person's role in creating the portfolio, as well as the customer issues that spawned the solutions. And the process doesn't have to be perfect from the beginning. Companies can reap benefits from this approach as soon as they begin using it, long before it becomes a well-oiled machine. Even if people in the company get an incomplete picture of customer needs, they can do their jobs more effectively than they could with no information. Unlike other processes, which may be divorced from the core concerns of the business, the course of action associated with the VIP approach to portfolio management is itself integral to the company's core success factors.

Supported by well-aligned goals, the portfolio is on its way to becoming a reality. In the next chapter, we take a closer look at the individuals who fulfill various roles within the company and the type of organization required for VIP success.

NOTES

1. Ralph G. Nichols, Leonard A. Stevens, Fernando Bartolome, and Chris Argyris, *Harvard Business Review on Effective Communication* (Boston: Harvard Business School Press, 1999).
2. According to a study by the Institute for the Future conducted for Pitney Bowes, an office worker sends and receives about 130 messages per day in the office.

7

ELEMENTS OF REALIZATION: THE ACTIONABLE PORTFOLIO

> "[Leaders] need to transform the airy cliché about people being their greatest asset into a guiding principle of business strategy."[1]

> "The way a team plays as a whole determines its success. You may have the greatest bunch of individual stars in the world, but if they don't play together, the club won't be worth a dime."
> —*Babe Ruth*

There are no great plans—only great executions. We don't remember the game plan of the Philadelphia Eagles in Super Bowl XXXIX; we recall the win of Bill Belichick, Tom Brady, and the New England Patriots. The plan of the German army for the Ardennes Offensive (commonly referred to as the Battle of the Bulge) is all but forgotten due to the actions of General George S. Patton and the U.S. Third Army when they suddenly left the front lines, performing one of the most amazing feats in U.S. military history by crossing mountainous terrain in a blinding snow storm to relieve the surrounded and trapped 101st Airborne Division at Bastogne.

Often, however, we recognize only the leaders for the successful achievements of the organization. In the late 1970s, Lee Iacocca joined Chrysler Corporation with the objective of rebuilding the company. He convinced

Congress to provide loan guarantees rather than cash to prevent Chrysler from going out of business. This inspired the workforce as the firm divested Peugeot and revamped the product line with release of small, fuel-efficient K-Cars. In 1983, Chrysler introduced the minivan, a product that continues to lead the automobile industry in sales. Iacocca became an icon, while many of the contributors—for example, Hal Sperlich, a subordinate of Iacocca's who came to Chrysler from Ford—remain in the shadows.

In 1981 Jack Welch became the youngest chairman and CEO of General Electric (GE) and made GE more competitive by improving productivity, reducing inefficiency, dismantling its bureaucracy, eliminating a stoic hierarchy, introducing Six Sigma quality, and modernizing by shifting its portfolio from manufacturing to services. *Fortune* magazine attributed the growth and transformation to Welch, naming him "Manager of the Century" in 1999.

What *Fortune* missed was recognizing the thousands of employees of GE as "Employees of the Century," just as many of us missed, in the shadow of the Super Bowl XXXIX triumph, that David Givens caught a touchdown pass to tie the score with 1:10 remaining in the first half of the game. The great accomplishments of organizations are the sum of the small achievements of each individual: each person contributing talents and skills, attitudes and motivations, and desire to be recognized and rewarded—working toward a shared goal. It takes the actions of an entire organization to realize the goal, from head coaches to equipment handlers, from generals to the enlistees.

This idea is the essence of the actionable portfolio. Getting from where you are today to a fully realized Value Innovation Portfolio means changing not only the way senior executives think about portfolio decisions, but changing the way everyone in the company thinks about their jobs and relationships. When the right people are working on the right tasks, following well-designed plans as part of competent and well-coordinated cross-functional teams, inspired and supported by senior management, the VIP becomes a reality.[2]

This chapter considers the organizational elements of manifesting a VIP. We examine the relationship of innovation to individual employees and the changes you may need to make within existing organizations such as the product development group to carry out the work you need to do. Using established frameworks for evaluating personality types and work styles, we look at whether your corporate organization may need to adjust to match your portfolio goals and at what is required of each level of management, from the C-level (CEOs, CFOs, CTOs, etc.) down to the shop-floor manager, to make it all happen. And we highlight a key difference in the VIP approach that can make your cross-functional teams more successful regardless of the personality types that compose them.

CHARACTERISTICS OF THE ACTIONABLE PORTFOLIO

The VIP, when properly executed, intertwines and integrates all parts of the firm—innovation, product development, sustaining or product maintenance, operations, sales, and administration—that deliver value to the customer through products and services. The *actionable* portfolio is concerned with releasing the potential energy in your organization to overcome obstacles and make execution more efficient. It's about getting from here to there. The actionable portfolio is based on industry best practices and recognizes that execution is a multifaceted transformation, starting with vague notions in a conceptual space and culminating, if successful, in the delivery of tangible products and services to the marketplace.

Introducing new products or services requires that the organization adapt to new strategies, processes, technologies, and skills. This very adaptation can itself introduce challenges. Social interactions among individuals change as people adjust to new work assignments. Newly appointed managers fumble to direct their groups. Alterations in reporting structures ruffle everyday routines. Political jockeying interrupts or obstructs projects. Developers struggle to become adept with new technologies, integrate new processes, or reach milestones using outdated methods. Leadership engagement is, as we have argued throughout this book, absolutely necessary to harness the actions of individuals and navigate potential obstacles to move the organization in the desired direction.

ATTRIBUTES FOR ACTION: PERSONALITY AND BEHAVIOR

Each of us is different, shaped by different forces: our parents, environment, knowledge, experiences, and DNA. Other people observe these forces at work through our behavior—that is, through the actions we take in different situations, and through our abilities. Some of us are creative; others are efficient. Some are good at marshalling and arranging resources, and a few of us are charismatic and persuasive. One individual maybe be good in science and math; another may have great verbal and conversational skills. While we often consider such abilities in the context of the workplace, we rarely look at natural talents—those that have contributed to success in our private lives—in relation to professional endeavors.

The first step toward realizing the VIP through making your portfolio actionable is to consider not just an individual's work persona but the entire human being. For example, a manufacturing company employed a machinist for many years. Outside of work, the machinist was a chess master who taught youngsters to play the game and win tournaments. His strengths in pattern matching helped him teach others how to make the right moves on the chess board. When his company tapped into this skill and had him teach young machinists how to optimize parts fabrication, the machine shop doubled its productivity. The entire organization benefited from lower piece-part costs, reduced cycle time, higher quality, and less redesign.

Understanding an individual's personality and why he or she behaves in a particular way allows an organization to unleash its employees' untapped potential and optimize the fit of people with actions, creating a powerful source of energy for moving the company forward.

Psychological Models of Behavior

There are many models of human behavior, from the psychoanalytic school of Sigmund Freud to cognition theory. The Myers-Briggs Type Indicator (MBTI),[3] based on the work of the psychiatrist Carl Jung,[4] is one method for understanding the differences among people. Jung believed that our behavior is rooted in intrinsic preferences that explain our attractions to some people, tasks, and things, as well as our repulsion from others. The MBTI theorizes four pairs of preferences:[5]

Extrovert/introvert. The extrovert is interested in the external world beyond the self, while the introvert finds meaning through introspection.

Sensing/intuitive. A sensor derives knowledge from the world through facts and experience and is good at observation. An intuitive discerns information by perceiving the unseen, how things are related, and by metaphor.

Thinking/feeling. Thinkers choose an objective, impersonal point of view when making choices. Feelers make subjective, personal choices. (A thinker pondering a layoff will decide based on the numbers, while a feeler will consider the impact on affected individuals.)

Judging/perceiving. Judgers want resolution, structure, and order. Perceivers are comfortable with alternatives, spontaneity, and adaptability.

These four pairs of preferences are traditionally arranged into the 16 types shown in Figure 7.1.[6,7] While this classification is helpful, it can be limiting, since the variation along each preference pair spectrum is practically infinite. A person's type may correlate well with some behaviors but may be way off in others. Our purpose in introducing the MBTI is to provide a framework for our discussion of the relationships among individuals working together and the relationship between people and the portfolio.

Putting Personality Insights to Work for VIP Success

Our discussion in Chapter 6 pointed out that shared goals are critical for VIP success. If a company can focus all actions in the same direction, movement toward a goal progresses efficiently. This alignment is complicated by the fact that people approach decision making (one aspect of behavior) differently depending on personality type. The decision-making style of one personality type may frustrate another. For example, judgers tend to make quick decisions and get on to what's next, while introvert-perceivers gather data and then reflect on the possibilities. Tension and frustration can arise when different personality types attempt to work together on teams, negatively affecting the organization and resulting in the potential loss of valuable contributions.

INFJ Dreamers, coaching, concern for others	**INTJ** Endless possibilities, "big-picture," follow-through	**ISTJ** Responsible, information oriented, pragmatic	**ISFJ** Orderly, sense of duty, obedient, protecting
INFP Strict in regimen, service to society, "idealists"	**INTP** Problem solvers, fits all the pieces into a complete picture	**ISTP** Skilled with hands, highly observant, willing to make the attempt	**ISFP** Relates to all harmoniously, nurturing, private and sharing little
ENTP "Inventive," big picture, risk taker, the entrepreneur	**ENFP** Enthusiastic, need to affirm / be affirmed, strong interpersonal skills	**ESTP** "Realist," relevant now focus, "doing something, not nothing"	**ESFP** Immediate gratification, accepting of others, circumvents conflict
ENFJ "Persuader", focusing and knowing the needs of others, able to size up the situation	**ENTJ** Confrontation and engaging, right but willing to be proved wrong, admirers others when new lesson is learned	**ESTJ** Administrator, organizer, need for control, adept at dealing with others	**ESFJ** Gregarious, caring, gentle nature but abrasive when routine is disrupted

Figure 7.1 The 16 personality types and their characteristics. (*Source:* Adapted from O. Kroeger and J. M. Thuesen, *Type Talk: The 16 Personality Types That Determine How We Live, Love, and Work,* New York: Dell Publishing, 1988.)

The value of having insight into an individual's behavior is that it allows you, as a manager, to match people to tasks and situations to maximize success. Give introverts time to gather the data and reflect, while providing extroverts with a forum to hash and rehash their intentions. Let sensors balance the rational with the daydreams of the intuitive. Expand the horizon of the thinker beyond the scientific and objective to the people affected by the thinker's actions.

Before the analytical types among you dismiss this as simply a fun parlor game, consider the impact on your organization as individuals consume time and energy in pursuits unrelated to the portfolio: positioning themselves for promotions, protecting turf, displaying egos, and establishing a pecking order. While all this is going on, your organization may miss great opportunities. The actionable portfolio must include some way to harness the positive aspects of individual behavior to assist in the creation of customer value. Individuals are the first tangible assets in the actionable portfolio.

Tapping the Potential of All Employees

Companies recognize those who excel for their productivity and their ability to transform intellectual capital into assets that bring value to customers. Whether you call these individuals rising stars, top performers, or protégés, it's in the interest of the VIP to make them part of your team rather then having them join the competition. But how do you help the individuals who don't achieve the enviable level of performance of rising stars transform their untapped talents in similarly admirable ways?

Conventional wisdom holds that people are born with certain innate talents that cannot be learned. However, both practical experience and scientific studies reveal that people do in fact grow and learn new skills, and even new ways of thinking and solving problems, given the right learning environment. Some people harbor latent talents that are revealed only when they learn something new *in a way best suited to their style.* This argues for ensuring that your organization offers the opportunity for employees to learn through a variety of educational techniques—workshop education, hands-on experience, mentoring, emulation of observed behavior or activity, and coaching.

Note that intelligence alone does not guarantee successful performance. On the contrary, very smart individuals can exhibit potentially isolating personality quirks. The competence necessary to solve a problem or accomplish a task often is unrelated to intellect and even to inborn talents. Look at the disappointing performance of skier Bode Miller at the 2006 Olympic Games. Unquestionably a skier of great talent, Miller apparently decided to rest on those talents rather than using discipline and hard work to garner a medal. In fact, individuals with less natural ability may be motivated to work harder and thus ultimately may be more successful. *Success* is the defining condition: whether an individual's attributes contribute to achieving or surpassing expectations. That success, as in the case of Miller, is not always determined by innate ability.

Individual Attributes for the Actionable Portfolio

We have identified the following attributes—which may be innate or learned—that enhance an individual's contribution to the actionable portfolio: *initiative, connection, commitment, leadership, teamwork, fit, finesse,* and *articulation.*

Initiative is the ability to eagerly take on responsibilities beyond an individual's job scope, demonstrating motivation to achieve a cause or a goal and a willingness to assume accountability.

Connection is the ability to interact and build relationships with colleagues to facilitate the exchange of knowledge, information, and feelings.

Commitment is a pledge to action or results that requires discipline and an ability to control attention and ignore distraction to focus on the given problem.

Leadership provides a vision that establishes goals and objectives and influences people's values, motives, and behaviors to accomplish results.

Collaboration is about sharing goals and responsibilities and coordinating efforts and interactions to achieve a desired outcome.

Fit is the ability to align with others by understanding not only your own viewpoint but also the context for that viewpoint and the perspectives of others.

Finesse involves interacting with the organization with style and tact to achieve results. More than interpersonal skills, this is street smarts—maintaining composure in difficult situations to negotiate a favorable outcome.

Articulation is exchanging ideas, knowledge, and emotion in written and oral presentation and performance formats to persuade others to actively engage, and communicating using the most appropriate format.

How many people in your organization are at the top of their form regarding each attribute on the list? How many are underperforming? Acquiring and strengthening these attributes develops the individual, not only for personal growth but to optimize team performance and engagement with the organization. Your organization can function at peak performance only when the *individuals* who compose it are at their best and engaged. It's the job of the senior managers responsible for the actionable portfolio to set the stage for optimal individual and group performance.

BRINGING INDIVIDUALS TOGETHER AS A TEAM

The world is far too complex and the pace too quick for organizations to rely on individuals—no matter how brilliant or well-rounded—working alone. Besides, no single individual possesses all the necessary attributes and preferences. The actionable portfolio recognizes individual variability and seeks to minimize weaknesses and advance strengths by constructing sets of people—teams—who, when working together, are optimized to tackle the tasks at hand.

At its most basic, a team is a collection of individuals recognized by the business organization. The business or project team is the subject of many articles and books and we take its value as a given. However, we note that—ironically, since teams are composed of people—*people* are the major cause of team failure![8] People issues cited include communication problems, the level of task engagement, people who are difficult to work with, reluctance to deal with challenging problems, unclear roles (that's-not-my-job syndrome), poor decision making, failed leadership, staff conflicts and resentments, unhealthy mood, lack of communication, and mistrust—by no means a trivial set of problems. Since you can't simply eliminate the cause of the problem without getting rid of the team itself, you need to figure out a way to design and work with teams to minimize these problems.

To stack the deck in favor of creating a team and identifying the predevelopment activities that can get a team up and running quickly, we turn to an approach for analyzing individual behavior based on William Marston's DISC behavior style.[9] Marston theorized that people act in response to the stimuli in their environments. He observed that antagonistic stimuli stir some individuals to activity while causing others to turn inward. You can visualize the

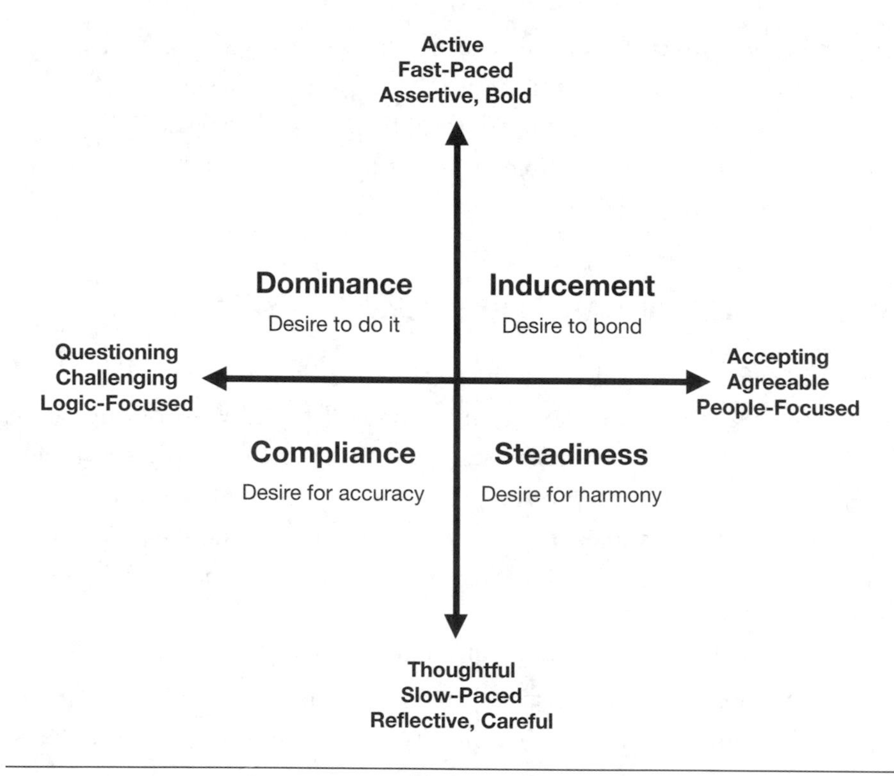

Figure 7.2 Marston's four individual styles.

theory by imagining an individual operating in one of four quadrants (see Figure 7.2).

The vertical scale represents the spectrum of activity, from fast-paced and assertive to slow-paced and reflective. The horizontal scale represents how the individual acts in the environment, which ranges from questioning the environment with a strong logical focus to accepting the environment with a people focus. The four styles (which can be described by their acronym, DISC) have the following characteristics:[10]

Dominance. Desire to *just do it*. Strong task orientation, exactness about time, and passion in pursuit of a cause. Prone to act in an antagonistic environment where bluntness may create tension.

Inducement. Enthusiasm to bond. Active orientation with a strong social focus, useful for persuasion and building team spirit. More active in an environment that has a favorable atmosphere but may not complete tasks in a timely manner.

Submission. Desire for harmony. Reflective, easygoing, and cooperative, but requiring a supportive environment to complete assigned tasks. Passivity occurs in a secure environment where the individual establishes a consistent routine with repetitive assignments.

Compliance. Desire for accuracy. Conscientious, strives for quality and accuracy. Enjoys detailed work if accompanied by well-defined instructions. Tending to limit interpersonal contact; will retreat inward in an antagonistic environment.

DISC theory is useful in team formation. It helps explain the interpersonal encounters—and potential conflicts—when individuals interact in meetings, share tasks, or participate on a project team.[11] A strong dominant individual can overwhelm a person with a steady style, creating conflict, resentment, frustration, and misunderstanding. Insights from the DISC behavioral model can create conditions for a successful cross-functional portfolio team, revealing individual motivations, eliminating obstacles that prevent communication, minimizing conflict, and allowing individuals to combine their personal attributes so the sum of individual contributions is greater than the whole.

The Value of Cross-Functional Teams

Cross-functional teams are the actionable portfolio's team of choice; the PDMA study we cited in Chapter 2 found they are the norm among development teams. Research has shown that when marketing and R&D work together on product definition, new products are more successful.[12] Firms have been forced—or have chosen as a route to competitive advantage—to outsource work to partners, perform product development and manufacturing at multiple global locations, and move innovation beyond the boundaries of R&D to engage the competency of the entire organization. Product development teams must accommodate this environment. They must extend beyond functional and firm boundaries to complete complex projects to deliver customer value.

The telecommunications firm Avaya puts together a cross-functional team early in the concept-development stage as part of its Global Solutions Process. Marketing and sales may have a more minor role early on. Once the company decides to move a concept forward into development, it forms a cross-functional team that includes people from sales, operations, marketing, and a variety of other functions. IBM does something similar with what it calls a Product Development Team (PDT)—a cross-functional team for a particular project that has representatives from sales, marketing, research, development, and other disciplines such as legal, fulfillment, and quality.

The increased functional diversity of project teams leads to more external communications, strengthens internal processes such as problem solving, and can produce innovations.[13] However, the same diversity can negatively affect performance compared to a homogeneous team, since the cross-functional team requires negotiation and conflict resolution skills that individuals may lack. The leaders and initiators of cross-functional teams need to help build these skills before launching into projects.

In the face of these challenges, the best way for a cross-functional team to build consensus around the VIP is to have the team conduct the one-on-one customer visits and observations we describe in Chapter 5, and then process the results of those visits *as a team* to decide on the key customer images and requirements. When the team makes decisions and recommendations, based on statistically significant and validated data, about how the portfolio should allocate its research and development dollars to solve the customer's problems, the team is more cohesive and the decisions are better. The team develops the ability to walk in the shoes of the customer. The consensus built as a result of this work takes the team above and beyond personality types and dispositions.

From a Team in Name to a Team in Fact

While an organization can form a team, the team doesn't act teamlike until all members *feel* they're a team. A successful team will go through the four stages: *Forming* is the time team members need to become accustomed to one another. *Storming* is the interval required to establish how the team will operate. *Norming* is the time for establishing roles and responsibilities and building trust. *Performing* is when the team realizes its maximum output. Since the team's progression through these stages actually depends on *individual* progression through them, the ideal team for creating an actionable portfolio includes individuals who can move through these stages quickly, either alone or working together.

The actionable portfolio is concerned with minimizing the initial stages of team development or eliminating them altogether to reach the performing stage and begin productive work from day one. The quicker a team can cycle through the preliminary stages, the more efficiently team members will be able to communicate and transfer knowledge in the performing stage, resulting in less conflict and a product with a better chance of meeting the customer's value criteria. Well-planned predevelopment activity reduces team stage cycle time, as does picking the right people for the team.

The predevelopment activities in the VIP process consist of articulating the team's charter or mission, defining the criteria for success, and identifying the attributes required to achieve the mission. For example, suppose a team's mission is to design a new line extension for a consumer product. The success criteria are (1) introduce the product through the existing distribution channel within six months, (2) develop a new channel within nine months, and (3) increase product quality. The attributes required to make this happen are a high sense of urgency, ability to negotiate with distribution channels, and the attention to detail necessary to create a high-quality product.

Given this mission and success criteria, the team should be composed of people who are fast-paced, precise, logical, people-focused, and accurate (dominant, compliant, and inducer styles, in Marston's parlance). Product designers would bring their logic skills to bear on creation of the product. Those who thrive in a fast-paced environment would bring a sense of urgency, while those with a focus on people bring the capabilities necessary to negotiate with the channels and those who are accurate would balance the fast pace to ensure a high-quality product. Incorporating all these perspectives makes for a better outcome and consensus.

You can even use information on individual and team styles and attributes as part of the radar chart we described in Chapter 4 when choreographing resources for potential projects. People, after all, are one of your major resources. Although the analysis of personality types and team attributes is somewhat more subjective than other input, this information could become another dimension along which you evaluate potential projects. Certain projects may require more of one attribute than another. Knowing where your teams are strong may help determine which projects to pursue or whether you need to invest in improvement or partnerships.

Sometimes the genius in managing a team comes from recognizing the gaps that need filling in the context of the team. The story of the team that put together Pixar Animation Studio's phenomenally successful movie *Toy Story* illustrates the implications of staffing decisions and what can be delivered when insightful and knowledgeable senior managers lead the decision-making process.

Prior to 1991, Pixar's main products for sale were computer animation software and hardware, although it had dabbled in making short films and commercials. Then, in July of that year, Pixar signed a three-film production deal with Disney and immediately restructured its staff, closing sales offices and beefing up the creative team to focus almost exclusively on the design and production of its first movie, *Toy Story*. Its staff of animators more than doubled, from fewer than a dozen to more than 25 as development got into high gear.[14]

But on November 19, 1993, disaster struck. On that day—later named "Black Friday" at Pixar—Disney questioned the film's creative direction, with Disney animation chief Peter Schneider saying, "It just isn't working." The key was that the Pixar staff, and particularly its creative head John Lasseter, were not trained or experienced in handling the development of feature-length films. Lasseter, an animator by background, had no experience writing screenplays for feature films and was struggling to create endearing characters. Yet seasoned Disney executive producer Bonnie Arnold did not terminate the project and disband the development team. She knew that a powerful team was the key to success and that tweaks were needed, not full-scale restaffing. She diverted the team of animators to commercial projects to keep them employed and sent Lasseter to a screenwriting course. Arnold stuck with the team until it was back on track. By April of 1994, Lasseter had successfully reworked the script and the animation crew rejoined the project. Full-scale production resumed and the movie launched on schedule, during Thanksgiving of 1995, to major critical and financial acclaim.

Teams and Innovation

Regardless of their composition, teams must have the authority to modify existing process or create new ones if the situation demands it. The actual process used for new product development (whether it's phase-gate or some other method) is unimportant. Assuming technical competency, correctly matching styles of team members to one another and to the project improves communication and interactions. A properly staffed team, when encountering an obstacle, is more likely to innovate and work together to overcome the obstacle, which is necessary because the likelihood of encountering such obstacles is extremely high. This empowerment is part of the innovation culture at Dow Chemical, says director for new business development Tony Frencham: "We empower our team leaders who are leading the project assessments to actively search for the fatal flaw of a project. It's their job . . . to look for what's the killer that's going to make this project unsuccessful." The team can then evaluate what's necessary for success or even, if the flaw is fatal, recommend killing the project.

When Cross-Functional Teams Aren't Appropriate

While cross-functional project teams are the foundation for the actionable portfolio, they may not be ideal for some special situations. When a crisis arises or an opportunity requires particularly fast action, a cross-functional team may not be able to overcome the obstacles to success. Instead of a cross-functional team, you may need a *squad*, which is a small collection of individuals specially selected to meet a particular challenge.

Analogies to the squad exist outside the business realm, such as police SWAT units or the U.S. Navy SEALs. Like a team, a squad has a mission, criteria for success, and attributes to complete the mission successfully. Unlike a team, however, its life span is short. Since it may not have time to cycle through the stages of team development, a squad must have a narrow mission and must consist of people with specific capabilities who are dedicated to the cause and to the squad. Squad members also must have commitment from

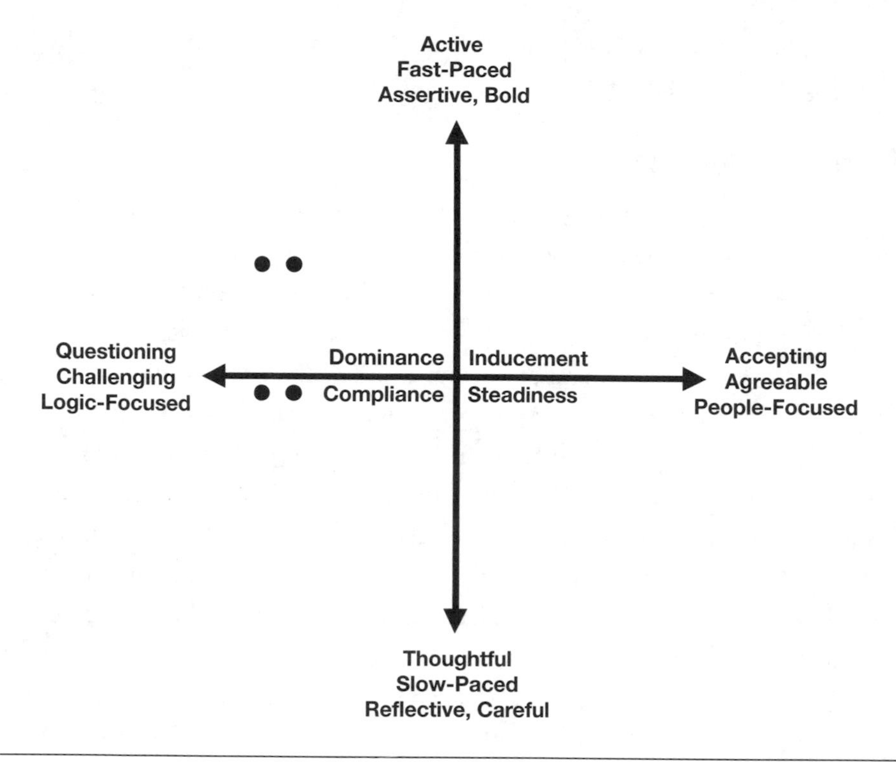

Figure 7.3 Squad composition example.

their home function or groups not to pull individuals away to other assignments until the squad completes its mission. Further, the squad must have the power to make decisions for functions it does not represent, since the mission is more critical and there may not be time for communication via traditional channels.

For example, suppose a medical device company encountered a Food and Drug Administration approval issue that stopped it from shipping its product. This would require the skills of a squad to resolve the problem quickly, since every day that goes by without resolution represents lost revenue and market share. The squad, whose makeup is shown in Figure 7.3, requires highly logic-focused individuals with a desire for accuracy and a sense of urgency. Note that the compliant types, selected for their quality orientation and high desire for accuracy, reside close to the neutral line between fast- and slow-paced. The further an individual's style is plotted from the horizontal axis (neutral line), the more reflective and slower paced he or she is. While this project requires accuracy and deliberation, its sense of urgency is, well, more urgent. A compliant, slow-paced style would both slow down the project and become a source of conflict with dominant individuals. While the situation demands accuracy and quality, getting the production line up and running quickly is the highest priority.

Squads and teams are the actionable portfolio's greatest weapons to generate competitive advantage. When carefully designed as part of the portfolio planning process, squads and teams optimize the interactions of individuals, encourage good decision making, maximize communications to disseminate information, resolve conflict through constructive dialogue, and provide leadership and direction to create a winning team.

Unfortunately, winning teams alone are not enough. Teams and individuals are part of the larger organization, and so another factor comes into play in the actionable portfolio: organizational design and culture.

ORGANIZATION AND CULTURE: THE FRAMEWORK FOR THE ACTIONABLE PORTFOLIO

Although scholars agree that culture evolves as it is learned and passed on, there is not a singular definition for culture. The best one we have found is by Edgar Schein, who defines culture as a collection of assumptions any given group creates "in learning to cope with its problem of external adaptation and internal integration, and that have worked well enough to be considered valid, and, therefore, to be taught to new members as the correct way to perceive, think, and feel in relations to those problems."[15]

An organization's culture, then, is the history of its successful problem solving. Since organizations solve problems every day, culture, at some level, changes daily. Introducing new processes forces the culture to change. This may be more apparent in fast cycle-time industries such as technology, but in the scope of this dynamic, transformation (progress or upheaval) also depends directly on dissemination of information throughout the organization and its acceptance as learning. The challenge for business organizations, even those in relatively slow-moving industries, is to remain competitive and grow in a world of intensifying global competition, scarcer resources, increased complexity, and ever-faster innovations. Often, there's no time to disperse new learning through the organization before yet another innovation renders it obsolete.

There is a long-standing debate over whether culture is a critical element due to its dynamic nature.[16] We won't take sides in the debate but instead will examine the potential impact of culture on the VIP.

The owners of a culture are those individuals with tenure at a company who realize the benefits of passing on solutions to new members. Having people with long tenure contributes to a culture's strength, as do the degree of homogeneity and stability and the intensity of shared experiences. Corporate organizations may have subcultures associated with functions, hierarchies, locations, and divisional units. This was true for the Bell System for nearly 100 years and for other multinational and multilocation companies today.

However, culture may or may not contribute to organizational effectiveness. Consider a strong culture like that of IBM of in the 1970s with its rigid dress code, long-tenured employees, and standing as a monolith of American industry, which nonetheless lost out to a young Microsoft Corporation's relaxed culture of technological inquisitiveness. The challenge for IBM was that its culture—the embedded and unconscious ways of solving problems, including the way it created solutions for customers through its product portfolio offerings—did not match, and in fact ran counter to, evolving market needs.

That was then, as the saying goes, and this is now. Today, according to IBM business transformation architect Tom Luin, the corporate IPD (Integrated Product Development) team has made a conscious commitment to cultural transformation. The way his team approaches what IBM calls "Horizon Three" projects (those involving emerging markets, new customers, new technologies, or new ways of applying technologies) "is not the mainstream [within IBM] and is somewhat unique. But other [groups] are starting to adopt it because we've been at it for four solid years with committed resources . . . We've come a long way in the last few years in terms of how we can work, with a significantly different way of thinking, evolving into an entrepreneurial culture that IBM didn't have before." Still, this culture has yet to pervade the company as a whole.

Transforming an organization's culture into one that matches current market challenges requires first that management recognize the mismatch. Then the organization needs to define the actions to take to correct the dissonance. The role of leadership is to change the structure of the organization to enable individuals to do the required work. Often, changing this structure is less a question of following some by-the-book procedure than understanding the characteristics of the organization that stand in the way and altering them to align with those required to realize the VIP.

Like individuals, organizations have styles.[17] For the actionable portfolio they include the following characteristics:

Performance-oriented. Dynamic, innovative, risk-taking, results-oriented with a passion to get the job done by leapfrogging the competition. These companies seek product leadership in their industries. (Apple, 3M)

Promotion-based. Market-centric, creating a customer experience rather than just selling products and services; interested in increasing market share and outpacing competitors. (Disney and Nike)

Protectionist. Focused on customer relationships; collaborative; strong commitment to producing harmony, security, and dependability; interested in securing customer loyalty to distance the competition. (IBM and Airborne)

Predictable. Focused on efficiency, achieving results through measurement, control, and governance procedures to deliver exceptional quality to customers. Managed through operational excellence. (Motorola and GE)

The quadrants in Figure 7.4 show where these types fall on axes from Marston's DISC model, which we apply here to companies rather than to individuals. A firm does not have to be identified with only one style. Microsoft, for example, demonstrates both product leadership and market focus. It seeks innovative products that provide a standard experience across its multiple

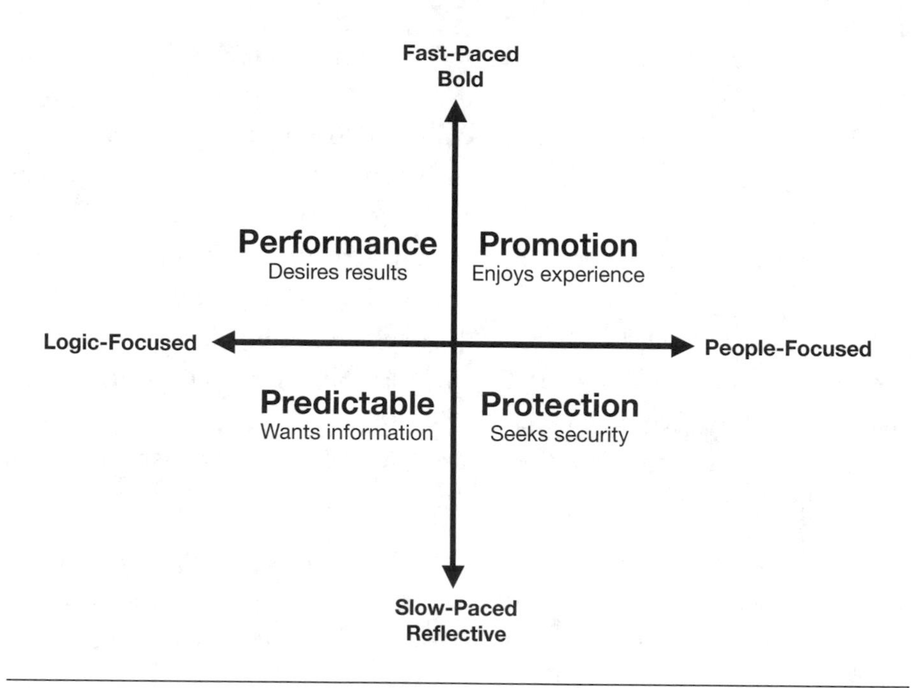

Figure 7.4 Types of organizational styles.

software products and services. Similarly, Maytag is customer-focused while exemplifying dependability; Motorola is innovative while delivering Six Sigma excellence. Organizations can exhibit aspects of all four styles, although one may prevail. As with culture, certain parts of the organization may operate with a style different from that of the corporation, either by accident or design. For example, Jonathan Hayes, design director at Microsoft, says in reference to the Xbox development organization, "We needed to develop a design culture apart from the Microsoft mainstream."[18]

As an example of how corporate culture and style needs to change to accomplish the VIP objective of providing customer value, consider the hypothetical case of a media and entertainment company we'll call Major Entertainment. The company begins as a promotion organization. The customer experience is crucial for the success of the company's products and services, but while the customer experience is intense, customer loyalty is lacking. Major Entertainment is always at work to maintain its market share.

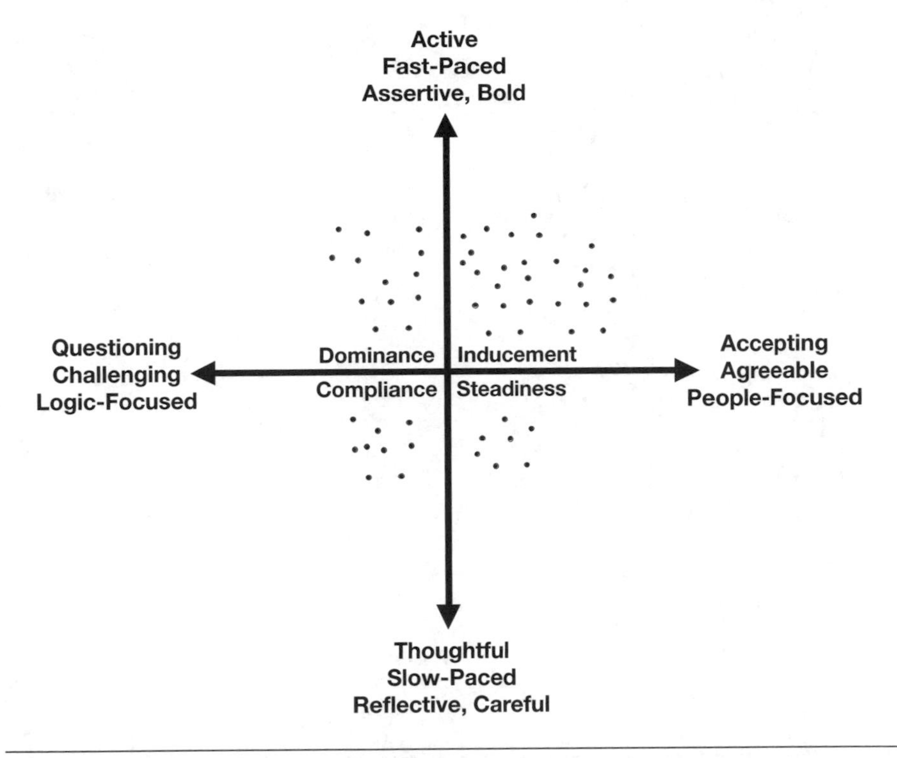

Figure 7.5 Organization population example—initial form.

Figure 7.5 shows the DISC style of the individuals who initially work at Major Entertainment. This organization is biased toward individual inducers who match the current actions of the organization. The predominance of this type of individual predisposes it to hire others with similar styles, since they will feel most comfortable in that environment.

In a just-concluded effort to gather data about customer value, Major Entertainment learned about a customer problem that required a highly creative innovation solution relying on the firm's core technology and competency. It also discovered via market intelligence that its chief rival was close to a solution highly valued by customers, which would give the competitor significant market share. Unless Major Entertainment were able to work with partners, its leadership would need to change either the structure and style of the organization to one that is biased toward performance or populate its promotion organization with individuals who have a dominant style (a predisposition to *just do it*).

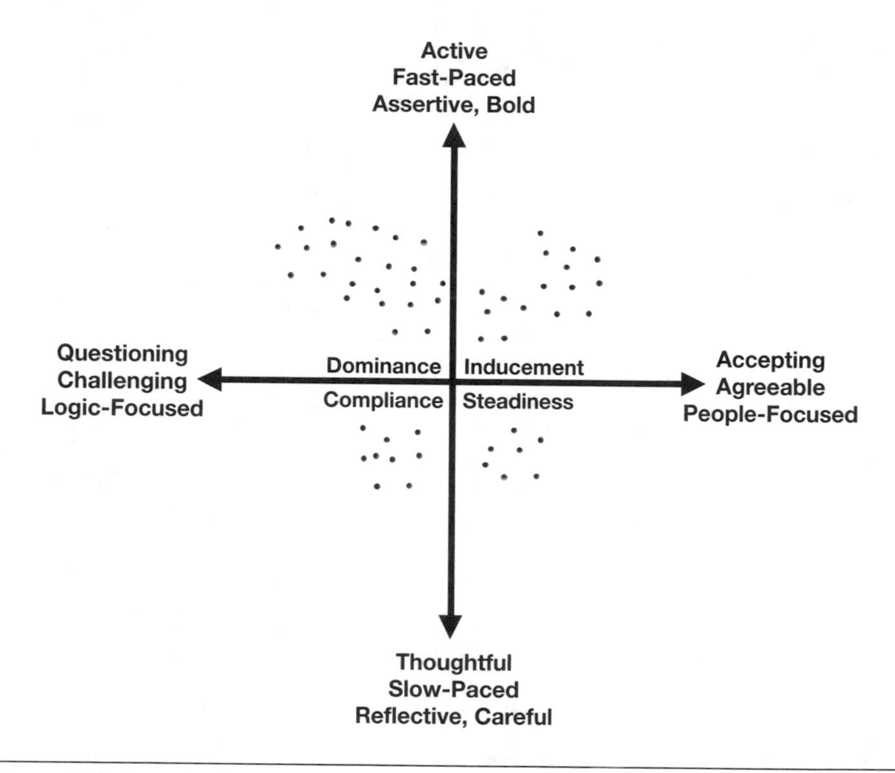

Figure 7.6 Organization population example—final form.

Constructing an action map of what it needed to accomplish, Major Entertainment decided to do the latter. It hired highly energetic innovators skilled in the company's core technology with a strong sense of urgency. At the same time, it shifted roles and responsibilities among team members to minimize conflicts based on different styles and personality types. To optimize communications and minimize organizational tension, the firm took three actions. First, it shifted some of its inducers, who had styles close to the dominant quadrant, into innovation roles and responsibilities. Second, it put its top inducer players into highly visible positions to reinforce its promotion organizational style. Third, it shifted the remaining inducers with styles close to the dominant category into liaison positions between the strong dominants and the strong inducers. The final form of the DISC style chart is shown in Figure 7.6. These actions, in conjunction with careful selection of product and services projects, delivered solutions valued by customers, increasing market share and stemming the competitive challenge.

ACCOUNTABILITY THROUGH MEASUREMENT

None of the wonderful benefits of teamwork, squad work, and alignment of corporate culture can occur without accountability and oversight, which is, of course, another responsibility of senior management. Whatever activity a company undertakes to advance the VIP—a development team designing a new product platform, a process team bringing in Six Sigma quality, individuals providing IT connectivity through the rollout of a database, or a person in finance negotiating a new agreement with the capital markets—there must be oversight to determine whether the activity needs to continue, be redirected, or be stopped.

You can reduce the complexity of monitoring the actions of the organization by taking a holistic approach. A steering team composed of leaders representing all relevant disciplines and hierarchies is a vital element of the actionable portfolio. The steering team's job is *to review a set of the organization's actions and communicate the progress, or lack of it,* for the VIP activities they oversee. The team must have accountability, decision-making authority, commitment, and the ability to communicate. The exact makeup of the team will be determined by each company's style and culture. At Dow Chemical, for example, the new business development (NBD) steering team assists in making portfolio-related decisions. The team is made up of people who own some of the resources used on individual projects, interested stakeholders (such as key scientists), intellectual capital partners, and finance partners.

THE ACTIONS OF LEADERSHIP

The value in understanding your firm's organizational style is that you can make internal shifts, as did our hypothetical company, Major Entertainment, to position the organization to deal with external forces. This translates into the initiatives you must include as part of the actionable portfolio. Of course, this doesn't happen on its own. Leadership is the motivating force as well as the glue for the VIP.

Leadership for the VIP is a *process*. The role of management changes as the action occurs. We can summarize these changes as follows. First, leadership decides that remaining at the current level of performance is not an option and that organizational optimization or realignment must occur. Even if this decision is prompted by knowledge arising from the lowest levels of the organization, there comes a moment when leadership recognizes its value. Executive leadership then *initiates* the action by setting new objectives and *communicates* the change to all members of the organization (as we described in Chapter 6). Senior managers take on the role of *instructor*, preparing the organization to act in a new way. As *director* of the action, leadership choreographs the activities and balances them with day-to-day operations and all the other items in the firm's portfolio, creating the portfolio roadmap we described in Chapter 4. As *facilitators*, corporate leaders eliminate obstacles that threaten to derail or prevent success. Finally, executive leadership *monitors* progress and takes corrective actions when the organization deviates from the path forward.

The actionable portfolio is about moving the organization to act—creating a memorable outcome, not just a game plan. Action by corporate leaders is the linchpin of the VIP: creating a mission and setting goals; providing the means to accomplish the goals; establishing criteria to measure progress; identifying the consequences, contingencies, and corrective action along the way; working through the challenges to align the individuals to the environment; clarifying the shared perceptions of the organization; building a sense of urgency to match the market's clock cycle; recognizing and using diversity; and building a corporate culture that matches the organization's goals.

This chapter focused on understanding one of the first assets in the portfolio—people—so you can bring them on board and use their talents to your best advantage. In the next chapter, we expand the discussion to examine how you bring other resources to bear, in the right levels and at the right time, on the problem of providing customer value.

NOTES

1. N. Moran, "Harnessing People Power: Most Companies See People as Their Greatest Asset," *The Financial Times Limited* (London), June 9, 2004.
2. S. L. Brown and K. M. Eisenhardt, "Product Development: Past Research, Present Findings, and Future Directions," *The Academy of Management Review* 20, no. 2 (1995): 343–378.
3. I. B. Myers and M. H. McCaully, *Manual: A Guide to the Development and the Use of the Myers-Briggs Type Indicator* (Palo Alto, CA: Consulting Psychologists Press, 1985).
4. C. F. Jung, *Psychological Types*, ed. R. F. C. Hull (Princeton, NJ: Princeton University Press, 1990).
5. O. Kroeger and J. M. Thuesen, *Type Talk: The 16 Personality Types That Determine How We Live, Love, and Work* (New York: Dell Publishing, 1988).
6. Ibid.
7. D. Keirsey and M. Bates, *Please Understand Me* (Del Mar, CA: Prometheus Nemesis Book Company, 1984).
8. Price-Waterhouse Change Integration Team, *The Paradox Principles* (Chicago: Irwin Publishing, 1996), p. 69.
9. W. Marston, *Emotions of Normal People* (London: Taylor & Francis Ltd., 1999); originally published in 1928.
10. M. K. Slowikowski, "Using the DISC Behavioral Instrument to Guide Leadership and Communication," *AORN Journal* 82, no. 5 (November 2005): 835–843.

11. The Myers-Briggs Type Indicator may also be used to form teams and construct organizations. We have chosen to use Myers-Briggs to explain understanding the individual in terms of process and attributes and Marston's DISC theory and its extension to culture for team performance, leadership, and organizational dynamics.

12. R. T. Hise, L. O'Neal, A. Parasuraman, and J. U. McNeal, "Marketing/R&D Interaction in New Product Development: Implications for New Product Success Rates," *Journal of Product Innovation Management* 7 (1990): 142–155.

13. D. G. Anacona and D. F. Caldwell, "Demographic and Design: Predictors of New Product Team Performance," *Organizational Science* 3 (August 1992): 321–341.
14. Catherine Crane, Will Johnson, Kitty Neumark, and Christopher Perrigo, under the supervision of Professor Allan Afuah, *University of Michigan Business School Case Study: Pixar 1996.* Published online at: www personal.umich.edu/~afuah/cases/case14.html.
15. E. H. Schein, "Coming to a New Awareness of Organizational Culture," *Sloan Management Review* 25, no. 2 (Winter 1984): 3–16.
16. This debate is discussed in some of the following:

    M. G. Patterson, M. G. West, V. J. Shackleton, J. F. Dawson, R. Lawthom, S. Maitlis, D. L. Robinson, and A. M. Wallace, "Validating the Organization Climate Measure: Links to Managerial Practices, Productivity, and Innovation," *Journal of Organizational Behavior* 26 (2005): 379–408.

    C. Stadler, and H. Hinterhuber, "Shell, Siemens, and DaimlerChrysler: Leading Change in Companies with Strong Values," *Long Range Planning* 38 (2005): 467–484.

    P. Bate, R. Khan, and A. Pye, "Towards a Culturally Sensitive Approach to Organizational Structuring: Where Organization Design Meets Organization Development," *Organizational Science* 11, no. 2 (2000): 197–211.

    C. Moorman and A. S. Miner, "The Impact of Organizational Memory on New Product Performance and Creativity," *Journal of Marketing Research* 34 (1997): 91–106.

    M. J. Hatch, "The Dynamics of Organizational Culture," *Acad. Management Review* 18 (1993): 657–693

    E. H. Schein, "Organizational Culture," *American Psychologist* 45, no. 2 (1990): 109–119.

    V. L. Meek, "Organizational Culture: Origins and Weaknesses," *Organizational Studies* 9, no. 3 (1988): 453–473.

E. H. Schein, "Coming to a New Awareness of Organizational Culture," *Sloan Management Review* 25, no. 2 (Winter 1984): 3–16.

T. E. Deal and A. A. Kennedy, *Corporate Cultures* (Reading, MA: Addison-Wesley, 1982).

17. Other authors suggest such classifications, which they describe in alternative words very similar to Marston's DISC definitions as applied to organizations. See:

K. S. Cameron and R. E. Quinn, *Diagnosing and Changing Organizational Culture: Based on the Competing Values Framework* (Reading, MA: Addison-Wesley, 1999).

W. E. Schneider, *The Reengineering Alternative: A Plan for Making Your Current Culture Work* (Burr Ridge, IL: Irwin Professional Publishing, 1994).

18. J. Hayes, "Re-conceptualizing the Xbox Platform," *Design Management Review Executive Summaries* 16, no. 4 (2005), Design Management Institute.

8

APPRECIATING INVESTMENT INTENSITY: THE FORTIFIED PORTFOLIO

"It does not take much strength to do things, but it requires great strength to decide on what to do."
—*Elbert Hubbard (1856–1915)*

When business strategist Chris Riley told marketing director Bill Spencer and Tom McAndrews—division director for DuPont's carpet fiber business—about researcher Armand Zinnato's discovery of the technology that would underpin DuPont's Certified Stainmaster carpet offering, McAndrews knew that the business was on to something really big. He had joined the business the prior year and had made a major strategic commitment to revitalize the residential carpet business, which was the largest but weakest of the four businesses in the company's portfolio. (Two of the other three businesses—commercial and auto carpeting—were in sound competitive shape at the time, and the third and smallest—rugs—was doing okay.) McAndrews commissioned in-depth market studies to see what this revitalization would take and discovered that a major consumer-focused advertising campaign with a to-be-specified new product in the portfolio could add significant market share.

Earlier consumer studies had shown that soil and stain resistance were some of the most sought-after characteristics of residential carpeting, but that existing commercial solutions fell far short of meeting consumer expectations. Until Stainmaster came along, consumers usually chose dark colors that wouldn't show stains. They were growing tired of foregoing color choices in an attempt to keep their carpets looking nice. The technology breakthrough McAndrews had in front of him offered a clear path to solve this nagging consumer pain point and so offered DuPont a clear path to hit the sweet spot for marketplace performance of a new residential carpet platform. As McAndrews said, the combination of this new product offering with the already conceptualized retail consumer advertising campaign created a perfect storm of an opportunity.[1]

But the DuPont carpet fibers team also knew that competitors like Monsanto were in hot pursuit of the same goal. If DuPont didn't act fast to develop and deliver a fully capable and robust solution in 18 months or so, DuPont would likely lose first-mover advantage and its associated benefits. It was clear to the team that DuPont Fibers would have to make major resource investments (both in development and in ongoing support after launch) if it wanted to fully exploit Zinnato's technology breakthrough. Resource commitments at the usual level might yield a profitable niche product, but only a rapidly executed, high-investment-intensity program would yield a dominant position in the marketplace. To achieve success, McAndrews's team knew DuPont needed to develop key technologies, design new treatment chemicals and carpet manufacturing processes, design and install new equipment, and plan and execute new consumer marketing communications programs.

The project called for high investment intensity and a commitment of resources well above usual levels. But the carpet fibers team knew that if applied effectively—and rapidly—this major resource investment could dramatically improve the profitability of DuPont's residential carpet business. As we share later in this chapter, McAndrews and his team early on made substantial investment intensity pledges, in particular committing to the largest consumer advertising campaign in DuPont's history to that point. But they made these decisions deliberately and with full exploration of both the risks and payoffs involved. In the end, they created a massive sweet spot for

DuPont's residential carpet fiber business, shifting it from a declining, low-margin, low-profit commodity business to a premium, branded, high-margin, high-profit one.

When you first identified the market sweet spot and began to construct your portfolio to target that sweet spot, you also considered the issue of portfolio balance. You evaluated possible portfolio solutions that arose from your innovation process or other sources using tools like the radar chart, where each of the axes represents a dimension to consider. You balanced the portfolio in terms of type of projects (i.e., some with short time to market, some with longer, some highly competitive, some risky) and included or excluded projects based on a number of criteria, including *investment intensity*—that is, the level of resources they would require for success—and the customer and strategic value this investment could create.

Investment intensity is an ongoing concern, important not only during portfolio planning but also during implementation. Investment intensity impinges on almost all areas of the company's operations, from manufacturing to customer support. It always involves balancing competing priorities, including customer value, as we first discussed in Chapter 4. Most companies can't simultaneously pursue several projects that demand high investment intensity; you may need to drop or delay some for which you have sufficient R&D funding but not enough advertising or manufacturing dollars to make them successful. Paying the proper level of attention to these supporting elements often spells the difference between an ongoing market winner and a marketplace failure. This chapter looks at these key supporting elements and their implications for the cross-functional team charged with making the portfolio a reality.

INVESTMENT INTENSITY PLANNING—WHAT ARE WE TALKING ABOUT?

Investment intensity planning encompasses more than simply deciding the total amount of resources—people, capital, material, and so forth—you need to completely develop a product and fully support its commercialization. It also is about choreographing those resources to create and capture customer value. Just as world-renowned dance master George Balanchine took the full dance troupe—from prima ballerinas to the extras—and directed their movements and placement to create a beautiful and powerful performance of the Nutcracker, business leadership must guide the movements of the full range of resources both inside and outside the organization to create a winning performance in the marketplace. Resource choreography is about transitioning from planning to doing. It is fully realized at the individual product or project level. While the major strategic resource choreography decisions are made at the portfolio or pipeline management level (you can look ahead to Figure 9.3 in the next chapter to see this), you must make decisions about the application of operational resources at the specific product operational level if a project is to move forward and stay on track.

Investment intensity planning is about investing the *right resources* at the *right time*, at the *right level* and focused in the *right areas*, so you can fully deliver the promised customer value for the purchasing volume you expect. Because you don't have unlimited resources, choreographing the application of those resources in a way that optimizes them is critical both for your chances of successful market launch and for the eventual payoff. If you dedicate too little investment (in the aggregate or in specific areas) or provide it too late, you may come up short in meeting customer requirements (see Figure 8.1). If you dedicate too much investment or invest too early, you can burden the project with more costs than it can support or slow the overall development process by diverting management attention to tasks that are not yet important. In fact, we believe a firm's *most critical asset* is the time and attention of its senior managers. Investing too early creates new programs and infrastructure that must be managed, potentially distracting senior managers from more crucial early stage tasks.

In the context of the VIP model, investment intensity planning includes thinking through what resources you need and when and where you will commit them. But it couples this with an ongoing assessment of what this resource investment will yield in terms of key knowledge (to guide whether to move forward) and in terms of customer and strategic value. Resource choreography then becomes the combination of planning and assessment around resources. Balancing investment intensity with market potential and the

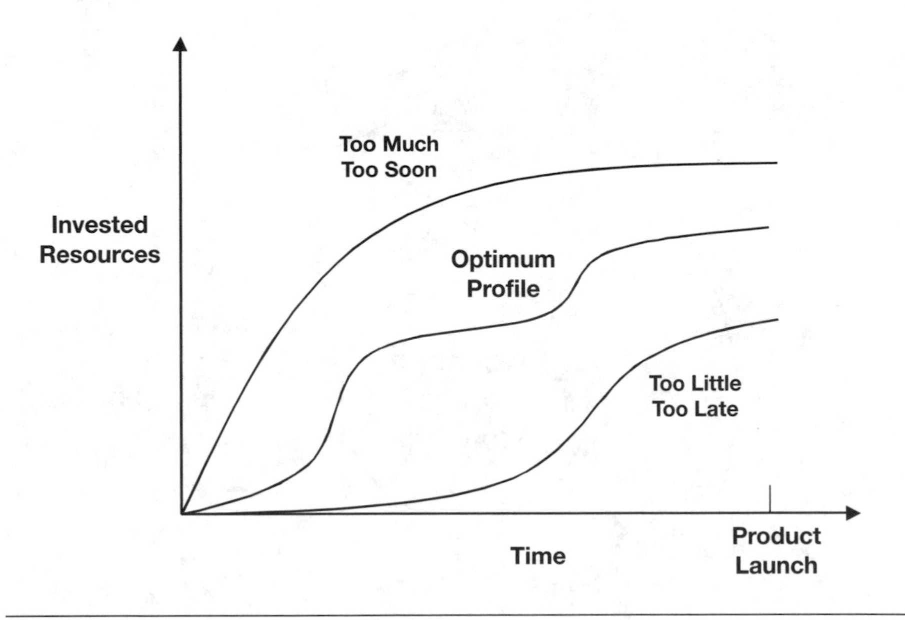

Figure 8.1 Investment intensity profile.

significance of the customer problem (statistically quantified as the percentage of people who say they want a better solution to their problem) is key. In the case of Stainmaster, for example, both the customer need (for carpets that would defy red wine spills) and the market potential (market size and the eagerness of competitors to enter the market) were high, offering balance to the huge investment in direct to consumer advertising DuPont would make.

Investment intensity planning must be *comprehensive* to ensure that you don't miss any key pieces that might cause the project to fail, and *properly timed* to meet key execution milestones while managing financial outlays to ensure profitable performance. Note that there are two kinds of investment: investment to learn (gathering voice of the customer data, determining value to the customer, validating potential solutions, and determining whether to proceed from ideation to validation) and investment to implement (putting in place capabilities to deliver and support the offering in volume).

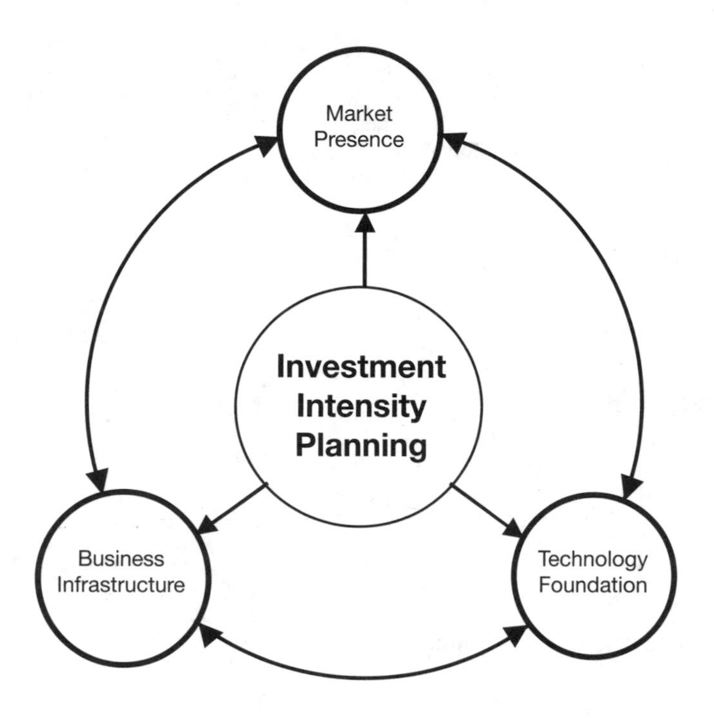

Figure 8.2 Investment intensity planning framework.

THE THREE ARENAS FOR INVESTMENT INTENSITY PLANNING

Investment intensity planning begins with a high-level look at the business—to determine the capabilities required to create market demand for your new product given the market needs you have uncovered—and at what capabilities you need to satisfy that demand. We have found three arenas, shown in Figure 8.2, where planning the right investment intensity is critical for portfolio success:

- **Building a robust technology foundation** that adds value to your offering
- **Constructing the full business process and operations infrastructure** needed to effectively (and profitably) sustain ongoing commercial activities
- **Establishing a powerful market presence**

BUILDING THE TECHNOLOGY FOUNDATION

Once DuPont was convinced that developing Stainmaster would provide value to customers, the Stainmaster commercialization steering team began in-depth exploration of the technologies needed for market entry. While successful launch would require little change in fiber spinning and coating operations, it would require significant new carpet treatment chemistries, which in fact had been at the heart of researcher Armand Zinnato's "aha" moment. It also would require application technologies for the carpet mills that were DuPont's direct customers, since DuPont did not actually make Stainmaster carpet but instead licensed mills that met its certification criteria to use the DuPont Certified Stainmaster label. The team, with support from senior management at DuPont Fibers, made the technology resource commitment it deemed necessary to develop and implement a robust and fully supportable technology base. This commitment eventually swelled the DuPont technology team, which engaged more than 20 people through the life of the project.

Identifying and Delivering the Golden Nuggets of Technology

For most new products or new product platforms, there are usually only a limited number of technologies that are key to delivering the customer value that drives a buy decision. As Anthony Carter, senior director of new business development for Motorola, told us, Motorola continually tries to understand, from a technology perspective, the one or two requirements that really compel customers to purchase their products. Identifying these attractives and evaluating the technology necessary to deliver them is a key part of implementing a VIP. We like to call these the *golden nuggets* of technology—the value innovation areas where you must effectively invest sufficient resources to define, develop, and embed in your offering if you want to win in the marketplace. (In Six Sigma terminology, these fulfill the most significant customer CTQs, customer critical-to-quality requirements.)

As a recent example, Carter cited Motorola's Canopy technology for high-speed wireless broadband communications that enables low cost and robust delivery of broadband Internet services to remote locations. Customers value having rapidly installed and relatively low-cost broadband capabilities that can reach them when they don't have easy access to land-line-based service.

The golden nugget in this case is Motorola's innovative use of transmitters that employ the unlicensed radio spectrum (initially at 5.3 and 5.8 GHz but expanded later to other unlicensed frequencies), readily supporting high-speed transmission while being free, clear, and available. This offering, which began as an idea within a business, is now a product line worth several hundred million dollars.

Another example is Stanley Works' recent addition to its automatic-doors line. As Will Hill described it, the highest value feature in an automatic door "is the sensor that opens and closes the door. It senses that someone is there—[it's] simple . . . but the actual sensing is critical, in terms of making sure the doors open as well as making sure the doors don't close until after the person passes through." Hill helped locate an individual who had the idea of using digital video camera technology to accomplish this task. This approach and the development of the digital video technology became the key to the door's success. Hill told us, "That particular technology is really the foundation—we doubled the business over three years after that technology came to the marketplace."

Completing the Full Enabling Technology Foundation

But while the golden nugget or value innovation technology may be the key to unlocking the major customer value in the marketplace, the business leadership team also must consider what it will take to build out the complete technology foundation required for successful marketplace entry before introducing a new product into the portfolio. In particular, it needs to consider the bundle of technologies that will be embedded in the product.

One of the most ubiquitous examples of this, given the proliferation of computer microprocessors into an ever-widening array of products, is the software technology required to enable a hardware product to meet all the customer's must-have needs. For example, in the Motorola Canopy wireless broadband offering we discussed earlier, the information management software technology not only had to handle a variety of interconnection issues but also had to include multiple layers of system security protocols to address customer concern over potential security flaws in wireless technology. There may also be needs for physical structure technologies, chemical performance technologies, mechanical control technologies, or whatever else is needed to make the product fully functional. Again, in the case of Canopy, fully realizing the product required such supporting technology as cost-effective and rugged outdoor enclosures and power systems, hardened Internet switches, and simple-to-use network connections. While investing in these may not yield product features with a big wow factor, they do yield must-have performance.

The technology base also must include the full range of enabling technologies required to successfully produce, deliver to the customer, and support a product (with its bundle of technologies). Manufacturing technologies are frequently significant here, as was the case for Gillette when it originally introduced the revolutionary twin-bladed Sensor razor and again when it made the quantum jump to the triple-bladed Mach 3. For both, Gillette used noncontact precision laser welding technologies to ensure pinpoint alignment of the multiple blades to deliver the phenomenal shaving experience that has made Gillette razors so popular with consumers.

Another example of the pivotal role of manufacturing technology is the success of fresh, not-from-concentrate (NFC) orange juice products such as Tropicana Pure Premium and Florida's Natural, which have become the fastest growing and most profitable segment of the orange juice market. For most of the last 60 years, NFCs were only a minor segment of the national orange juice market, which was dominated by frozen concentrates. Not until the mid-1980s, when the industry developed new aseptic (sterile) equipment technologies, did sales of the product take off. These technologies allowed large-scale and cost-effective processing and long-term storage of single-strength (not concentrated) juice, ensuring a microbiologically stable and commercially sterile juice. Ever since, NFCs have steadily displaced frozen concentrate and reconstituted products on the grocery shelves, reaching 51 percent of the market in 1998. In fact, Tropicana Pure Premium orange juice is the number three most sold item in America's grocery stores today.

A different example of the critical role of production technology is the story of Pixar Animation Studios. Over a 13-year period, Pixar created and produced six of the most successful and beloved animated films of all times, beginning with *Toy Story* in 1995 (discussed in Chapter 7 in the context of applying people resources) and continuing through *The Incredibles* in 2004 and *Cars* in 2006. The key to this success has been a string of powerful, breakthrough technologies for computer animation. According to a corporate overview appearing on the Pixar Web site, the company believes "that its proprietary technology, which enables animators to precisely control the motion of characters and the sets in each frame, represents a breakthrough in the art of animation. The result is a new 'look and feel' with images of quality, richness and vibrancy that are unique in the industry." These technologies have received numerous awards and continue to be developed and improved.

BUILDING THE BUSINESS INFRASTRUCTURE

Defining the full business process infrastructure needed for full commercialization is the next critical step in investment intensity planning. The DuPont Stainmaster team found all sorts of processes and capabilities would have to be in place for a successful market launch. Correctly producing the carpet treatment chemicals required modified chemical manufacturing processes at one of DuPont's plants, as well as new application equipment and processes and new performance certification procedures at all partnering carpet mills. Convincing skeptical customers about stain-resistant performance required new warranty support systems and toll-free customer call banks. Protection against counterfeiting required new tracking and testing processes. And the Stainmaster team needed to implement these capabilities rapidly to beat Monsanto and AlliedSignal to market.

The portfolio must incorporate the full range of actions that position a company to win in the market. Frequently, this means portfolios contain not only the product but also the infrastructure required to produce, distribute, and support the product. (Dell Inc.'s direct computer sales are one good example of this. Before Dell's model of selling and delivering directly to customers would work, the information technology infrastructure had to be in place to enable fast communication and customization of each machine.) The organization must effectively support the customer through the entire consumption chain for the product, from selection to purchase and delivery through use and servicing to final disposal. To do this, the business must invest in effectively managing the entire supply chain and consumption life cycle, as Figure

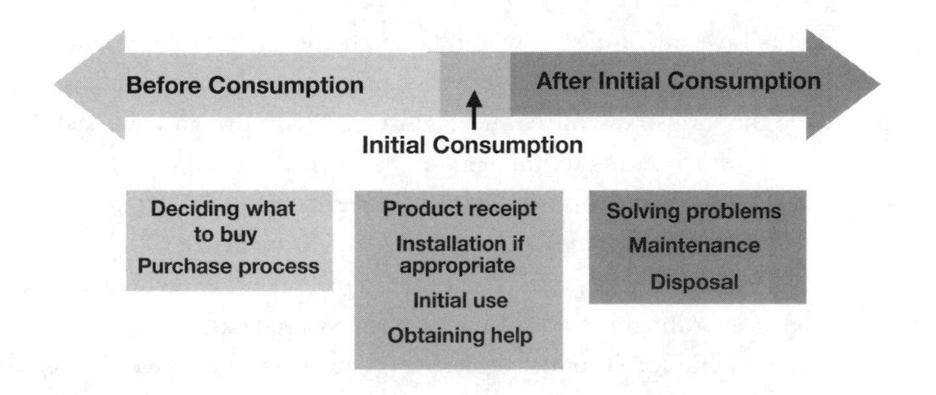

Figure 8.3 Consumption life cycle.

8.3 illustrates. For example, as consumers become more comfortable in general with online ordering, many companies in traditional businesses have had to quickly implement online ordering and tracking systems. In some cases, this new wrinkle in the supply chain appeared so quickly that companies have had to reassess how they are investing in their portfolios. Suddenly, they needed to divert funds to an area that previously required little investment.

Production/Manufacturing

For companies building physical products, manufacturing/production (which includes sourcing) capabilities can be the major driver in marketplace performance of their product portfolios. It also can be far and away *the* biggest investment they will make to bring new products to market. Engaging experienced and knowledgeable production design engineers and facilities construction professionals early in the process of investment intensity planning is particularly important for such companies.

The semiconductor/microprocessor industry, dominated by Intel, is a case study in the importance of early, thorough investment intensity planning. The cost of constructing semiconductor fabs (the fabrication facilities that manufacture semiconductor devices) has been escalating dramatically over the decades and is now in the billions of dollars. (Intel announced in July 2005 that it will invest $3 billion in its Arizona campus for new manufacturing facilities to enable next-generation technology, while in October 2004 Advanced Micro Devices recently opened its new Dresden Germany Fab 36 facility with expected total investment of $2.5 billion through 2007. According to an article in CNET News, "Though chip designers often get most of the attention and glory in the industry, semiconductors rise and fall through manufacturing. Efficient manufacturing techniques and its meticulous 'copy exactly' philosophy for building [microprocessor] fabs have been significant pillars in Intel's rise according to, among others, chairman Craig Barrett."[2] Without these, Intel would not be the profit powerhouse it is. The article goes on to cite chip maker AMD's difficulties in the manufacturing arena as one of its major failings, accountable for "product delays, chip shortages and huge financial losses."

Another example of the significance of production infrastructure as a factor in investment intensity planning is Pixar's major investment to deliver on the capability of its computer animation technologies. Each frame of Pixar's first major animated movie, *Toy Story*, required a farm of 117 Sun Microsystems computers. The movie contained more than 100,000 frames and in total required 1,000 CD-ROMs to hold all the data. For its next two movies—*A Bug's Life* and *Toy Story 2*—Pixar increased its computer farm size by more than a factor of 10. These may seem like astronomical investments, but they paid off in enormous box office success. Without them, the movies never could have been made, and thus never could have reaped the huge returns that they did. (*Toy Story 2* brought in box office returns of more than $245 million.)

Distribution

Distribution—getting your product to customers when and where they want it—includes the physical movement (shipment and delivery) of products. For consumer products, distribution often goes through a retailer. But distribution takes on broader meaning when you include offerings like financial services and the theatrical experience of full-length feature movies. In all cases, setting up an effective distribution process is a critical item to evaluate for investment intensity decision making. If poorly planned and executed, the distribution process can sink a new offering—by adding too much cost, by failing to get the product to customers in a way that meets their needs after purchase, by falling short of distributor requirements, or by failing even to get the product in front of the customer so they can make a purchase decision.

The Stainmaster story offers a simple but particularly pointed example of the importance of proper distribution for all items of your offering. The most critical step in the manufacturing of certified Stainmaster carpet is the application of the right kind of DuPont manufactured treatment chemicals to the finished carpet. DuPont knew that the carpet mills, as a group, were cost-driven and would be tempted to obtain similar but less expensive chemicals from other suppliers to trim costs. To reduce the tendency for mills to apply other chemicals or to apply less than the recommended amounts, DuPont decided to *automatically and at no charge* package and ship its stain-resistant chemicals with its premium carpet fiber.

A different perspective on distribution comes from Pixar again. When Pixar CEO Steve Jobs signed the original three-film production agreement with Disney, he agreed to take a relatively modest share of the box-office and video revenues (estimated at 10 to 15 percent of film profits) because he wanted access to Disney's extensive distribution network in addition to its noted marketing capabilities. As a result of Disney's clout with theater chains, Pixar's six animated movies were all box-office smashes, grossing well over 3 billion dollars worldwide, something that would have been unthinkable for Pixar as an unknown.

Information Technology (IT)

IT is ubiquitous throughout the business world. It plays a major role in virtually every industry worldwide and has a dominant position in the minds of many executives as they make investment decisions. To quote Nicholas Carr of Harvard Business School: "Today no one would dispute that information technology has become the backbone of commerce. It underpins the operations of individual companies, ties together far-flung supply chains and increasingly links businesses to [customers] . . . As IT's power and presence have expanded, companies have come to view it as a resource critical to their success."[4] By the end of the 1990s nearly 50 percent of the capital expenditures of American companies went into information technology. So it is clear that portfolio managers and individual product development teams need to

IN AN INDUSTRY BUILT LARGELY ON DISTRIBUTION, DISTRIBUTION IS A PORTFOLIO ISSUE

Distribution is particularly important in the beverage industry. Quoted in an article in the *Wall Street Journal Online*, John Sicher, editor and publisher of *Beverage Digest*, said: "If in the real-estate business it's all about location, location, location, then in the beverage business it's all about distribution, distribution, distribution. Coke, Pepsi and Cadbury with their bottling networks can get into almost every venue in the country."[3]

For smaller beverage companies—and particularly those trying to break in with new products—lining up distribution is not so easy. In the case of J. Darius Bikoff and his company Energy Brands, Inc., this was a major challenge to making his company's line of enhanced waters a success. Energy Brands launched its first product (Glaceau Smartwater, which contained extra electrolytes) in 1996. While Bikoff had been around the beverage industry for 20 years, first as an employee and later as CEO of an aluminum fabrication business that made beverage cans, he had no major clout within the industry. But by starting small, focusing personal attention on independent stores in New York City and personally arranging for shipment to these stores, he was able to get Smartwater—and his next product, Fruitwater—into natural food stores in the Big Apple and then moving nationwide as a niche product. When Bikoff stumbled upon his third and most successful product—Vitaminwater—he followed basically the same path, albeit targeting mainstream mom-and-pop shops rather than health food stores. In this way, he flew below the radar of the big beverage companies and got his waters placed in a steadily growing number of locations in New York. Once firmly established in multiple venues there, he had the credibility to use his considerable personal charm to cultivate targeted players among the pool of independent beverage distributors in the United States who could provide him access to a broad range of retail outlets across the country and set Energy Brands up for growth. With this strategy in place, Glaceau grew from a standing start in 1998 to a $350 million/year enterprise by the end of 2005.

The not-from-concentrate orange juice business offers another example of the importance and payoff of distribution investment intensity planning. Tropicana Pure Premium—the leading product in the category and now owned by PepsiCo—has its own distribution network and so does not have to go through the travails that Glaceau did. However, the high shipping costs (up to 20 percent of the wholesale price) associated with transporting something that is 75 percent water significantly impacted its financial performance. (For comparison, frozen concentrate is concentrated by a factor of seven.)

Tropicana has a history of working to make its transportation process more efficient and cost-effective, by doing such things as continuously improving tracking of its bulk trucking fleet, developing 22,000 gallon super-tankers for rail transport, and finding better port facilities to support its European trade. Tropicana now has the lowest nationwide shipping costs among U.S.-based juice producers.

The latest major competitive twist in the orange juice industry has resulted from distribution/shipping investment in Brazil. Brazil is the largest and lowest-cost producer of orange juice in the world and over the years has taken a major share in the U.S. frozen concentrate business despite the presence of a large U.S.-imposed tariff. But Florida growers felt confident in their control of the NFC market because of the high cost of shipping the (mostly water) single-strength juice. However, in 2003, Florida growers were shocked when Citrosuco, Brazil's largest citrus processing and exporting company, launched a new generation of large (8-million-gallon) super-tanker refrigerated ships. With these ships, Citrosuco could move and unload NFC so fast that the projected cost for delivery of Brazilian orange juice to the northeast United States is lower than the cost of delivery from Florida-based suppliers—even with the tariff.

* * * *

consider what IT investment intensity is appropriate to enable the marketplace success of their offerings, if only because senior management will expect it.

One of the biggest users of IT as part of the introduction of new products to the marketplace is the financial services industry. From personal online accounts to major investment portfolio products to currency exchange products, IT is the critical capability that makes new products viable in this information-intensive industry. In fact, some financial institutions think of their IT software/hardware development effort as synonymous with their product development effort.

But IT can still play a major enabling role even in industries where management of transaction information is not so critical. Whether it is in providing process simulation capability for the chemical industry or vehicle CAD/CAM design capabilities for autos or the tracking of product distribution for electronics companies, IT can make the difference between success and failure. IT's role is often underplayed *and* crucial.

So IT investment can be a major enabler of marketplace success. But—and this is a big but—IT investments have a history of major failure. Depending on what articles you read, anywhere from 40 to 80 percent of all major software implementation projects fail. According to IT consultancy IT Cortex, an IT project is more likely to be unsuccessful than successful; only about one out of five IT projects is likely to "bring full satisfaction."[5] Statistics have shown that in all industries, there is no correlation between level of IT investment and financial performance. The goal is wise investing: consciously and thoughtfully to explore exactly what capabilities are needed and what you can successfully execute.

Customer Support

Most companies recognize the importance of investing in the right customer service and support infrastructure to sustain a product in the marketplace. It's one of the most thoroughly discussed areas in the business literature. (A recent search on Amazon.com yielded more than 5,000 books on the subject.) The number and type of customer service approaches is massive and growing: call in help desks, online product support tools, automatic problem diagnosis systems, customer-problem-solving SWAT teams, and on and on. We will not attempt to cover the options available to you; for that we suggest you peruse some of the books catalogued in our Amazon.com search. But we do note that a discussion of what is the appropriate investment intensity needs to be a critical part of the investment intensity planning effort for your portfolio or for individual products. The goal is to be systematic, balancing the need to make the customer's experience of your product after purchase an acceptable one with the cost and resource commitment required to develop and provide it.

An example again comes from DuPont's Stainmaster introduction. It was clear to the Stainmaster steering team that there needed to be a major change in the whole consumer experience of buying and owning carpet. As Tom McAndrews put it: "We wanted to change the carpet buying experience to become a source of comfort in what had been an unpleasant experience. We wanted to sell confidence and quality so we set up a whole set of consumer

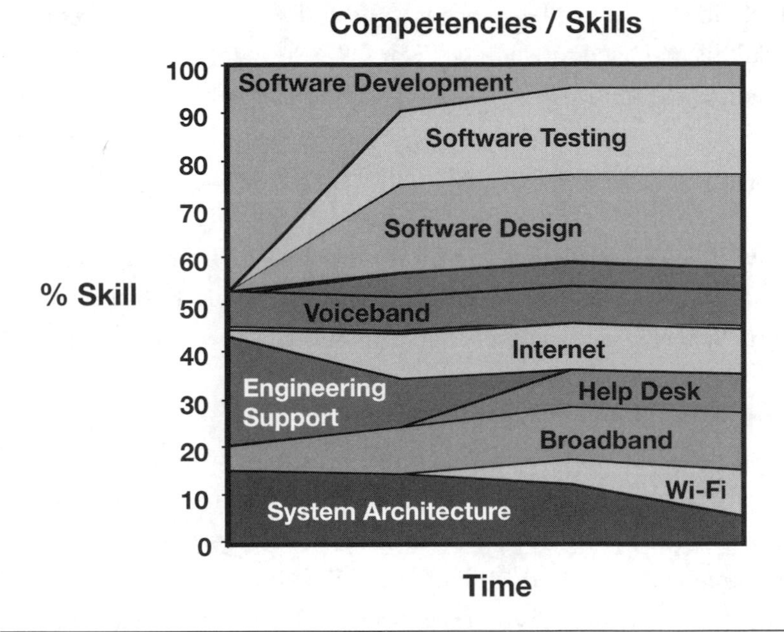

Figure 8.4 Staff balancing.

services to give [customers] confidence in the product." This program included a five-year repair-or-replace warranty (a first for the industry), a toll-free number tended by people knowledgeable in carpet-stain treatments (again, a first for the industry), negotiated agreements with Stanley Steemer to provide rapid response for on-site cleaning services, and agreements with carpet installers to replace carpet that could not be cleaned. The team recognized that the best way to keep customer service requirements low was to sell only product that met specifications, so the program also included an aggressive zero-defect-tolerance program to monitor carpet mill performance and, where appropriate, publicly sanction carpet mills that did not follow DuPont's specifications.

Staffing Levels

Appropriate staffing, both in the development stage and for full commercial operations, is critical to portfolio and product success. For VIP management, we like to say that the goal is to get the *right number* of the *right people* in the *right jobs* at the *right time*, as shown in Figure 8.4.

The portfolio staffing challenge needs to be addressed at the highest level to ensure that it is managed for success. Pixar CEO Steve Jobs wrote in his letter to shareholders in June 1998 (18 months after the release of the blockbuster movie *Toy Story* and just before the release of its next hit, *A Bug's Life*) that the company had added 100 people in the past year, bringing total staff to 400. "In many ways, these are the most important decisions we make . . . we strongly believe that 'you are who you hire.' Our size has doubled in the last two years and we are now close to having the talent in place to meet what promises to be a very demanding production schedule over the next several years."

A dialogue around the people component of investment intensity planning is probably one of the first discussions a portfolio planning team will have, since staffing of the development team often is senior management's first priority when adding a product to the portfolio. Effective staffing and structure of development teams, both at start-up and as the development moves forward, is another topic that has been well explored in the business literature and that we discussed in detail in Chapter 7.

For staffing of ongoing operations it is important to think through both the needs and the timing required to satisfy the needs. The investment intensity planning should incorporate the people resources required to handle all the enabling business infrastructure and technology activities discussed in the previous sections as well as the market presence activities we will discuss next. (Refer to Chapter 7 for an in-depth discussion of ways of evaluating people resources to determine where they will most benefit the VIP.) Planning needs to be predicated on success. In the case of Stainmaster, it immediately became clear that sales would far exceed even the most optimistic estimates, with DuPont's phones literally ringing off the hooks after the first major TV commercials were shown. (Initially, the thought was that Stainmaster would be only one of several carpet products in the residential carpet line, but within two months the Stainmaster fiber lines were sold out and it became clear that Stainmaster products would make up 100 percent of the residential portfolio.) The team had to respond, quickly bringing on board and training people to create a bank of capable phone operators (who had to have personally tested and cleaned Stainmaster carpets) to handle customer calls, beefing up the carpet mill audit team to stay on top of sold-out manufacturers, committing major DuPont engineering resources to design and build new fiber lines, and especially continuing to engage creative talent at its advertising firm BBDO to get even more TV ads completed and on the air. As Tom McAndrews said, "When the signs were clear that we had a major hit on our hands in early December (about six weeks after the first TV commercials appeared) I told the team 'Let's pour gasoline on the fire! Here's another ten million dollars to spend on advertising.'" The team stayed on top of this bucking bronco and was able to manage the onslaught of orders to continue to grow market share.

BUILDING MARKET PRESENCE

The DuPont Stainmaster team began detailed planning for the marketplace introduction of its Stainmaster line of products more than nine months ahead of the launch. The team built the launch around a broad-based consumer advertising campaign that included major broadcast network commercials (one of which went on to win a Clio award), point-of-purchase displays at carpet retailers, and major trade publication advertisements. The planned first-year budget alone for this campaign exceeded $30 million, more than six times what the nearest competitor was spending, a huge sum for any chemical company product introduction and truly unusual in the floor-covering industry. The result was one of the most successful product introductions in DuPont history that yielded a dominant brand awareness position for Stainmaster and a revitalization of the previously moribund residential carpet business that lasted many years.

There are three components to building a powerful market presence:

- **Developing a compelling story** to tell
- **Getting that story heard** and remembered above the din from the marketplace
- **Being present for purchase** when the customer makes the decision to buy

Developing a Compelling Story

Mark Hughes, author of *Buzzmarketing*, has said, "The goal with products is to give people a great story to tell, so they can tell two friends, and they tell two friends, and so on. Being new is a great advantage on this front."[6] The key is to have a story to tell that brings something fresh and new to the listener (customer) and does it in a way that virtually compels them to pay attention. It has a framing or a context or a positioning that can command attention. Before any development team launches a market communication or advertising campaign, it is imperative that they invest first to make sure they have something to say. The image diagram described in Chapter 5 is a powerful tool not only for understanding customer problems but also for building the marketing messages that will resonate with customers after a product has launched. PR and marketing people can use these images and stories to create campaigns that target the biggest, most pressing problems customers experience.

One of the key drivers of the Stainmaster success was that it did in fact provide a dramatic, measurable improvement in stain resistance performance—that is, the Stainmaster team did have something meaningful and quantifiable to say. What the team needed was to find a way to turn that into a clear and compelling story. The team worked with advertising agency BBDO to come up with a range of ways to communicate the stain resistance performance to key players in the game. DuPont committed to pay for the carpet treatment equipment needed at the carpet mills to help show that DuPont was committed to the carpet mills winning. The company developed technical data sheets to share with the carpet dealers cataloguing quantitative performance characteristic. It created a display unit that allowed customers to dip swizzle sticks, some with treated Stainmaster carpet tufts and some with untreated tufts, in various substances to see the difference in stain resistance. And it created TV spots using actual Stainmaster carpet that showed off what Stainmaster could do. Finally, to make the story even more compelling to consumers, DuPont implemented a five-year no-cost repair-or-replace warranty program to show the consumer that DuPont was willing to put its money behind Stainmaster's performance.

Getting Heard

There is an immense amount of noise in the marketplace today. We get hit from every angle, in both our professional roles and in our personal sphere, with messages about products and services we should buy. A company that wants its portfolio to succeed in the marketplace must be heard above this noise. Capturing share of mind or share of attention span ensures that potential customers will hear and remember your message. Most of the many avenues for getting your message out—especially conducting major advertising or marketing communication campaigns—cost big bucks. As with other areas of investment intensity, this means putting a premium on thoughtfully assessing exactly what you need before investing. The payoff from this investment, if done right, can be a major and powerful force in your portfolio's success.

A classic example of how *not* doing this right can lose a company its first-mover advantage is the story of portable MP3 players, a market now dominated by Apple's iPod. Creative Technology Ltd. (a Singapore-based company known best for its Sound Blaster audio cards for personal computers) launched the first portable MP3 player with a tiny hard drive that could store hours of music almost two years before Apple introduced the iPod. Unfortunately, Creative Technology did not appreciate the significance of its product or what it needed to fully exploit its innovation. The company never placed ads on TV or in newspapers but instead ran all advertising in computer trade magazines using in-house-designed copy. When Apple arrived on the scene with its massive (and creative) print, poster, and TV marketing campaign, it ran rings around Creative Technologies, even in the firm's home market. As the *Wall Street Journal* said: "Creative had little understanding of the often-subtle and always expensive marketing tactics a company like Apple uses to sell its products. And so—as often happens with innovative Asian manufacturers—the Creative MP3 player has been a modest hit while the iPod has become a global sensation."[7]

The story of Glide dental floss, developed and commercialized by the W.L. Gore Company (of GORE-TEX fame), offers a different perspective on how to approach this and shows that you don't always have to invest massive resources to win in your target market. At the time of Glide's launch, Gore had a major position in such businesses as medical products, fabrics and fibers, wire and cable, and filtration, but was new to the consumer packaged-goods market, which encompasses direct-to-consumer products such as dental floss. Consequently, it had neither the existing resource base nor the experience to communicate a direct-to-consumer message. Given this lack, John Spencer, who led the commercialization effort for Gore, was not in a position to get funds to compete head-to-head in consumer advertising with the major consumer goods players like Johnson & Johnson. Spencer hit on the strategy of going after the customer in a very targeted setting: the dentist's office. Consumers, he reasoned, would be receptive to a Glide message when seated in the dentist's chair. The best way to reach them in that chair would be through the person they spend most time with in the dental office: the dental hygienist. He hired his sister (who was a dental hygienist) as a marketing resource and set out to recruit dental hygienists as sales agents by pitching Glide's value in improving patient compliance around flossing (because of its easy slide between teeth it made flossing a lot less uncomfortable). He made up samples for hygienists to give to patients and wooed them at major conferences. In the end, this stealth and low-cost approach gained Gore's Glide a nationwide foothold that was helped by a brief article in *New York* magazine and its appearance in an episode of Seinfeld. Spencer skillfully exploited this publicity to get into major retail outlets. Within 18 months, Glide became the best-selling dental floss in the United States.

Spencer recognized a huge opportunity for Glide in the Gore portfolio. He also knew that marketing would be an enormous component of a potential success, but understood that Gore would not commit the resources required. So he found a way to achieve the same ends with a much smaller investment.

Being Available

The last element required to create sustainable market presence is what we call *availability to buy*—having your portfolio of products present and available when the customer is ready to purchase. In the past, the investment needed to create this availability was a huge deterrent to the launch of niche products, whose producers had to work extra hard to get into purchasing venues like retail outlets or distributors' catalogues. The rise of the Internet and low-cost shipping by UPS, FedEx, and others has minimized the investment required to be available for direct purchase. However, for a large-scale launch, this investment remains significant. Most consumer packaged-goods companies still need to fight—and pay—for shelf space in supermarkets, discount stores, and drugstores.

It's especially important to pay attention to this element of portfolio planning when you put a lot into getting heard and creating demand. Perhaps the only thing worse than an unnoticed product is one that customers are clamoring for but can't get. Except in rare cases, if a product is not available for purchase when a customer is ready to buy, you lose immediate sales but, perhaps more significantly, you may lose the future interest and goodwill of potential customers. For example, many toy and game companies become victims of their own success at holiday time, when stores run out of inventory on the hot new item and parents leave stores empty-handed and often with a bad feeling about the toymaker. (The Toyota Prius may be an exception to this rule, with customers signing up at dealerships for cars in colors not of their choosing, to be delivered after months-long waits.) So it behooves the development team and portfolio management leadership to plan this investment carefully.

SOME CONCLUDING PERSPECTIVES ON THE ROLE OF LEADERSHIP

How a business invests resources to capture business opportunities through its product portfolio determines whether the portfolio succeeds or fails in delivering customer value and enhancing company strategic value. As we said in the beginning, the key is having the right balance of investment intensity across the portfolio, knowing that too little or misapplied investment and the business opportunity can be lost and too much investment can dig a resource/cash hole so deep it swallows the product and, sometimes, the whole business. Senior leadership must ensure that investment intensity is front and center in the portfolio planning process. It must provide the structured tools and frameworks introduced in this chapter to effectively address investment intensity. It must assemble the cross-functional teams that offer the best insights into investment intensity issues and provide the environment (training, organizational) for those teams to succeed.

This means, as with other elements of the portfolio management process, that senior leadership must in fact lead investment intensity planning. Senior managers must

- Be fully engaged in the process, committing meaningful calendar time and energy
- Hold the development organization and itself accountable for using the structured tools and frameworks it has put in place
- Respond decisively to resource requests from the development teams driving the portfolio of products

Senior leadership must be bold and innovative in finding to ways to resource and support its development organization when the going gets tough. And it must be brutally honest in cases where watered-down commitments are worse than none at all. Believing you can cut the advertising budget for a new concept and still get a small return from the product is like believing you can be partially pregnant. Don't waste your development dollars if you're unable to make the other investments necessary for the product to succeed.

A final vignette from the Stainmaster story illustrates the level of commitment that can be required for success. As we described earlier, having a carpet that actually lived up to the advertising hype on stain resistance was imperative to a successful launch, and the key to that performance level was having a robust chemical treatment process in place at all the carpet mills that were launch partners. As the launch date neared, the Stainmaster team realized it might not get the mill processes fully under control by the launch. So Tom McAndrews made a striking resource commitment. For a two-week period, he put DuPont's fleet of corporate executive jets at the disposal of the lead technical services manager to use as needed so he and his team could reach a mill partner site trouble spot within hours of a problem showing up. With this rapid-response capability, the first carpets were certified just weeks before the Stainmaster introduction.

We challenge any company that wants a VIP success story to show this kind of leadership. In the next chapter, we look at extending this leadership to keep the portfolio alive and able to adapt to constantly changing market forces.

NOTES

1. The Stainmaster example used throughout this chapter, and quotes appearing in association with it, are based on personal interviews with DuPont staff: Bob Axtell (business leader for Residential Carpet Fiber), Bob Shellenbarger (end-use research manager), Tom McAndrews (division director, DuPont Carpet Fibers) and John Hesselberth (technical director, DuPont Carpet Fibers). Information also came from: Case 1-2, "Stainmaster" by Bette Collins, James D. Culley, and Paul W. Farris, published in *Cases in Advertising and Promotion Management*, 4th ed., John A. Quelch and Paul W. Farris, eds. (Burr Ridge, IL: Irwin Publishing, 1994), pp. 22–42.
2. Michael Kanellos, "New AMD Factory Ups the Ante against Intel," *CNET News.com*, October 14, 2005.
3. Gwendolyn Bounds, "Winning Shelf Space in a Competitive Market," *Wall Street Journal*, January 30, 2006.
4. Nicholas T. Carr, "Why IT Doesn't Matter Any More," *SearchCIO.com*, June 11, 2003.
5. From the IT Cortex Web site: (www.it-cortex.com/Stat_ Failure_ Rate.htm).
6. Bounds, "Winning Shelf Space."
7. Chris Prystay, "When Being Doesn't Make You Number 1," *Wall Street Journal*, August 12, 2004.

Additional Sources

Motorola., Inc. Web site (press releases and technical PowerPoint presentation for Canopy information).

Floor Focus Magazine Web site (Article on the carpet market: www.floordaily.net/features/FeatBrand0402.htm).

Bill Bane, "Testing Stainmaster Carpet," *Bane-Clene Professional Cleaning Digest* 33, no. 1 (Winter 2003): 6.

Harold Brubaker, "USA: DuPont's Goal—Change Nature of Its Business," *Philadelphia Inquirer*, September 2, 2001.

Dell Inc. Web site, section on innovation at Dell.

9

KEEPING THE FIRES BURNING: THE DYNAMIC PORTFOLIO

> "Whereas in 1900 the train carried almost all long-distance travelers, in 2000 such travelers almost all went by car or airplane . . . [T]he real story after 1945 was the quickly disappearing railroad passenger."
> —*From "American Railways in the 20th Century"*[1]

The story of passenger rail travel over the last 150 years is often cited to illustrate the dangers of failing to understand what business you're in. The railroads, the argument goes, continued steadfastly to believe that they were in the railroad business rather than the transportation business, and thus fell victim to the steep decline in passenger rail travel as people increasingly took to highways in cars and to the air in planes.

The story, often-cited though it may be, underscores the importance maintaining a dynamic portfolio that can adapt to changing market forces. The changes may not always be as dramatic as the rise of the interstate highway system and Americans' concomitant love affair with the automobile, but failure to adapt may be every bit as devastating.

A portfolio must be dynamic because it exists in a world in flux. Like the railroads, which continued offering a portfolio of rail travel while the technology and competitive landscape transformed around them, your company may be blindsided without a dynamic portfolio review process. This chapter is about that process and about what's necessary to ensure that the portfolio, ablaze with possibility at the moment of inception, can adapt and thrive in a changing world. What changes in thinking are required to ensure that the portfolio doesn't end up, like an untended fire, as a useless mound of cold ash? What's necessary to build synergies among projects and develop a culture that accommodates the dynamic nature of VIP management? We introduce the idea of dynamic governance, a process for making portfolio management part of a company's day-to-day operations, and revisit the deployment tree introduced in Chapter 6 as it pertains to evaluating portfolio performance.

DYNAMIC GOVERNANCE: MANAGING THE VIP IN A WORLD OF CHANGE

In ecology, an ecosystem is defined as a group of organisms living together within an environment, forming a dynamic and interactive unit. Plants exchange oxygen and carbon dioxide with the atmosphere, and insects transform waste into fuel. Actions by any part of the ecosystem affect every other part in some way; in fact, this interplay among an ecosystem's elements sustains life. A business ecosystem consists of similarly interdependent entities: corporations, divisions, business units, competitors, and the economic and regulatory environment. Organizations, like living organisms, change and react in response to changes that occur elsewhere in the system.

Many different types of external events affect a portfolio over time. Disruptions and surprises can come from anywhere, at any moment. They may occur suddenly (like Hurricane Katrina, which directly and immediately affected the portfolio plans of automobile companies) or may build over time. Changes in technology, disruptive competition, radical shifts in public opinion, or new legislation—events taking place *outside* an organization—all impact what occurs *inside* the company's portfolio. For example, imagine that your company lays out its portfolio strategy for the coming year at a high-level year-end meeting. On February 1 of the new portfolio year, a competitor introduces a product that will provide more customer value than your planned product, essentially making obsolete a product not yet created. The ecosystem has changed. Through no doing of the company, its portfolio plan for the year is now inadequate. The market need you thought the portfolio would fill will no longer exist when the product is introduced. You must reevaluate the portfolio.

Disruptive competition is an external event that demands an immediate response within the portfolio. Similar reevaluations need to occur in response to other external forces. Changes in consumers' attitudes toward smoking have forced tobacco companies to find other businesses. Rising oil prices compelled automakers to rethink their approaches to producing SUVs and other fuel-inefficient vehicles.

Without a formal portfolio review process, responding to any of these events would be impossible. Such a review process, which we refer to as dynamic governance, allows the portfolio to evolve in response to the activities and changes of the larger environment. It includes measurement tools that are themselves dynamic. And, like creation of the portfolio, it should be a concern of senior management.

Establishing a sensible and effective review process (including formulating criteria and a mechanism for the out-of-bounds review) and establishing metrics by which to evaluate the portfolio are part of *dynamic governance* of the portfolio. Any portfolio assessment must provide decision makers with not only a roadmap of how to execute against objectives but also with insights into the trade-offs and risks associated with their decisions. Therefore, successful governance of the VIP consists of targets and reviews. A target is an objective projection of where the portfolio performance should be throughout the implementation period. You need to monitor progress regularly along the way, since, without a formal governance system, too much depends on hope and heroes. The company needs to conduct frequent, periodic reviews at a project level to minimize bureaucracy, but these reviews must be done in a structured manner (see Figure 9.1).

The discussions around project progress toward the targets result in individual project actions to keep the overall portfolio on track. These are the portfolio *predictive process reviews*, which will predict progress toward the desired results. A higher-level review of the results also must occur to ensure success, but less frequently. The results review either reconfirms that the

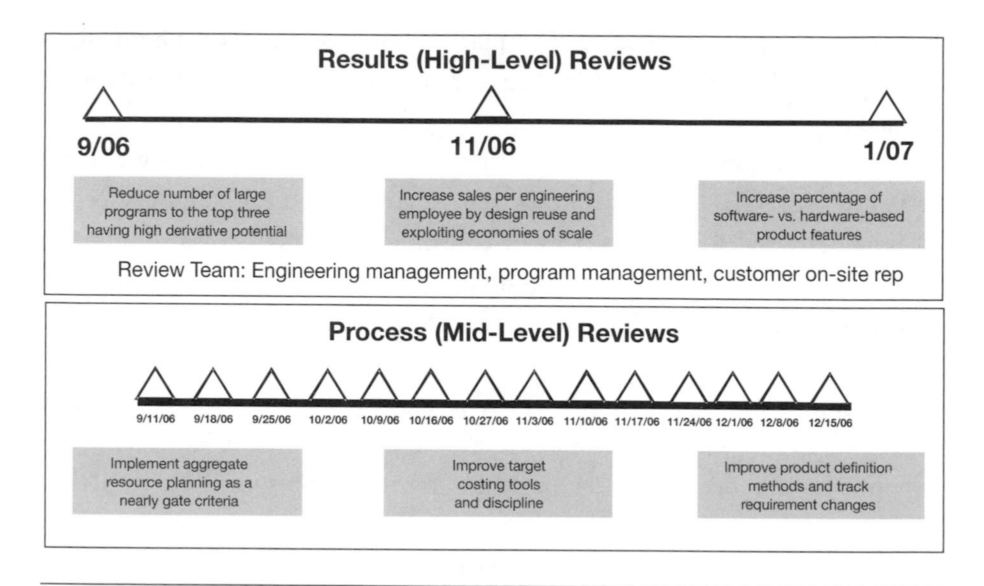

Figure 9.1 High-level and mid-level reviews take place at different frequencies.

portfolio is exactly on target or identifies changes that must be made. Both project- and executive-level staff participate in the portfolio results review.

The remainder of this chapter talks in more detail about what dynamic governance looks like and about ways of setting it up to ensure that day-to-day activities contribute to the long-term health and well-being of the portfolio.

TWO LEVELS OF PORTFOLIO REVIEW

Clearly, an annual portfolio review meeting is not adequate to accommodate the intense rate of change in the business world. Would an interval of six months be adequate? Three? Two? One? Once a week? The answer depends on the level at which the review takes place (executive, tactical) and the industry cycle time for a particular company. We believe that every company needs at least two levels of review, with different frequencies, to enable it to respond appropriately to change.

A formal, executive-level review can take place quarterly or even twice a year or annually. This is where strategy meets the portfolio. David Miller, vice president and general manager for DuPont Electronic Technologies, describes his process: "We have a yearly strategy review process . . . objectives for the year flow out of that strategy review. We might say 'Look, the semiconductor market's going to copper. You don't have a copper remover or CMP slurry, you need a copper product.' So one of the critical operating tasks for '05, or '04, or whatever year is: we've got to get a copper offering."

Informal portfolio reviews must take place more frequently—at least monthly, we believe, and, in some cases, even weekly—because you may need to make portfolio adjustments much more frequently in response to marketplace events or new discoveries. Most of the companies we spoke with in writing this book touch their portfolios at least monthly. At Hewlett-Packard, for example, the portfolio review process is ongoing, occurring almost constantly. "[We don't] look at it once a year and then everybody goes and does their jobs," says Deborah Nelson, VP of marketing and alliances for HP's Technology Solutions Group. "It's looked at constantly—more than monthly—for adjustments and incorporating new things that we've learned. That doesn't mean that the major milestones . . . shift, but maybe how we're thinking about other elements around those products can be adjusted. [W]e are constantly looking at our portfolio and our roadmap. You know how much technology changes . . . so it is a living, breathing, ongoing, real-time process."

At DuPont Electronic Technologies, the annual strategy review flows down into monthly reviews. "We have monthly execution reviews for each business unit," DuPont's Miller says. "We'll sit down with the business leader and his CFO and planning person for two hours once a month [to ask] 'What's going on? How are your financials? How are these projects going? How are your critical operating tasks going?' . . . [T]hat process is more of an auditing in real time. In these monthly reviews you might say, 'Hey, something's changed. We need a new offering.' That will be the process where we'll talk about doing it or not."

THE OUT-OF-BOUNDS REVIEW

While full-blown, formal review meetings sometimes require lots of time and preparation, informal reviews can occur quickly, allowing quick response to ripples in the marketplace or any other changes. The benefit of frequent reviews is that they allow you to attend to potential problems before they rage out of control like a house fire that could have been contained if it had been caught when it was a smoldering in a wastebasket.

Mid-level executives are responsible for these reviews, and it's important to have clear directives about their scope of responsibility and a mechanism for escalating problems. They may be able to highlight a disruptive problem and schedule a higher-level review, but they probably won't be charged with the dealing with situations that are either much worse or much better than anticipated—situations that are out-of-bounds in relation to the initial portfolio plan. When out-of-bounds conditions occur, senior management must respond. Will Hill of The Stanley Works is adamant about the role of senior management in the portfolio review process. "I talked about the management commitment of the senior leadership, but the other thing that's fundamental is the process you use to manage this . . . [W]e had product development reviews, which were monthly meetings that included the president of the businesses. There were also regular new product reviews with the CEO and the overall corporate management team who met on this quarterly and reviewed progress of the projects. The actual project work was done by project teams that met anywhere from weekly to daily. This was done in the context of an annual worldwide product plan, which was reviewed once a year over three days by the senior management team."

A variety of conditions may trigger an *out-of-bounds* review, as shown in Figure 9.2. One company we worked with called an out-of-bounds review in April because it realized it would not be able to meet its delivery schedule for the end of May and would need an additional two months. (Resources had been diverted from the team to another emergency project.) The out-of-bounds review gave management an early warning and an opportunity to make a decision about which project was more important, and the team was able to negotiate a compromise that resulted in completing the project at the end of June.

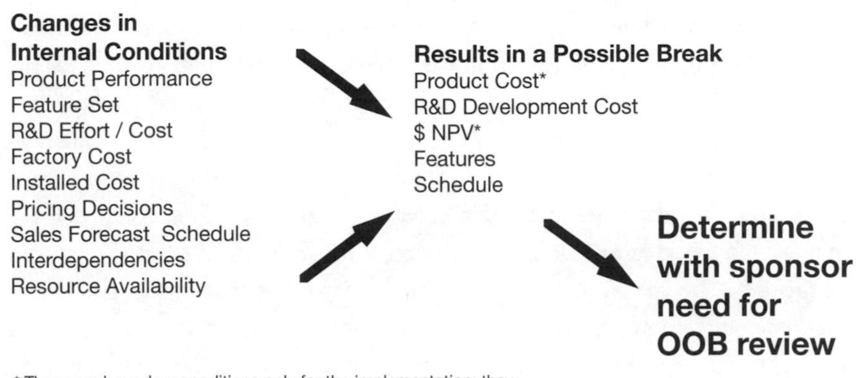

Figure 9.2 Out-of-bounds trigger events.

It's important to remember what the out-of-bounds review is not. It is

Not usually optional; not a judgment call. The team's experience and judgment were exercised earlier, in the definition or implementation phase review, which occurred when there was no possible crisis brewing.

Not being called on the carpet. The purpose is to objectively assess the situation and reestablish agreement with management on the project plan.

Not an occasion for a simple "We'll try harder." Teams need to dig deep and analyze causes and effects so management has confidence that the project won't continue off track.

Not an elaborate presentation that takes weeks to prepare. Almost always, earlier correction is better than delayed correction (putting out the smoldering wastebasket fire, not the raging house fire).

TERADYNE'S RIGOROUS REVIEW PROCESS

Teradyne, Inc.'s Broadband Test Division, a provider of automatic test solutions for the communications industry, has developed a rigorous portfolio review process that has turned around the company's performance ratings with customers. The process includes all the elements we just mentioned: regularity, appropriate frequency, the participation of management, and escalation when out-of-bounds conditions occur. According to Frank Bauer, who manages Teradyne's Broadband Test Division advanced development organization, these review practices have brought much greater predictability to product delivery, which, in the Broadband Test Division's case, is mostly software. Bauer describes the reviews: "We've developed a mechanism that takes those requirements, as we define then, from customer interaction and put them into a system of releases—software releases that occur every three months. Each release has a particular cycle of gates—call them gates, if you like, or milestones—that start with the definition phase and move through a series of steps that continues to get further agreement from all the cross-functional groups inside the company . . . [w]hen the software is delivered to our own internal system verification team, when it's available for field trial, when it's fully available for customer acceptance, and then when it's released as a product. That whole cycle actually takes six months. But because we need a software release every three months, we actually have two teams that operate in parallel. They're offset by a factor of three months. So we'll set one team in motion, and then three months later set the second team in motion, and they'll continually cycle off of one release and onto the next. That way, each three months we have a software release."

Information gathered from customers at the beginning of a project goes through an initial management review, then flows into a funnel for a roll-in to the releases. "So we have always a year of funnel in front of us that shows which release is carrying which features, and which items for which customer. Those get reviewed once a month—not only the projects that are in progress, but also the projects that are upcoming. Although we've built the funnel a year out, as we get closer to them, obviously they get refined. And we go through to make sure we've got the right features for the timeframe that we need. At the end of that entire cycle, of course, we release the product.

"Management business reviews occur once a month. There are also weekly core team meetings. Each release has a core team at the level of those that are implementing, rather than managing the release. A further extension of representation would not only include sales, marketing, and engineering, but also our operations team, our manufacturing team, and so forth. They get together once a week with quite a bit of tracking around the project. We have an earned value system that tracks quantitatively the progress of development, so each week we get a snapshot of where we are against the plan, and then work the deviation. [For example,] if the execution on a weekly basis deviates from plan by more than three days, then it's escalated to the next level of management. If it deviates by more than a week, then it has to be escalated to the general manager . . . he then gets involved, along with any other appropriate managers, to see what we can do to pull the release back in on plan."

Bauer continues, "This release process works particularly well because it's forced us to get very organized with the input side. We've been using this now for two years and it's been very successful for us, in that we can very much predict with a high degree of accuracy when we can deliver something and what can deliver." Before putting in place this process, Teradyne often heard complaints from customers about performance. Customers "would tend to say that we delivered a very good product, but we were generally late. We were not predictable about when that product would be delivered. That problem has gone away, now. We have not only a very good product that we deliver, but it's very predictable when we are able to provide it. So that part of the process I think works very well for us, and it's also very efficient, in terms of the use of engineering resources and so forth. Engineers can schedule their work, know when it's going to be completed and know when they're going to work on the next project. So across the organization and for our customers, I think it's a terrific process and working very well."

* * * *

GOING BEYOND PHASES AND GATES

The phased development approach (also known as phased project planning, or PPD, phase-gate, or by Robert Cooper's proprietary Stage-Gate terminology) is a popular approach to managing new product development. As Preston Smith and Donald Reinertsen point out, this approach endures at many organizations because it's comfortable.[2] The phase-gate process measures budget and schedules with respect to milestones in the development process. If used as the primary framework for the VIP, however—or if isolated

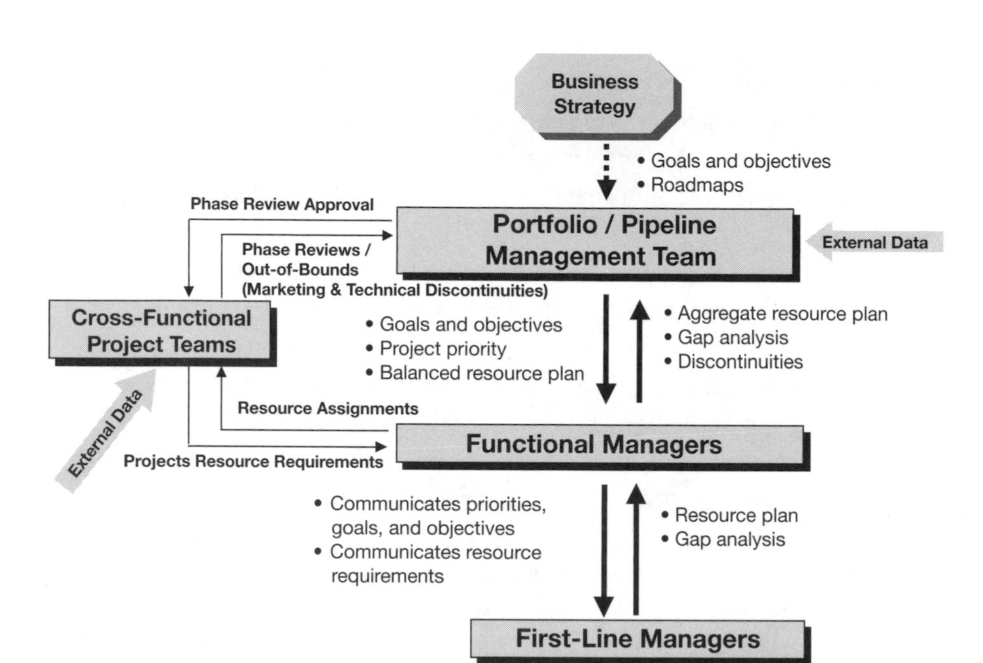

Figure 9.3 Pipeline management integrated with portfolio management.

from other parts of the process—phases and gates have some shortcomings. The focus on *process* usually does not consider the holistic effects on the portfolio or address the impact of one project on others in the portfolio. Furthermore, it does not consider external events that may affect development.

We believe that senior management needs to own and oversee three distinct but integrated areas: pipeline management (phases and gates), portfolio management, and process management (see Figure 9.3). An integrated approach ensures that your portfolio doesn't fall victim to the waiting game—where you delay work on some parts of a project while waiting for other parts to reach a predetermined end point. Integrating pipeline management with the VIP process also ensures that the measurements used to evaluate progress are customer-based rather than financial. Using the VIP approach, you continue to obtain and analyze customer and competitive data even as your project moves into different phases, allowing you to respond to what is happening in the real world rather than rigidly adhering to a predetermined go/no-go decision point.

Finally, integrating pipeline management with portfolio management provides the formal mechanisms, often lacking in a phase-gate process alone, for dealing with issues *outside* of the portfolio. These fluctuating, messy, real-world ecosystem issues can have a huge impact on the portfolio and are the triggers for the out-of-bounds review discussed earlier in this chapter.

MEASURING THE DYNAMIC PORTFOLIO

Regular review can keep portfolio activities on track. But without some form of assessment, a business will never know whether those activities are the right ones—whether the portfolio is fulfilling the goals that were defined when a company used the deployment tree introduced in Chapter 6. Measurement is key. "You've got to measure things, you absolutely have to have metrics in place," says Steve Sichak of BD Diagnostics. "The adage, 'That which is not measured, is not managed' is absolutely true. You need to be disciplined if you're going to be successful. You need to rely on data. Disciplined, meaning you've got a good process that's in place and followed regularly, and data, meaning that it's fact-based decisions, and not opinion-based, with broad participation from the management team whereby the management team has a common agenda that is agreed upon and followed. That way you don't have individual functions off doing things that are not aligned with the overall direction of the business."

The portfolio—as well as the company, the competition, and the world—are not the same today as they were yesterday. They cannot be managed or measured using processes or metrics that are not themselves dynamic, just as a scientist cannot apply the same units of measure as a substance changes state from solid to liquid to gas. Yet, traditionally, businesses have used static measurements to evaluate portfolio performance and keep projects on track. These results-based metrics, such as sales figures, market share, or return-on-investment, come after the fact. They tell you only that you have *already* succeeded or failed. They offer no meaningful data about the direction you are currently going in, whether you are headed for a train wreck, and whether you can avoid that wreck by taking action now.

Just as metrics such as rising profits, increases in stock price, or overhead rate have limited utility in selecting products for the portfolio, they also are limited in measuring portfolio success. The VIP uses customer value not only as the criterion for selecting products and as a common language to communicate about the portfolio *but also for measuring every task conducted by the company in the course if its business.*

This may seem like a tall order. Yet over the years our interviews with metrics assessment managers have revealed consistent dissatisfaction with both the effectiveness and efficiency of existing metrics. Given this dissatisfaction, what company wouldn't like to institute metrics that are simpler, better understood by those who need to use them, and more effective in bringing about the desired results? Implementing the metrics that flow from the deployment tree is easier because the metrics are already in a language people understand.

The deployment tree we introduced in Chapter 6 works almost as automatically as a measurement tool as it does in its strategy deployment and communication role. At every level of the tree, you can establish metrics around the goals related to realizing the portfolio. Remember that establishing a deployment tree involves setting appropriate goals at each level of the organization. To add a metrics capability to the tree, you simply ask questions related to each goal such as *how much? when? how good?* For example, suppose you are creating a new electronic device. As part of the development process, the engineering department has as a goal to prove the viability of a new semiconductor technology. To add measurement capability to the tree, you associate a time with the goal: prove viability by March 31. If March 31 comes and goes without that happening, you know the overall project schedule is likely to slip. Being attentive to the small actions described as part of the deployment tree creates a framework that builds on itself and ultimately rolls up into larger and larger projects and, finally, into corporate objectives.

Too often, companies treat assessment as a mechanical or arbitrary process or a necessary evil that inhibits creativity. Such a view is at odds with the dynamic nature of the VIP. As we discussed in the previous section, assessment, and the metrics associated with assessment, need not be complex. Ethicon Endo-Surgery (EES), for example, uses the same surveys it develops for assessing the importance of requirements in the portfolio definition stage

THE SUBLIMINAL MESSAGE OF MEASUREMENTS

The job of project manager represents the crucible where strategy is transformed into action. Each morning, arriving at her desk, the project manager in a company's hypothetical consumer software division works on a variety of activities: coordinating code revisions, reviewing marketing copy for the product packaging, scheduling beta testing.

If the company employs a financial approach to metrics, the VP of the consumer software division may be evaluated on her products' contribution to revenue. To attain that contribution, she may make decisions such as moving resources from one project to another or cutting functionality to remain on time and within budget. The project manager who works for her understands that money and time are paramount. She approaches her daily tasks with that mindset. When the development team presents two alternatives for building security into the software, she will pick the one that requires the smallest investment, since that's how she and her boss are evaluated.

Now imagine the scenario with different ground rules. Before the project launched, everyone involved learns about the customer need that led to selection of this particular product for the portfolio. Business planning determines the larger questions around the project manager's daily tasks (Are they the right ones? What actions will cause this project to be successful?). The company measures individual performance not by contribution to revenue but by the extent to which it contributes to meeting that customer need. The company benchmarks all its activities against the value the company is delivering to its customer. Faced with the same two alternatives for addressing the security feature, the project manager will now look at the customer's need for information security as defined in the project mission and ask, "To what level must the product address that need in order to provide value?" She may use a process such as market-driven product definition to evaluate the relative value customers place on various requirements. She may take a very different path with customer value, not money, as her yardstick.

* * * *

to analyze portfolio performance after a product's launch. "We use that same survey throughout the development process. We needed a predictive tool for product performance at a high level. These surveys give us insight to the level of preference or satisfaction with our product. We survey customers to understand their current satisfaction level with products; we measure their satisfaction now, then ask again with written or actual concepts to predict their success. We confirm that we hit the mark with the product post-launch survey as well."

As part of this evaluation, EES uses what it calls *spider charts* (these are akin to the radar charts we introduced in Chapter 4). "We use spider charts also to assess metrics or technical specifications, as well as the importance/satisfaction . . . to develop predictive performance from the voice of customer at the highest requirement levels. [We use them] through the whole process . . . And if there are any design trade-offs that need to be made we'll reassess importance/satisfaction. Pre-launch, again, we do labs or hands on, we assess it, and then post-launch, after the customers have actually used a product." In this way, metrics become an integrated and organic part of the VIP process.

Of course, this will only work if you pay attention to what the measurements are telling you. As in the case of out-of-bounds conditions, management must pay attention to bad news—and take early action to correct the underlying problems generating the bad news. Ignoring early signals about schedule slips and believing that you can make up time at the end of the process is almost always wasteful folly. You must be prepared to act immediately to change the conditions that are leading the portfolio off track.

LIVING, BREATHING, AND GROWING

Unlike the railroads, Verizon Wireless, a communications giant created from the merger of Bell Atlantic Corp. and GTE Corp. in 2000, recognized itself to be in the communications business rather than in the land-based phone business from which it was born. It grew aggressively through acquisition and in its first five years invested more than $72 billion to maintain, upgrade, and expand its technology infrastructure.[3] Such growth happens not accidentally but by creating a portfolio of products that match the state of the world and the needs of consumers and putting processes in place that keep the portfolio alive.

Once you have taken steps to ensure that your portfolio is a living, breathing entity that permeates every part of your organization, you can go on to ensure that the VIP process itself becomes part of the corporate culture. Institutionalizing the process, as we explain in the next chapter, means that the VIP process will become a vital part of the way your company operates long after its champions are gone.

NOTES

1. "American Railroads in the 20th Century," from the National Museum of America History Web site (http://americanhistory.si.edu/onthemove/themes/story_42_1.html).
2. Preston G. Smith and Donald G. Reinertsen, *Developing Products in Half the Time: New Rules, New Tools, 2nd ed.* (New York: John Wiley & Sons, October 1997).
3. "The History of Verizon Communications," from Verizon corporate Web site (http://investor.verizon.com/profile/history).

10

A TALENT FOR CHANGE: THE SUSTAINABLE PORTFOLIO

> "Plans are nothing; planning is everything."
> —*Dwight D. Eisenhower*

> "We already know how to do our jobs better than we do them now. We don't lack great ideas. Instead, I'd characterize our problem as 'Pilot-itis'. . . islands of successful change in a sea of opportunity."
> —*President of a large company struggling to institutionalize business process change*

In the science fiction television series *Star Trek: The Next Generation*, whenever the crew decides to chart a new course, Captain Jean-Luc Picard speaks three little words with great authority: "Make it so."

Changing the business procedures and processes of any organization is a major undertaking, and few managers can summon change simply by announcing their intentions. In fact, one of the few business processes that fails more than new product introductions is the introduction of new business processes!

You know the drill. An executive attends a conference or reads a book like this one and learns about an exciting new way of doing business that can save money, save time, improve profitability, and enhance customer acceptance. A pilot project takes shape. Staff is assigned, and work gets underway. A year later, the new process is heralded a success and rolled out across the organization. A year after that, it has disappeared entirely, never to be seen again. The president of a large company we worked with once expressed his frustration this way: "The problem isn't that I don't have enough ideas about how to make my business run better. The problem is getting the ideas to work." There's no shortage of good ideas about how to change business processes. The shortage is in the tools and ability to incorporate change into a company's daily operations.

Some kinds of change catch on all by themselves. To get employees to use e-mail, nobody needed to "implement a program" other than putting the infrastructure in place and providing minimal training. Such so-called viral innovations are so compelling they hardly need management or a rigorous process to become popular and widely accepted. Introducing the VIP approach to managing a company's portfolio of products is undoubtedly a big change. Yet a new approach to portfolio management, unlike some new technologies, probably isn't exciting enough to spread on its own. Just as it's up to senior managers to recognize the benefits of the VIP, it's up to them to ensure that the pieces are in place to actually implement the change.

Success with VIP management requires more than simply recognizing it as a good idea. It requires a new approach to planning, executing, and measuring change. In Chapter 6, we discussed a method for propagating the VIP approach throughout the organization, communicating it to everyone, and automatically linking it to business strategy. This chapter looks at the larger issue of introducing change to an organization. We examine ways to that ensure your new portfolio management process makes it beyond the pilot stage by making your organization adept at the process of change itself. We look at how institutionalizing the VIP approach allows it to live on beyond its originators. This chapter is about the actions that lie behind the intention to "make it so."

PILOT-ITIS: THE PROBLEM WITH THE STANDARD APPROACH TO INSTITUTING CHANGE

When considering a fresh idea or way of doing business, many companies turn first to the time-honored pilot project, reasoning that trying something new on a small scale is a good way to work out the kinks before introducing it more widely. While conducting a test run is wise, and pilot projects themselves often are successful, failure regularly follows as companies attempt to roll the pilot project out more broadly.

What happens after a successful pilot project is a syndrome we call *pilot-itis.* The basic story line goes something like this: A company identifies a new approach or opportunity for improvement. It assembles a team of heroes—the best and the brightest, who know how to get things done and are well connected within the organization—to carry out a pilot project. No expense is spared; the team receives whatever resources it needs and lots of attention from management. With the best talent, lots of money, and support from senior management, the project is wildly successful.

At this stage, new business processes such as VIP are like plants started in a greenhouse. They have germinated in an ideal environment. In the pilot stage, they receive copious water and fertilizer, as well as the undivided attention of the master gardener. But what happens next? The heroes move on to the next project, leaving the ordinary folks to try to replicate the pilot project's results, often by adopting completely new ways of doing their jobs. Senior management (the master gardener) turns its attention to the Next Big Thing. Funding (water and fertilizer) dries up. The ordinary folks encounter all the real-world barriers that the pilot team never faced. The traditional model of the change process, shown in Figure 10.1, leaves the institutionalization of change to chance. *Maybe* people will remain committed to change . . . if the obstacles aren't too great. More likely, without understanding what worked or why, they will become frustrated and overwhelmed and return to the old way of doing business.

As always, executive leadership can make the difference, as tool and security manufacturer The Stanley Works discovered when it began changing its approach to product development. "We had an organization with some pockets of excellence in new product development, but they really had very little air

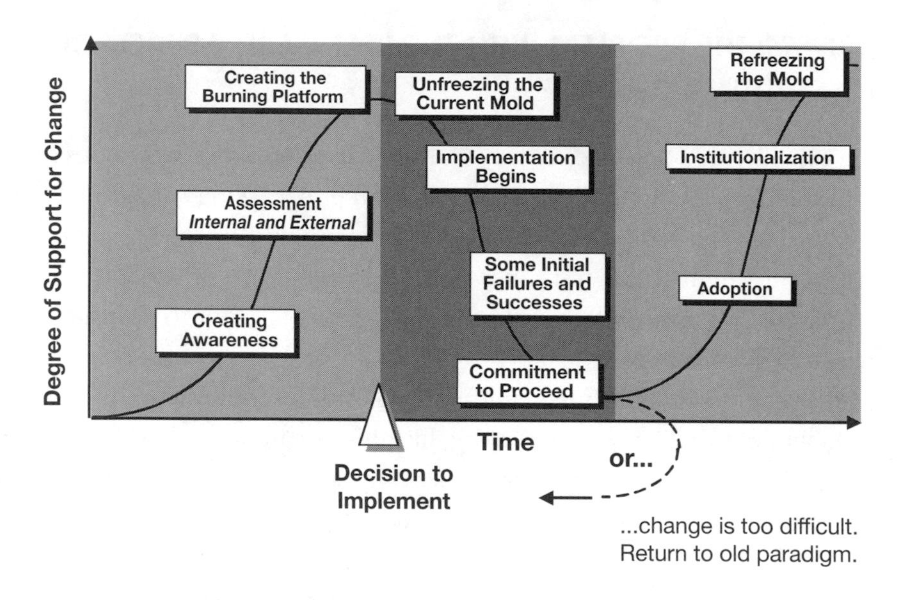

Figure 10.1 Traditional change model.

cover from the leadership in the organization," says Will Hill. These groups were "more guerilla warfare efforts trying to do innovative things. I use the analogy that product development innovation is like planting seeds . . . in the spring, you do the work and you plant the grass seed and it just pops up miraculously. [But] if you don't protect it, if you don't water it every day, it quickly dies. It's very vulnerable in that stage until it gets established and the roots get down. Innovation is the same way . . . a guerrilla group can start it and they can prepare the ground, but if they don't have help to water it and protect it, it's just going to get crushed."

Transplanting a delicate pilot project to the rough environment of the corporation can kill it before it ever takes root. It's no wonder that such a small percentage of all new business initiatives ever become part of the fabric of the organization. Even one successful VIP project within a division won't guarantee ongoing success throughout the company.

So what explicit steps must senior management take to make sure the VIP approach to portfolio management becomes an established part of the corporate culture? PDC has found there are three key elements to institutionalizing any change, particularly ones that occur rapidly. Figure 10.2 illustrates these:

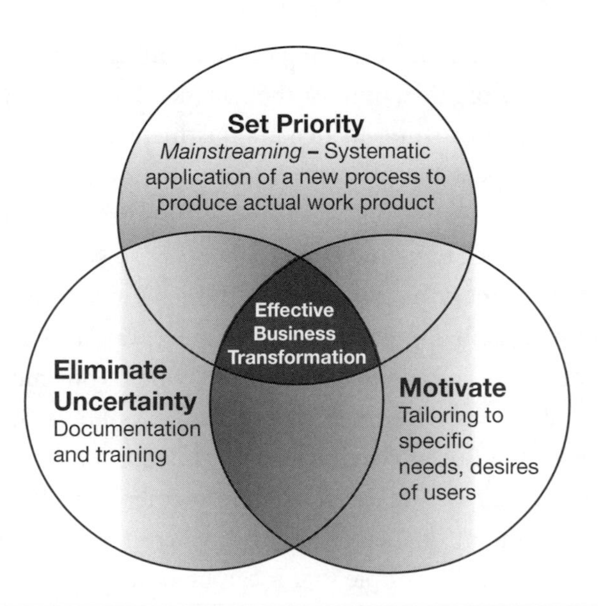

Figure 10.2 Key elements of rapid change.

setting priorities to produce actual work while the change is initiated, eliminating uncertainty and barriers to adoption through effective training, and motivating participants by tailoring programs to their needs.

IGNORE THE MIDDLE STAGE AT YOUR PERIL

In an effort to get to market more quickly or simply to keep up with what they perceive as an accelerated business environment, companies often ignore a critical middle stage in the process of implementing change: the time between discovering a new way of doing business and fully deploying it as a habit. It may seem counterintuitive that moving more quickly involves additional steps. Yet ignoring this middle stage, and the steps that should occur within it, actually *prolongs* the time it takes to fully deploy the VIP approach and ultimately leads organizations to settle back into old habits and practices. Missteps take more time than middle steps, and the erosion of confidence that occurs with failures requires many more subsequent successes to eliminate the sour taste of failure.

This middle stage, like the hardening off of seedlings before setting them outdoors, prepares the organization for the hard work of sticking with a new way of doing things. It's a time to make adjustments, dissect exactly what makes the process repeatable, identify barriers to implementation, devise practical ways around those barriers, and guide teams through the first implementation. It involves engaging the heroes who were so successful during the pilot stage to lead ordinary people through the new way of doing business. Once people are successful doing something in a new way, the change becomes part of the business. "It is nice to put your money where your mouth is and be able to apply what you developed to a program," says Lucia Buehler, group product director of the Breast Care Division at Ethicon Endo-Surgery of the design excellence process she was involved in implementing. "It's good to have the philosophy and intent of the process and program behind you. It's even better to then apply it, show people that it can be done, and demonstrate the real success in dollars and time!"

We have identified several critical factors surrounding the middle step in the implementation of business process change.[1] The ideas are simple:

People learn by doing. Identifying a member of the pilot project willing to coach the teams going through the new process for the first time is often the best way to help people learn.

The change process should focus on outcome. *Delivering real work* while making a change happen.

Metrics are critical. Objectively measuring whether the change occurs provides invaluable feedback about what works and what doesn't.

Incremental rather than wholesale change is easier to manage. Expanding a successful pilot to a slightly wider group initially works better than rolling it out companywide right away.

Simple as they may be, these ideas have profound implications for how a business approaches change. For example, we have noted two common maladies, often related to pilot-itis syndrome, afflict companies attempting to change their business processes: *planning-itis* and *training-itis*. While the staff is figuring out how to do things differently, teams are consumed by making plans and attending training sessions. Day-to-day work gets short shrift and deadlines slip.

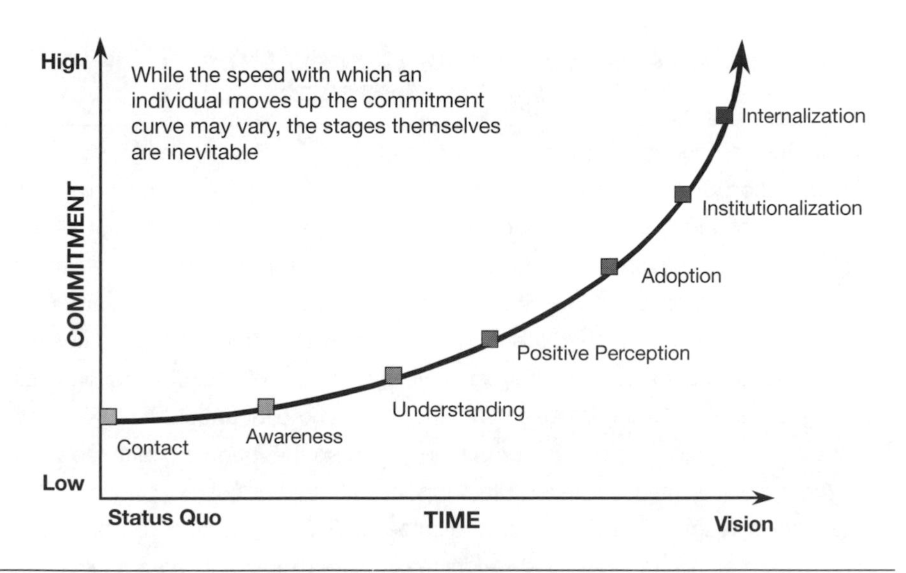

Figure 10.3 People are ready, willing, and able at different rates and travel up a commitment curve that defines the stages for building personal commitment to change. (*Source*: Used with permission from Ethicon Endo-Surgery, Inc., a Johnson & Johnson Company.)

To avoid turning project people into process improvement people, planning and training must be *outcome-based*. These activities must advance current projects and produce real work. Instead of attending training sessions while projects sit undone back at their desks, people should be actually doing their jobs in the new way. The learning should be the sidelight and the doing should be the highlight. Think of it as just-enough training—only what's required to do the work at hand. Identifying an individual who was part of the pilot project who can disseminate knowledge about how to institute change through workshops, seminars, or one-on-one meetings helps get real work done while people are learning. Ideally, this person not only understands the challenges and roadblocks but also has enough standing in the organization to modify the process to make it work.

Finally, instituting change requires sensitivity to the individuals who will be carrying it out. EES, whose implementation of a major initiative is profiled in the accompanying sidebar, has created a commitment curve, shown in Figure 10.3, showing the stages required for building personal commitment to change.

IMPLEMENTING DESIGN EXCELLENCE AT ETHICON ENDO-SURGERY

Lucia Buehler, currently group product director of the Breast Care Division at Ethicon Endo-Surgery, describes her company's commitment to managing the process of change during the introduction of a new approach to product development. At the time, she was marketing product director and had been selected with two colleagues to serve on the design excellence implementation team. EES used a model for change that it termed a "change management adoption curve," which, according to Buehler, helped drive awareness of the change process throughout the organization. "We had pilot teams and pilot projects, but we also created a curriculum for the senior management, so that people could see what we were doing at the team level with support from the top down."

Buehler's team, which included dedicated staff from operations, marketing, and R&D, worked together to develop the required tools and communication. "We did a lot of workshops. We identified the pilot teams. At the director level we had what I would call our sponsors, and then at the board level we had the commitment around education and creating awareness.

"We branded and developed the communication plan . . . we created posters, banners, and process maps [so] that people could see the language and understand the intent of the program. Then we developed subject matter experts who could coach individual teams and we developed groups called the synchronization teams. We had three synchronization teams that went through the whole process, from transitioning the front end into R&D. We had a group that looked at design intent and requirements development. The last group was the V&V group, our validation and verification group."

EES made extensive use of internal coaches. "We had the dedicated pilot teams and then we identified the subject matter experts. For the different phases of the project, they would be what we called a kind of 'yellow pages.' If you had a question on, say, image diagramming, there would be three or four subject matter experts you could call up and say, 'I'm in this phase of Design Excellence, and I need to find out how to do this.' Or, 'I'm struggling with this concept, can you help me?'"

Assessment was another key element of the process at EES, which assembled assessment teams that included sponsors of the initiative to go out and interview and evaluate implementation teams. "So not only did we provide this infrastructure," Buehler says, "but we went back out with a team of senior managers and sat down with teams. It was pretty informal, but the team would walk us through at a high level what they had done, and then the assessment team would interview, ask questions." This feedback tool showed exactly how the teams were moving along the commitment curve.

The key elements of the process—developing a common language via the branding of design excellence, creating the infrastructure reference tools and procedures, identifying coaches, and putting in place assessment teams—ensured that what is now called "new product development excellence" became an established way of doing business at EES.

* * * *

The only way to know whether change is taking place, and what the results are, is to set up an *objective* system of measurement—in other words, metrics. It's not enough to casually observe that things seem to be progressing faster or that product quality seems to have improved. We described in Chapter 9 how critical metrics are for evaluating the success of the portfolio. They are no less critical for evaluating the success of the VIP *process*—the means by which you achieved the portfolio. Tangible measurements also let you compare outcomes with best practices from other companies.

The proper development and application of metrics could be the topic for an entire book. Suffice it to say here that these metrics need not be complicated, but the people developing and applying them ought to be the same people who are engaged in the activities to make the change happen. Something as simple as defining the desired outcome and time frame, then reviewing the outcome regularly, ensures that you stay on track. Suppose a company's issue is that it is having trouble applying the right resources to its small research projects (a common problem), causing these projects to remain underresourced for months without anyone noticing until deadlines have been missed and schedules slip. To avoid this, the company simply needs an appropriate metric—for example, resources on the job as a percentage of originally planned resources—that it evaluates regularly. As the number moves downward from 100 percent, the company knows it may have a problem brewing. With the early feedback from this simple process of measuring and evaluating, it can avoid a potentially large problem down the road.

TAKING AIM AT CHANGE

The Accelerated Implementation Model (AIM®) is a machine designed for repeatable success. Using it, companies can implement change such as introducing a VIP in systematic steps that

- Break down the VIP management process into discrete steps.
- Define the potential workshops to address those steps.
- Identify the critical few areas where the VIP approach may fail without intervention.
- Develop custom workshops to address the weak spots.
- Implement the workshop program at all levels in the organization.
- Measure the effectiveness of the change process.

Lest executives flee the room on hearing the word *workshop*, we hasten to say that, like many other actions and initiatives we recommend in this book, the AIM workshop is not intended to add a layer of complexity. Instead, these workshops are *part of the process of getting the work done.* While participating in a workshop, team members actually accomplish the tasks they were charged with doing. They simply do so in an environment that includes additional support (in the form of the expert who has already been through the process) and scrutiny (in the form of measurement and analysis of how well the new process is working). Appendix C describes in more detail the components of Production Development Consulting's AIM process. (The MDPD workshops described in Appendix A also are part of the AIM process, in that they are about executing real work while implementing a new approach.)

* * * *

Trying to implement a change throughout an entire organization immediately also can derail the process. Gradually expanding a successful pilot project by introducing it to several groups—enough to be sure that you're representing different types of projects and teams but not so many that you lose control of the process—results in an almost automatic institutionalization of the process. Once four or five groups have been successful with the new way of doing business, it becomes part of the fabric of the company.

Finally, note that the middle stage ought not to go on forever and is designed to self-destruct. As soon as everyone involved knows how to do the new process the right way and the change becomes a habit, the middle stage—with its additional staff and processes—simply goes away.

THE IMPORTANCE OF INSTITUTIONAL MEMORY

We have stated throughout this book that VIP management needs one or more champions to bring it into the organization and make it real. Apart from adopting a model that institutionalizes change, companies can take some specific steps to improve the corporate repository of knowledge about portfolio management and ensure that the VIP approach doesn't vanish from the company with the departure of a key executive or team member. Becton Dickinson, for example, has begun using technology to help manage project knowledge. "We're trying to assemble a database [of projects]," says Steve Sichak, president of BD Diagnostics, Preanalytical Systems. "The idea would be over time to compile a database and to make sure that this is available for future generations. It would become, if you will, the first place [people] would look, rather than the last place they look." The idea behind a database of information on projects is that, rather than having team members start from scratch with research, they can "look at the database first and only if they can't answer their questions in the database [do] they move on and do project-specific work." Companies like Hewlett-Packard, with a well-developed system for collecting and managing customer data related to products, have great flexibility and can achieve great efficiencies.

TURNING THE CAPACITY FOR CHANGE INTO A COMPETITIVE ADVANTAGE

Adopting a system to implement change—whether it's something like the Accelerated Implementation Model or another systematic approach—offers another benefit. Since the world doesn't stand still, companies that must reinvent their approach to implementing change each time change is required are at a great competitive disadvantage. When companies begin thinking strategically about *global change management* or *change as a process*, they institute systems that develop a core competency in the process of change itself—*any* kind of change, from a new way to design a product or organize a supply chain to a new approach to portfolio management. When companies develop and mature the capacity to handle change, they can welcome change and use it to their competitive advantage. Automobile club AAA went through this maturation when introducing a portfolio management process, according to San Retna, the chief portfolio officer at AAA. The initial reaction from senior managers to instituting portfolio management was "We don't do PM and we won't do it here." Retna described how his company was able to implement a portfolio management process by first working with the senior mangers to find out what problems they had with their current approach.[2] AAA's capacity for change was expanded by the realization that senior management commitment emanated from a focus on what areas needed improvement, rather than on process for process's sake.

THE ROLE OF COMMUNICATION IN BUSINESS PROCESS CHANGE

We discussed the importance of communications in Chapter 6. Here we want to reemphasize the importance of communicating the change initiative undertaken by management in as many forms and venues—both internal and external—as possible to the constituencies involved: Face-to-face meetings, speeches, internal communications media, the Web site, advertising, press releases, investor and public relations, the annual report, company bulletin boards, posters, and videotapes or DVDs. Companies often undertake activities such as changing a slogan or tag line or redesigning the company logo. These activities signal change, but they are only an outward manifestation of the underlying shift.

As the VIP approach rolls out through an organization and becomes an established part of business practices, *everyone* will be involved to some degree. Because successful implementation of the business process change initiative rests with the employees who will carry the load and do the heavy lifting, *the execution of the communication strategy is as critical as the proposed business process change.* The repetition of the new vision, mission, or strategy demonstrates senior management's commitment to change. A well-executed communications strategy dispels the notion that the VIP approach is just another business phase or management style *du jour*, but rather is a fundamental change requiring total employee commitment.

While the line managers and staff are the ones who will turn the vision of a value-based portfolio into a reality, high-level attention is absolutely required at the outset and must be part of the ongoing oversight of the VIP. For example, when the communication division of Bolt, Beranek and Newman (BBN) first implemented cross-functional teams in 1991 as a new approach to doing product development, middle managers, who felt most threatened by the change, almost derailed the process. The senior management team had to get the line managers together in a regular forum to help them understand how to manage in the new environment so they could see their roles, what they had to do to make the cross-functional team process work, and how that was a critical component of the change. High-level attention was crucial to making this happen. Including the critical middle step in the change process ensures that the lines of communication between the initiators of change (management) and executors of change (staff) remain open.

COMPLETING THE PICTURE: THE FULLY REALIZED VIP

What will your company look like and how will it act after you adopt the approaches we outline in this book and make the necessary changes in company culture and business practices? Some of the characteristics of a company that has fully realized the VIP approach to portfolio management include the following:

Executives are involved in portfolio management. This isn't something you delegate to others. It is the heart and soul of your company's ability to meet its goals.

Products in your portfolio offer a high degree of customer value. You won't waste time and valuable resources on developing products that don't provide high customer value. If you want to be a leader in your industry, you'll get out of the office and develop an in-depth understanding of what motivates the people who do or would use your future products. Find out what makes them tick, what inspires them, what drives them crazy, and what gets in the way of them achieving their own goals.

Your portfolio is aligned with strategic value. You develop your strategy as your way of achieving your mission and vision. A VIP portfolio fully supports that strategy and, during development, may influence shifts in strategy. You take an active role in this alignment, since just wishing for synchronicity won't make it happen.

Your portfolio is balanced and fits within the budget boundaries of the strategic plan. You are realistic about what you can accomplish. If an opportunity were too large to walk away from and requires greater investment than you can afford, you would find a partner. You understand that funding a portfolio is not just allocating dollars to research and technology but balancing the advertising budget, manufacturing capital requirements, distribution investment, training or retooling, sales, and customer service.

The organization is aligned with the VIP. Everybody in the company understands the concept of customer value and how it relates to his or her job. Communicating in a way that engenders this understanding avoids chaos and ensures that the organization will march in a single direction to create the products in the portfolio.

The portfolio management process includes a mechanism for addressing market and technological change. The world doesn't stand still. As a practitioner of the VIP approach, you are nimble and flexible as you learn about changes. Instead of keeping your head in the sand, disregarding the real world and hoping for the best, you actively seek to understand, embrace, and plan for change.

The VIP process is institutionalized. It is part of the fabric of the organization and doesn't depend on a single champion. The return on your investment in the VIP grows as you continue to use it. It represents not a one-time activity, but a fundamental change in the way you think about investment decision making and how you achieve your goals.

The ideas in this book are achievable. Pursuing the path to VIP management will empower everyone in your organization with an understanding of customer value and how their individual actions can create innovative solutions to provide this value. While often the voyage—the discussions, the thinking, the brainstorming, the learning—provides the greatest value, we're confident you'll find the results worth your effort. Incorporating the VIP into your approach to delivering innovative products and services is the first step to bringing double-digit growth to your company. Enjoy the journey *and* the destination.

NOTES

1. These factors compose PDC's Accelerated Implementation Model (AIM), described in more detail in Appendix C.
2. Presentation at the IIR/PDMA best practices event, Strategic and Operational Portfolio Management Conference, February 27–March 1, 2006, Fort Lauderdale, FL.

This book has free material available for download from the Web Added Value™ resource center at *www.jrosspub.com*

APPENDIX A: USING MARKET-DRIVEN PRODUCT DEFINITION (MDPD) TO CAPTURE THE VOICE OF THE CUSTOMER

As we discuss in Chapter 5, companies should derive customer value using a best-practices voice-of-the-customer process such as PDC's MDPD approach. Sheila Mello's previous book, *Customer-Centric Product Definition: The Key to Great Product Development* (PDC Professional Publishing, 2003) provides an in-depth look at MDPD; this appendix offers a brief overview of the process.

MDPD is about defining products based on what customers value. It takes you from concept to idea generation and product specification. Like other product definition processes, MDPD generally occurs at the front end of a typical product development or phase-gate process (see Figure A.1). Its output also feeds into the VIP management process.

Companies use MDPD to develop an in-depth understanding of the issues customers face. The methodology allows cross-functional product development teams to capture the unmet needs and requirements of represen-

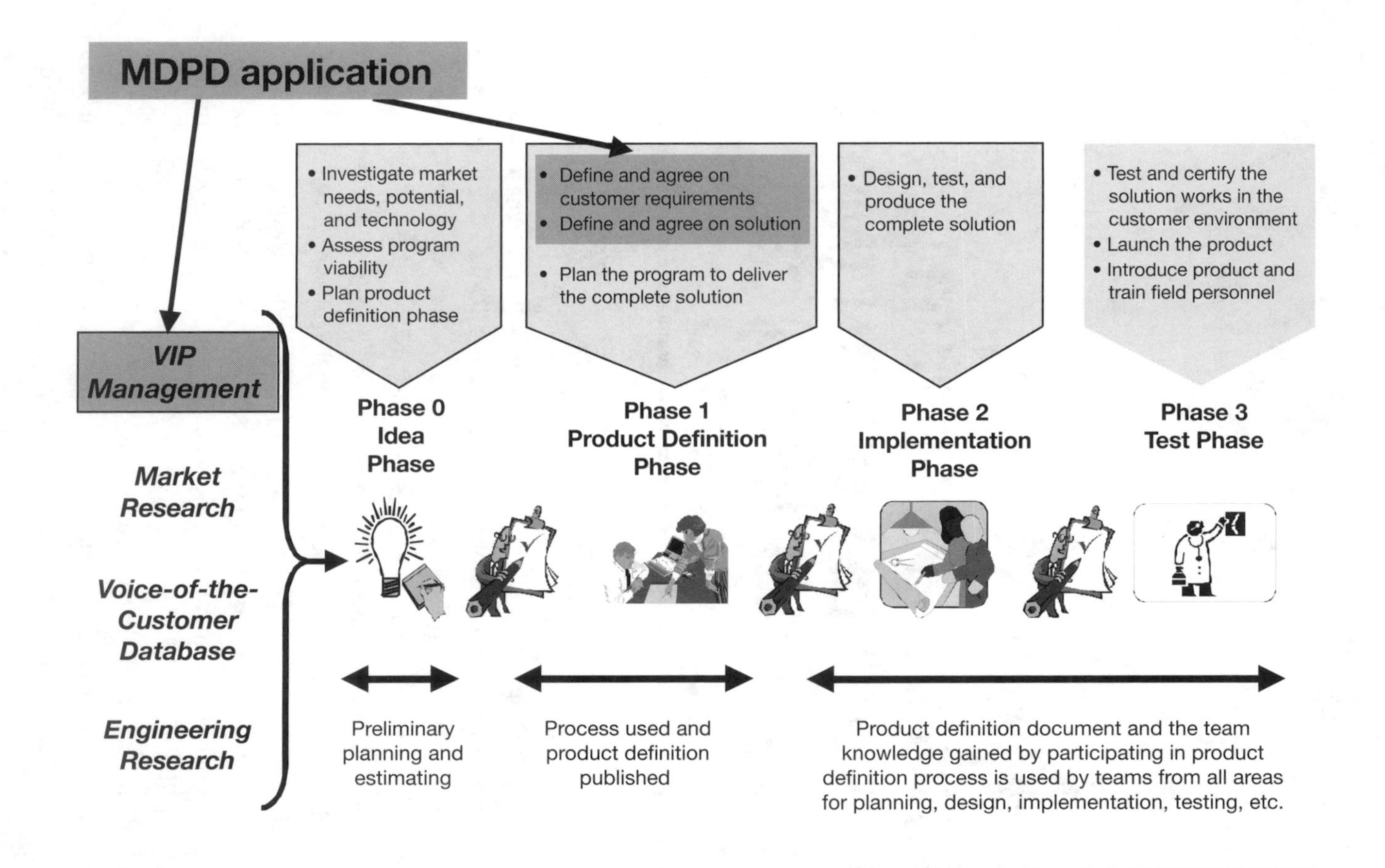

Figure A.1 Where defining customer requirements fits into new product development.

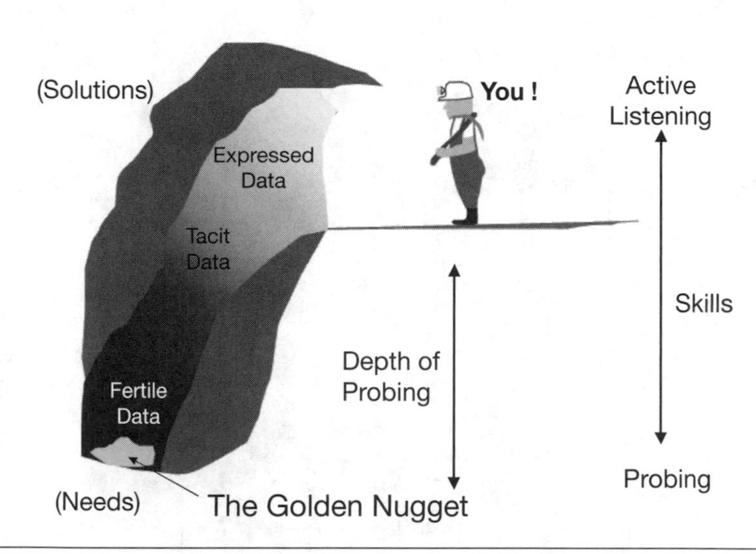

Figure A.2 The old-mine principle.

tative customers in target markets. It provides a context for making trade-off decisions and improves time to market because using it means fewer changes during the course of the project, less feature creep, and fewer late additions of features. Also, because the team has a common basis for understanding what needs to be done, it can better react to problems and adjust concepts to address any technical challenges that may arise. The data captured through this process often is far more valuable than that captured through other traditional customer research methods. As Figure A.2 shows, the really valuable data about customer needs, like gold deeply buried in an old mine, requires particular skills to unearth.

The implementation of MDPD starts with the formation of a cross-functional team composed at the very least of representatives from product marketing and engineering, with other support functions (e.g., manufacturing, service, regulatory, quality) added as appropriate. Based on our experience, a team size of six to eight individuals is ideal.

Since the flow of activities involved in the MDPD process drives the rest of the portfolio process, it's important to understand these activities and how they fit together. Figure A.3 shows the sequence of events in the MDPD process.

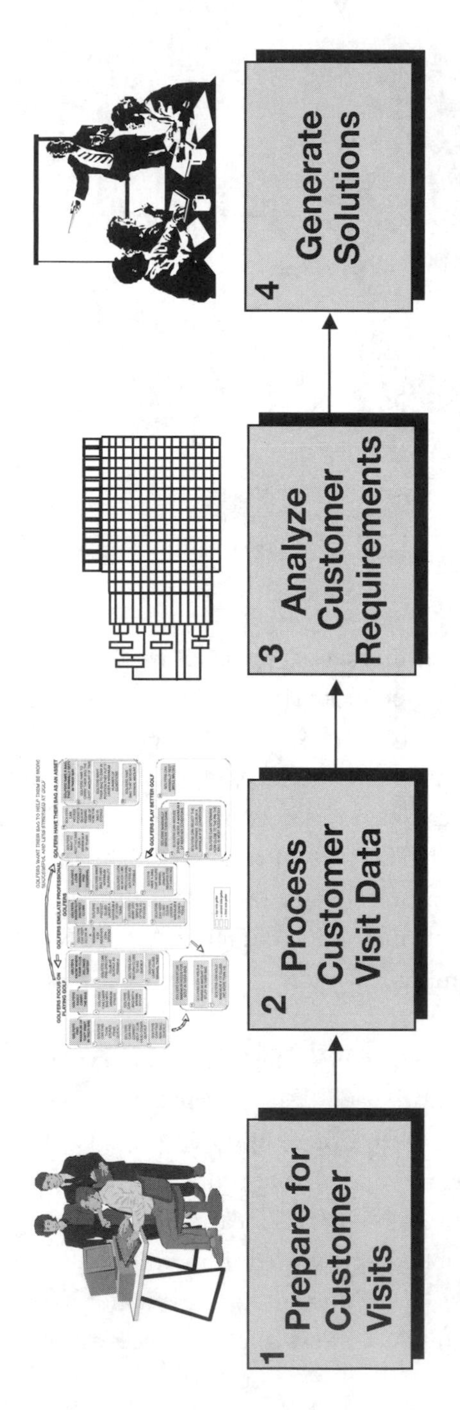

Figure A.3 MDPD high-level flow.

Stage One: Prepare for Customer Visits

The MDPD process fully prepares functionally diverse groups to undertake in-depth, ethnographic-type research. During this stage, teams formulate interview guides and learn how to conduct customer interviews in a manner that elicits insights about the customer's world. These insights are the key to developing innovative new products.

Stage Two: Process Customer Visit Data

One of the most difficult tasks development teams face when conducting qualitative research using other methods is distilling data around the customer experience into a usable form. MDPD is a systematic, repeatable way to process such experiential data. During stage two, the team synthesizes information, draws conclusions about the target customers' environment, and unearths unmet needs and future product requirements. During this stage, the team reaches consensus on the critical customer requirements.

Stage Three: Analyze Customer Requirements

The team gathers quantitative data regarding the identified measurable customer requirements. Using a unique market research technique, the team collects data that is statistically significant and establishes market segmentation. The findings are used to rate new concepts as well as to rate competitive offerings.

Stage Four: Generate Solutions

In the final stage, teams translate the customer requirements into product features. The team engages in creative generation of ideas, evaluates potential solutions, and uses a robust process for weighting and selecting a winning product concept.

Understanding some terminology will help in understanding the MDPD approach. *Voices* are the raw language data from customer interview transcripts that may include requirements, solutions, images, and other statements. Voices are anything the customer says. *Images* are the descriptions that evoke the sense of being in the environment of the user. They may be rich portrayals of the context for use of the intended product or service and usually are emotional evocations of the physical or psychological environment. *Requirements* are statements of what functionality a product or service possesses to satisfy or delight customers. Customer value is the manifestation of the requirements. *Features* are the elements of a product that are embodied in a specific form to meet the customer requirement.

As we discussed in Chapter 10, to institutionalize a process in your organization, you need to make it repeatable. The MDPD process is broken up into 16 workshops, each addressing a component of the process required to reach the ultimate goal of an unambiguous set of customer-requirements-driving concepts that provide customer value. Conducting individual workshops that address specific components of the process fosters repeatability and develops subject matter expertise among team members. Figure A.4 details the 16-step MDPD process, which, when implemented, has delivered impressive results for new product development with revenue increases and increased profits.

The text that follows details the objectives of each stage of the MDPD process.

STAGE ONE: PREPARE FOR CUSTOMER VISITS

Workshop 1. Define the project mission, decide which categories of customers and relevant functions to visit, and confirm the product scope, project staffing, budget, and schedule.

Workshop 2. Develop interview guides for each different type of user you plan to visit based on Workshop 1.

Workshop 3. Learn how to successfully conduct customer interviews and practice interviewing to test and hone new skills.

Workshop 4. Review transcripts of first several completed interviews and suggest adjustments to interviewing techniques and to the interview guide based on actual usage.

STAGE TWO: PROCESS CUSTOMER VISIT DATA

Workshop 5. Develop an image diagram by identifying and selecting the key customer images.

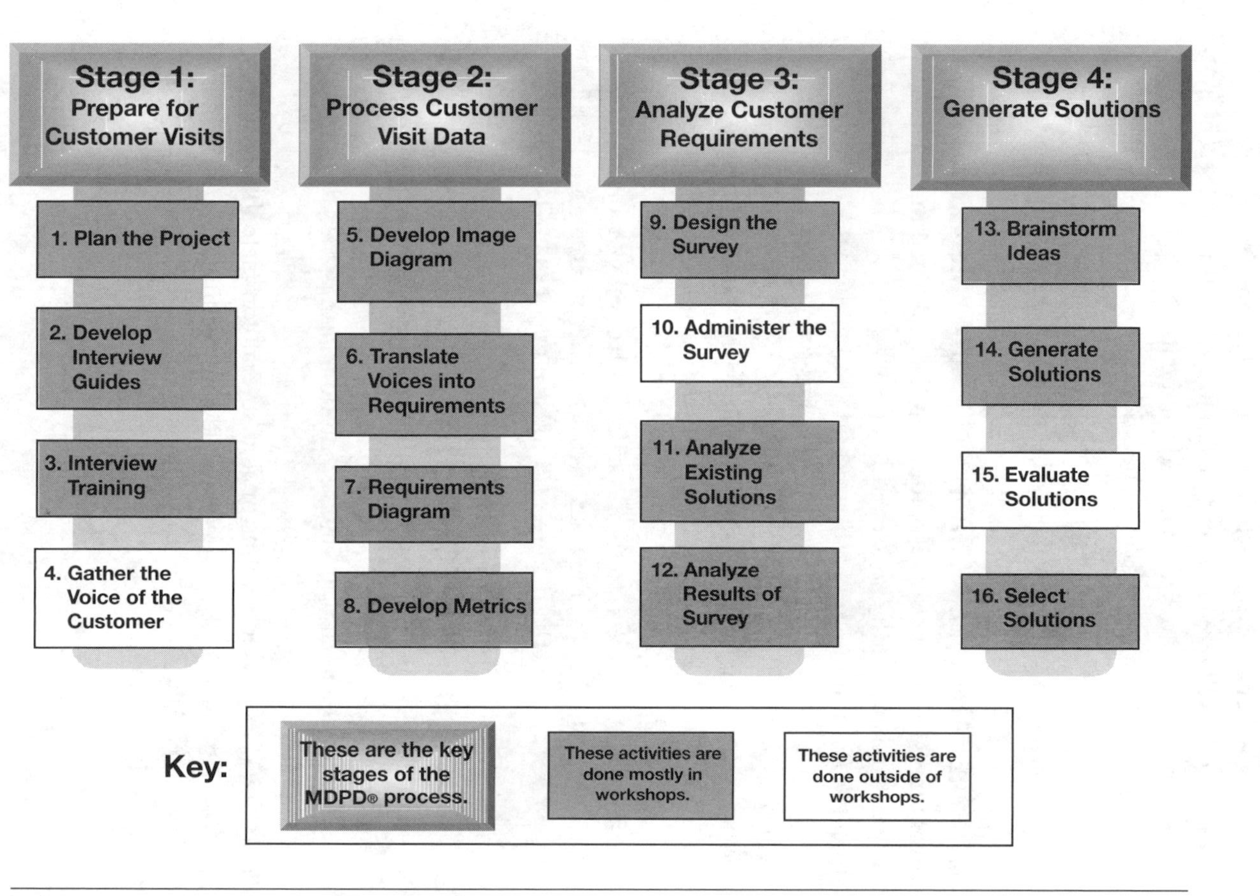

Figure A.4 MDPD process flow.

Workshop 6. Translate voices into requirements—combine customer voices and key images to define customer requirements.

Workshop 7. Develop requirements diagram by selecting and reaching consensus on the key customer requirements.

Workshop 8. Develop metrics and operational definitions for requirements to understand quantitatively when the customer requirements have been met.

STAGE THREE: ANALYZE CUSTOMER REQUIREMENTS

Workshop 9. Design the surveys—develop the self-stated importance, reflected sum of the ranks, and Kano surveys.

Workshop 10. Administer the surveys and analyze the data to validate, prioritize, and select the requirements and determine where responses differ by market segment.

Workshop 11. Analyze existing solutions based on a requirements matrix rating competitors and existing solutions on performance against each requirement.

Workshop 12. Analyze results of survey and develop requirement-weighting factors for the assessment of concept strength. Identify the priorities of each requirement in each major market segment.

STAGE FOUR: GENERATE SOLUTIONS

Workshop 13. Brainstorm ideas for each requirement that will support the requirement approach defined in Workshop 12.

Workshop 14. Generate alternative solutions using the ideas from Workshop 13.

Workshop 15. Evaluate solutions based on technical feasibility, cost, staffing requirements, and other internal constraints.

Workshop 16. Analyze trade-offs using weighted selection criteria to arrive at solutions.

APPENDIX B: MANAGING INVESTMENT INTENSITY IN THE VIP

Investment intensity is one of the critical components of VIP management. In making investment intensity decisions, the organization gets serious: about validating the data supporting the opportunity, making its portfolio decisions into reality—and committing to spend money. As we said in Chapter 8, the goal of the VIP process is to commit the *right resources* at the *right time*, at the *right level* and focused in the *right areas*. By doing so, you build the capabilities to fully deliver the promised customer value at the expected purchasing volume, enabling you to hit the market sweet spot.

Investment intensity planning—how you choreograph resources—focuses on two areas: (1) investing to establish needed capabilities in the arenas of technology foundation, market presence, and business infrastructure and (2) investing to acquire the insights and data to effectively guide planning and implementation as you move toward and into full commercialization. The big-dollar investments usually fall in the former category, but the latter yields the most leverage. This appendix offers perspectives on some of the elements required to successfully manage investment intensity in the VIP and examines, through a case study example, the dynamics that affect investment intensity decision making.

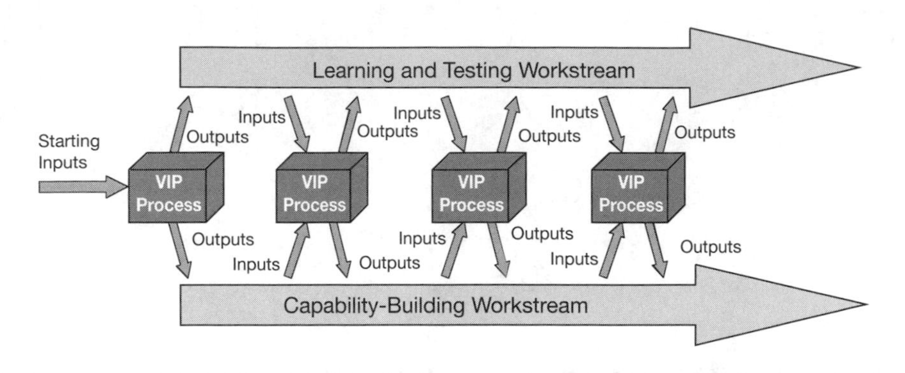

Figure B.1 The two work streams, with inputs and outputs.

AN ONGOING PORTFOLIO PROCESS

Investment intensity is part of the VIP dynamic governance framework we described in Chapter 9 and so is not a one-time event. It is an ongoing process whereby organizational leadership regularly adjusts resource commitments in response to new information, whether from internal sources (e.g., the results of a technology development program or new directions on resource availability) or external sources (e.g., an unexpected competitive signal in the marketplace or the results of a prototype test in the field). (See Figure B.1.) This allocation decision making—that is, resource choreography—can be done in the context of a formal executive-level portfolio review, at an informal review, at an event-triggered out-of-bounds review, in the context of a project-specific phase/gate review, or as part of a project-specific team process. While a company may look at this as predominantly a top-down process in which portfolio decisions determine investment intensity, many of the inputs that drive investment decision making—particularly new market and internal development or capability insights—must bubble up from the project level. Consequently, you must explicitly design and structure the linkage between the investment and project management. To maximize business success, investments cannot be solely a top-management activity.

A significant question is how to differentiate investment intensity planning from ongoing project management and planning. In the VIP model, investment intensity planning clearly is an activity that encompasses both portfolio-level resource investment decisions and resource decision making at the project/product team level. It includes senior management's framework for deciding how to allocate and assign resources across the portfolio—that is, the balancing process we discussed earlier in Chapter 4—and the flow down of those investment decisions to individual cross-functional project teams and functional managers (see Chapter 9). But it also includes the dance of resources at the project/product level that turns those portfolio decisions into events or objects with marketplace impact. The out-of-bounds review process as defined in Chapter 9 is the means by which discontinuities percolate up to senior management.

DEFINING WHAT IT TAKES TO WIN

One of the first things a new product/project team must do to prepare for investment decision making is to define *what it takes to win*—that is, to paint a picture of the capabilities it must have in three arenas (market presence, business infrastructure, and technology foundation) to win in the marketplace. At kickoff, this picture is painted with broad-brush strokes to provide general guidance. As the project drives toward commercialization, the picture is painted in increasingly fine detail and with revised or updated content. With this picture in hand, the team can map current capabilities against the winning position and can define the gaps. Investment decision making then comes down to deciding how to choreograph the deployment of resources to close those gaps. The team regularly revisits these gaps analysis and the resource choreography during the project's lifetime as the team receives fresh input resulting from the dynamic VIP governance process, as it builds capabilities to support the project, and as the picture of what it takes to win evolves with new information from internal and external sources.

RESOURCE CHOREOGRAPHY

We introduced the term *resource choreography* early in the book and then briefly outlined what we mean by it in Chapter 8. We prefer this term to the more common expression *resource allocation* because the former more effectively captures the essence of the dynamic nature of investment intensity management in the VIP and the dynamic way resources and capabilities must interact to win in the marketplace. A master choreographer preparing for the premier of a new ballet starts with an overall concept for the work, but in the end must get down to planning and detailing the exact placement and movement of the resources at his or her disposal—that is, the members of the dance troupe, from prima ballerinas to the supporting cast. The choreographer then must work with the troupe to execute against this plan: training, preparing, and rehearsing while making corrections and adjustments as the concept becomes real on the rehearsal stage. The choreography involves all the activities that lead to the performance as much as the final performance itself.

Like a master dance choreographer, the leadership of a business using VIP management must choreograph the resources and capabilities at its disposal, both for the final marketplace performance and for the resource commitment needed to prepare for that performance. Like the dance choreographer, business leadership needs to work its broad-brush business concept down to the specific placement and movement of resources, both those actually appearing on the marketplace stage and those used to prepare for the show.

The resource choreographer must keep in mind three important points when initiating the effort to plan and coordinate the application of resources:

- Think through and thoughtfully design the relationship and interaction of resources and capabilities so they work together in a seamless fashion during the on-stage performance.
- Always be aware of the "score" to which the resources will be "dancing" and be sure to shift if the score changes; that is, understand the market environment and make adjustments in reaction to (or better yet, in anticipation of) changes in the environment.
- Be appropriately sensitive to the role of the supporting cast. Don't focus so exclusively on your star resources that critical but lower-profile resources and capabilities receive inadequate attention and ruin the performance.

A noteworthy dynamic around resource choreography is the interplay between the work of the portfolio team and that of the project/product teams.

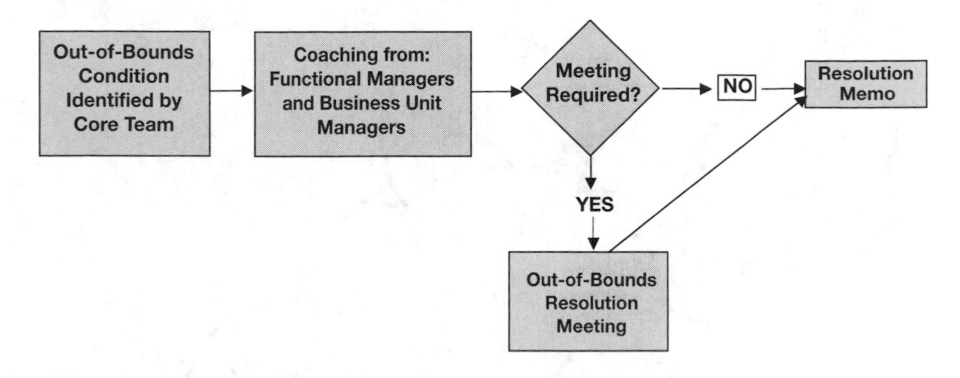

Figure B.2 The resource choreography management loop.

The portfolio team is responsible for directing and guiding the broad-brush choreography of resources across the portfolio to address the overall business strategy, while individual product/project teams must choreograph their available resources to meet their specific targets. We discussed the review process framework in Chapter 9. Of all of the reviews we discussed, one of the most important is the *out-of-bounds review*, which provides a mechanism to resolve major issues that fall outside the boundaries of the team. (See Figure B.2.)

While full-blown, formal review meetings require lots of time and preparation, informal reviews can occur quickly, allowing rapid response to ripples in the marketplace or any other changes requiring prompt attention before a potential problem can rage out of control. Figure B.3 shows a schematic of the process loop that engages the portfolio team and the core team in resource rechoreography through out-of-bounds reviews.

A CASE STUDY: VIP IN ACTION IN THE DUPONT STAINMASTER INITIATIVE

Chapter 8 discussed the DuPont Certified Stainmaster Carpet initiative in some detail, describing many of the investment intensity decisions and actions that the Stainmaster team took.[2] We now look at the planning and investing process the company used and how it maps to the planning and managing frameworks we discuss here and elsewhere in the book.

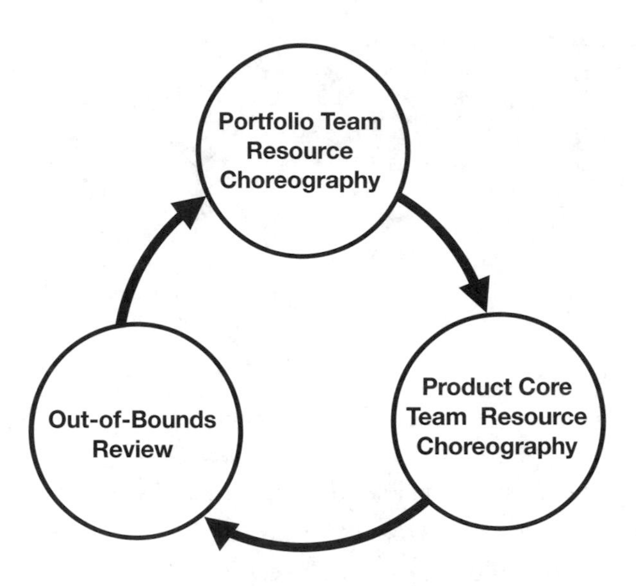

Figure B.3 Relationship of the portfolio team to the product team.

The Stainmaster Development Effort: What It Looked Like

As we said in Chapter 8, a year before the Stainmaster technology breakthrough, the DuPont Carpet Fibers management made a strategic portfolio decision to invest to revitalize its residential carpet fiber business—the largest business in the carpet fiber portfolio (and the weakest competitively). DuPont learned early on in that revitalization effort that launching a major consumer advertising campaign coupled with a significant new product announcement could dramatically improve the residential carpet business. So when Tom McAndrews, then the head of the DuPont Carpet Fibers business, learned of the technology discovery that would underpin the DuPont Certified Stainmaster Carpet product, he knew that a lot of money was at stake around commercializing it. He realized from the start that getting the Stainmaster platform of products to market ahead of the competition with a powerful consumer brand message would take an intense, focused, and costly effort on DuPont's part. But he also realized that the profit payoff for the company could be even larger.

USING BACKCASTING TO ENLARGE YOUR STARTING KNOWLEDGE

One of the most challenging parts of successful investment intensity planning and resource choreography is developing a comprehensive and thoughtful list of issues, uncertainties, and assumptions. While it's impossible to begin planning with complete knowledge—and you will be making decisions before you have all the facts you'd ultimately like—it's particularly critical to dig out the hidden assumptions that may be hard to uncover because they are so ingrained that people *know* they are true.

We have found a modified version of the technique called *backcasting*[1] useful for getting beyond surface knowledge. We assemble the team and first ask them to develop a starter list of issues, uncertainties, and assumptions. Then we take a break. Upon returning, we pose the following provocation: "Pretend that it is now x years or y months in the future. At this point, your initiative should be fully launched and making pots of money. Unfortunately, your business initiative has crashed and burned—either because you never could get it launched or because it failed miserably in the marketplace when you did launch it. Now tell me what happened."

The first reaction of the team on hearing this is usually a sharp intake of breath; they don't want to conceive of their baby dying. But once over the initial shock, the team invariably loosens up and offers all sorts of scenarios on what could go wrong. Among this rich set of possible negative scenarios, you may discover many critical hidden issues that need to be resolved going forward.

* * * *

With this assessment in mind, McAndrews established an ongoing management and planning process to guide the initiative. An ad hoc Stainmaster core team was formed that took the lead for this development and commercialization effort. Bob Axtell, soon-to-be head of the residential carpet business, provided strong and critical leadership for the team that included business, marketing, market research, technical, and market liaison staff in the residential carpet business (both from within and outside DuPont). Although McAndrews was not an official member of the team, he frequently attended meetings and assumed the critical roles of resource provider, chief encourager, and overseer of strict confidentiality both inside and outside the company.

This steering team met weekly, sometimes for several days at a time, from its inception until well after commercial launch and focused on detailed project planning, management of the multitude of project tasks, and making decisions on the correct investment intensity.

A Carpet Fibers leadership team that included the leaders of the four business units in the division as well as the several divisional functional leaders from technical, manufacturing, human resources, and marketing was already in place, led by McAndrews. This body also met weekly and provided overall direction and decision making for the Carpet Fibers business and its business portfolio. Axtell was a member of this team and would give program updates and get guidance from the team members at these meetings. But members of the leadership team (from business, manufacturing, R&D, and marketing) all worked together in a building in downtown Wilmington, Delaware. This made it easy to arrange quick, ad hoc meetings of Carpet Fibers leadership. When Axtell encountered an out-of-bounds issue requiring a senior Carpet Fibers leadership decision—for example, shifting R&D resources—he would walk into McAndrews's office and they would round up the necessary cross-functional players to address the issue. "We were in and out of each others offices all the time," Bob Axtell said.

With weekly scheduled meetings and a continuing series of ad hoc meetings, the planning and decision-making cycle was rapid and the business was able to respond quickly to new information. For example, the team moved up the scheduled market launch date shortly after seeing a trade press article about a competitor that was working on a stain-resistant carpet and added resources quickly when demand exceeded expectations after launch. Further, unlike many businesses, the Carpet Fibers business at the time was in a position to round up all the necessary resources without major impact on other businesses in the portfolio. McAndrews in particular exercised his responsibility to authorize the funds for the large pool of external advertising, market research, trade support, and customer call center staff. As Bob Axtell said: "I could always get what I wanted from McAndrews!"

The business developed the basic elements of a vision for what it would take to win with a stain-resistant residential carpet offering very early on. These elements included knowing the major customer value of *true* stain resistance, the importance of new treatment chemistry and application technologies to guarantee stain resistance performance, the impact of direct-to-consumer advertising, the critical role of the carpet mills that would apply the stain-resistant chemicals, and the importance of speed to market. The broad strokes of the picture stayed remarkably constant during the run-up to launch, even as more and more data came in and the team learned more, which was not surprising given the maturity of the residential carpet market in the United States and the experience level of the DuPont staff. This consistency of vision was a powerful aligning force and enabled the team to stay focused.

As development went forward, it became clear that the single biggest technology development and operational issues were the carpet treatment chemicals and the treatment process to be used by the carpet mills. The focused teams handling technology development and mill implementation were beefed up as needed. This intense and focused effort resulted in getting the selected test mills ready just weeks before launch. But while the carpet mill treatment represented the most challenging element, focused development teams were in place across the whole spectrum of activities. These included teams to establish a comprehensive retail programs for the carpet dealers, to develop and schedule consumer TV advertising spots and publications, to establish a consumer warranty program, and as the launch rolled out, to implement a large and sophisticated call center.

The Stainmaster Development Effort: The Outcome

Stainmaster was announced to the trade press on September 1, 1986, and the first commercials appeared on national TV on October 13 of that year during the National League baseball playoffs. The response was overwhelming. Consumers were excited. The demand was so high that the Stainmaster team had to scramble to supply the fiber and treatment chemicals needed and to manage the allocation process while capacity was increased, to staff up the customer call center to handle the flood of calls, to expand the number of certified mills, and to provide more support materials to the carpet retailers.

DuPont's carpet fiber manufacturing facilities sold out within two months, and the profitability of the business soared. The original expectation was that Stainmaster would be only one of several products in the product line But within four months of launch—when it was clear that the intense market excitement was continuing to increase—the Carpet Fibers leadership made the major portfolio decision that 100 percent of the residential carpet fiber product line would be Stainmaster and that they would make the capital investments and manufacturing and technical resources shifts to make that happen. Several competitors entered the market within weeks of DuPont's announcement but were unable to match DuPont's advertising punch. Stainmaster became—and remains today— the most recognized carpet brand name in the United States. With this huge success, the portfolio planning effort shifted to expanding fiber capacity to meet demand and to improving treatment chemistries and application technologies to support wider adoption.

THE STAINMASTER DEVELOPMENT EFFORT: MAPPING TO THE VIP PROCESS

Although the Stainmaster team could not have used VIP management process because it did not exist at the time, the team did apply many of the principles that underlie the model as it made investments.

Customer Value

The Stainmaster team started with a clear understanding of the customer value and the power of communicating about that value. This knowledge was solidly grounded on market data the company already had developed on what consumers valued and on the potential impact of an aggressive direct-to-consumer advertising campaign. One thing the team did not do as it moved forward was to aggressively test its assumptions on the size of the opportunity. It believed the opportunity to be limited to particular market segments, such as households with kids that wanted family room carpeting. Had the team tested the power of the new value proposition very broadly, it might not have been caught by surprise when sales exploded and it had to scramble (successfully, as it turned out) to meet this unexpected demand. In the end, things turned out very well for the business (profitability more than doubled in the year after introduction). However, being forced to let competitors fill this demand could have been a serious blow to market share.

Management and Governance Structure

The Stainmaster steering team and Carpet Fibers leadership team structure that Tom McAndrews put in place effectively engaged all the decision makers. We believe such engagement is critical to successful portfolio management (Figure 9.3 in Chapter 9 illustrates this). Because of the program's potential impact and urgency, these teams met at weekly intervals, bringing together everyone (business leadership, functional managers, and team leaders) needed to make on-the-spot decisions to eliminate potential waiting-game issues and keep the program on schedule. This is consistent with our belief that companies need to make portfolio adjustments frequently in response to marketplace events and new discoveries.

The heavy involvement of the business unit head (McAndrews) in a specific program and his attendance at many of the weekly Stainmaster team meetings was not common in DuPont at the time, but it was critical to keep this rapidly moving, high-impact, transformative program on track. (Steve Jobs is reported to have done the same with the development of the iPod at Apple.) This role is not the norm in the application of our dynamic governance model, but it is consistent with our principle that senior managers must own the portfolio process and involve themselves at a sufficient level to make it successful. At DuPont, when the intense surge of launch and immediate post-launch activity ended, the weekly meetings of the steering team shifted to a different focus more in line with the usual portfolio management process as the company deliberately exploited its initial gains and enhanced its technology and market position.

Covering the Key Arenas

The Stainmaster team clearly addressed the three investment intensity arenas (market presence, business infrastructure, and technology foundation) we identified in Chapter 8 and did so aggressively and thoughtfully. Team members developed a clear picture of what it would take to win in these arenas and systematically put the pieces in place. They understood early on the scope of a winning market communications campaign and implemented it, vastly outspending competition in consumer advertising and effectively drowning out the competitive message in the marketplace. They identified all the business infrastructure elements they needed (including uncommon items for DuPont, like a consumer warranty and replacement program and a certification program with strong quality enforcement features for the carpet mills) and methodically put them in place. And they defined from the start the technology pieces needed to provide a consistent, quality offering that had robust stain resistance performance—and then developed and implemented them.

Planning and Resource Choreography

Here, too, the team applied the principles we recommend. It planned in depth to initiate the effort, carefully choreographed resource commitments to realize its picture of what it takes to win, and then continuously monitored progress to ensure activities were on track as it drove toward commercialization. The focus of the in-depth planning and resource choreography (and rechoreography) was clearly at the Stainmaster core team level. However, an ongoing stream of informal reviews and meetings with the Carpet Fibers Division leadership ensured that resource issues were addressed rapidly and were handled with a full Carpet Fibers perspective (i.e., not limited to the branded residential business).

In summary, the Stainmaster effort offers an excellent example of the kind of effective capability building the VIP model enables.

NOTES

1. "[Backcasting] involves working backwards from a particular desirable future end-point to the present in order to determine the physical feasibility of that future and what policy measures [and actions] would be required to reach that point." (J. Robinson, *Futures* 22, no. 9 (1990): 820–844.
2. The Stainmaster case study, and quotes appearing within it, are based on personal interviews with DuPont staff: Bob Axtell (business manager, Residential Flooring), Bob Shellenbarger (end-use

research manager), Tom McAndrews (worldwide division director, DuPont Carpet Fibers), and John Hesselberth (technical director, DuPont Carpet Fibers).

APPENDIX C: THE ACCELERATED IMPLEMENTATION MODEL (AIM) FOR CHANGE

The road to deploying potentially great new business processes across the enterprise is littered with disappointments. Like the hurried test taker who thinks he can finish quicker by diving right into answering questions and misses reading important information in the directions, the company that dives into a new way of doing business (such as VIP management) without adequate planning often finds that the process takes longer and produces poorer outcomes. Once any new way of doing business is decided upon, deeply seeding it in the enterprise requires proactive direction.

PDC's Accelerated Implementation Model (AIM), which we described briefly in Chapter 10, is based on the beliefs that learning through experience—that is, real work, not just empty workshops and training sessions—must occur during the implementation of a change and that all attempts at change must be measured.

AIM is a three-faceted tool that encompasses planning, implementation, and management. In its role as a *planning tool*, it compartmentalizes each of the most challenging aspects of the change into separate work sessions. This generally bypasses the common missteps found in a prior pilot implementation. In the aggregate, these work sessions become a concrete list of workshops, organized in a simple matrix by time and responsibility (see Figure C.1). Part of the plan includes a full definition of what happens in each workshop.

	Interviewing	Images	Requirements	Verification	Concepts
Project Management	1) Mission Statement 2) Program Plan	8) Interview Transcription 9) Images on Post-its	14) Requirement Statement Scrub	20) Acquisition of Customer Lists 21) Competitive Requirements Evaluation	26) Concept Constraint Analysis 27) Business Case
Marketing	3) Customer Visit Matrix 4) Interview Guide 5) Set-up Interviews	10) Language Analysis	15) Language Analysis	22) Kano Survey 23) Self-Stated Importance Survey	28) Marketing Risk 29) Competitive Sustainability
Development Team	6) Interview Training 7) Interviews	11) Extract Images 12) Red Dotting 13) Image Diagram	16) Create Customer Requirements 17) Red Dotting 18) Requirements 19) Requirement Metrics	24) Best-in-Class Decisions 25) Setting Targets	30) Idea Generation 31) Concept Generation 32) Concept Selection

Figure C.1 AIM planning tool—VOC example.

#13 Image Diagram Workshop	
	3 hours
Image and language analysis training:	**.5 hrs**
Initial image grouping evaluation:	**1 hrs**
Higher-level label generation:	**1 hr**
Cause/effect analysis and summary:	**.5 hrs**

Figure C.2 Implementation tool example—VOC workshop 13 image diagram.

As an *implementation tool*, AIM workshops are opportunities for people on an actual project to do real work. The format is a facilitated workshop (see Figure C.2), usually between three hours and one day long, providing just-in-time training, evaluation, data preparation, and decision making. The output of the process is work product to advance the project. The key to overcoming the challenge of succeeding in a new way of doing business is to harness the talents of a skilled facilitator that ensures that new practitioners are successful in their initial attempt. This pays a second important dividend as well: the avoidance of negative internal publicity and less baggage to overcome around the too-common protest of teams: "But we're different—this new process just doesn't work for us."

As a *measurement tool*, AIM capitalizes on the compartmentalization of the workshops to offer a simple, objective evaluation of how well the change is being implemented. Because real work is preplanned and executed in the workshops, you can score your progress against your plan (see Figure C.3). This can be done at each phase of the project and helps detect problems early on, before they become unwieldy. The remaining workshops can then be tailored to bolster weak areas and ensure project success.

Once the execution of the workshops on several projects reveals the most challenging aspects of the new way of doing business, you can phase out the AIM workshops. The AIM system is designed to put itself out of business. This marks completion of the middle step of change, allowing the new way of business to run on its own into the future. Initial discovery became success, success spread through facilitated workshops, and the new approach then became

$$\text{“Improvement Aim”} = \frac{12 \text{ (sum of block scores)}}{18 \text{ (best possible score)}} = 67\%$$

	Interviewing	Images	Requirements	Verification	Concepts
Project Management		1	14) Requirement Statement Scrub	20) Acquisition of Customer Lists 21) Competitive Requirements Evaluation	26) Concept Constraint Analysis 27) Business Case
Marketing	2		15) Language Analysis	22) Kano Survey 23) Self-Stated Importance Survey	28) Marketing Risk 29) Competitive Sustainability
Development Team		0	16) Create Customer Requirements 17) Red Dotting 18) Requirements 19) Requirement Metrics	24) Best-in-Class Decisions 25) Setting Targets	30) Idea Generation 31) Concept Generation 32) Concept Selection

Sum of block scores = 12 = 3+2+3+1+3+0
Best-possible score = 18 = 6 x 3

Figure C.3 Metric: end of images phase—how well is the project executing the new approach?

an everyday work habit. The transition is now complete. This doesn't imply that you never again conduct a workshop; some of the activities, such as building the image diagram in Figure C.2, are always best carried out in a workshop setting. However, after the completion of the AIM process, a subject matter expert does not necessarily need to attend each workshop.

INDEX

C

D

N